Short Changed

Transnational Institute Series

The Transnational Institute is an independent fellowship of researchers and activists living in different parts of the world, who develop innovative analyses of world affairs.

It serves no government, political party or interest group.

Other titles in the TNI series:

People and Poer in the Pacific
The Struggle for the Post-Cold War Order
Walden Bello

The Debt Boomerang
How Third World Debt Harms us All
Susan George

Revolution of the Right
Simon Gunn

Paradigms Lost
The Post Cold War Era
*Edited by Chester Hartman
and Pedro Vilanova*

About the Authors

Michael Barratt Brown is chair of the Third World Information Network (TWIN) and Twin Trading. He is author of numerous well known studies on Third World Development, most recently *Fair Trade: Reforming the International Trading System* (1992).

Pauline Tiffen is a fellow of the Transnational Institute in Amsterdam and Director of the Third World Information Network (TWIN).

TWIN is a London-based charity which works with organisations of small-scale producers in Africa and Latin America to help them get a better deal for their produce in the marketplace. TWIN's associate, Twin Trading, is directly engaged in the marketing of mineral and agricultural products from the Third World.

Short Changed

Africa and World Trade

Michael Barratt Brown and Pauline Tiffen

Foreword by Susan George

Pluto **Press**
London • Boulder, Colorado
with the Transnational Institute (TNI)

First published 1992 by Pluto Press
345 Archway Road, London N6 5AA
and 5500 Central Avenue
Boulder, Colorado 80301, USA

in association with the Transnational Institute
Paulus Potterstraat 20, 1071 DA Amsterdam

Distributed in the Netherlands by the
Transnational Institute

British Library Cataloguing in Publication Data
A catalogue record for this book is available from the British Library

ISBN 0 7453 0694 2 (hbk)
ISBN 0 7453 0699 3 (pbk)

Typeset in Stone by Stanford DTP, Milton Keynes
Printed and bound in Great Britain

Contents

Tables and Charts in Text

Statistical Annexe: Tables and Charts

Abbreviations

ACP	African, Caribbean and Pacific countries
AIDS	Acquired Immune Deficiency Syndrome (see HIV)
ASEAN	Association of South East Asian Nations
CAP	Common Agricultural Policy
CAR	Central African Republic
CEAO	West African Economic Community
CEPGL	Economic Community of the Great Lakes
DDA	Swiss Development Cooperation Authority
ECOWAS	Economic Community of West African States
FAO	Food and Agriculture Organisation
FRG	Federal Republic of Germany
GATT	General Agreement on Tariffs and Trade
GDP	Gross Domestic Product
GNP	Gross National Product
GSP	General System of Preferences
HFCS	High Fructose Corn Syrup
HIV	the virus that causes AIDS
ICA	International Cocoa Agreement
ICCO	International Cocoa Organisation
ICO	International Coffee Organisation
IDA	International Development Association
IMF	International Monetary Fund
INRA	International Rubber Agreement
ISCOS	Instituto Sindacale per la Cooperazione Allo Sviluppo
ITO	International Trade Organisation
ITTO	International Tropical Timber Association
LDC	Least Developed Country
LDDC	Least Developed Developing Country
MARIUN	Mano River Union
MFA	Multi-Fibre Arrangement
MFN	Most Favoured Nation
NIC	Newly Industrialised Country
NNPC	Nigerian National Petroleum Company
ODI	Overseas Development Institute, London
OECD	Organisation for Economic Cooperation and Development

OEM	Original Equipment Manufacture
OPEC	Organisation of Petroleum Exporting Countries
RSA	Republic of South Africa
SADCC	Southern African Development Coordination Conference
SAL	Structural Adjustment Loan
SCP	Single Cell Protein
SDR	Special Deposit Reserve (IMF currency)
SSA	Sub-Saharan Africa
TNC	Transnational company
TNI	Transnational Institute, Amsterdam
TWIN	Third World Information Network, London
UDEAC	Union Douanière et Économique de l'Afrique Centrale
UN	United Nations
UNCTAD	UN Conference on Trade and Development
UNCTC	UN Centre for Transnational Corporations
UNDP	UN Development Programme
UNECA	UN Economic Commission for Africa
UNESCO	UN Education and Scientific body
UNICEF	UN Children's Emergency Fund
UNIDO	UN Industrial Development Organisation
UNPAAERD	UN Programme of Action for African Economic Recovery
USDA	US Department of Agriculture

Acknowledgements

This book is a project of the Transnational Institute (TNI), Amsterdam. It is a critical study of the export-led development strategy proposed to bring sub-Saharan Africa out of its crisis. TNI's goal is to contribute to a constructive reappraisal of this policy for Africa's future, leading to a reassessment of what realistically can be done.

The project would not have been possible without the vision and determination of Susan George and Dan Smith, respectively Associate Director and Director of TNI. The DDA (the Swiss government's Development Cooperation Authority) and ISCOS (the Third World cooperation arm of the Italian trade union, CISL) funded the extensive and original research which underpins the arguments behind *Short Changed: Africa and World Trade*, but leaving TNI full independence. They are not responsible for the analysis or conclusions.

Material was provided by several experts commissioned by TNI: Cameron Duncan, formerly of the Institute for Policy Studies, Washington, now head of the Multilateral Development Bank's programme at Greenpeace; Lev Gonick of Wilfrid Laurier University, Ontario; Gerd Junne and Henk Kox of the Free University of Amsterdam; Julia Mazza of Third World Information Network (TWIN), London. The research material for the chapter on oil was contributed by Abubakar Siddique Muhammad of the Department of Economics, Ahmadu Bello University, Zaria, Nigeria. These contributors' statistics are noted. Traders in London, New York, Canada and Nigeria were interviewed during 1990 under the seal of confidentiality. They are not referenced.

Henrietta Cooke, of TWIN, worked unstintingly at text and charts to bring the book together. TNI is responsible for the final editing.

Foreword: Exported To Death – the World Bank and Africa

Susan George

The World Bank walks on two legs. Though such a Maoist metaphor would doubtless displease the neo-classical economists of 1818 H Street NW, Washington DC, it nonetheless encapsulates the truth. The first leg is reliance on the marketplace, which is believed capable of satisfying virtually all humankind's needs, both economic and social. The second leg is integration – all countries should participate in the world economy to the fullest possible extent. Standing on these unvarying principles, the Bank has, for nearly half a century, straddled the world. They are part of the Bank's structure and the pillars of its doctrine: the technical measures the Bank implements in one country or another all derive from them in some way. Asking the Bank to 'change' them would be about as realistic as expecting a horse to canter on webbed feet.

Although the twin doctrines – market forces and maximum integration – are usually presented in the abstract, without reference to particular historical or geographical circumstances, it is clear that they are not preached in a vacuum. In the late twentieth century, and whatever the talk of 'level playing fields' or 'the international community', it is also clear that some participants in the world economy are more equal than others. The stronger members of this 'community' can observe whichever parts of the doctrine suit their purposes while ignoring the rest. The weaker ones are not afforded this luxury. Thus, for example, powerful countries can maintain tariff and non-tariff trade barriers against competition from goods manufactured in weak countries, while still dumping their own industrial or farm products on more vulnerable countries.

Various international institutional arrangements exist for the implementation of the basic doctrine. The standard wisdom proclaims that goods should flow freely across frontiers. Ensuring the proper conditions for such flows and providing them with a legal framework is the specific task of the General Agreement on Tariffs and Trade (GATT). Today, however, with increasing frequency, countries may be hampered from full participation in the world economy for sheer lack of cash. In such cases, the International Monetary Fund (IMF) exists to provide – at a financial and political price – 'balance of payments support'. Its loans come with increasingly strict conditions attached as a country's deficit and consequent borrowing needs increase. The IMF is not supposed to be a 'development' organisation and its Articles of Agreement make clear that its vocation is to finance trade.

In the free market, integrationist worldview, merchandise – whether in the form of goods or services – and money must, then, be free to cross borders. The same rules do not apply to all factors of production, however, for example, stopping noticeably short of demanding the same freedom for labour.

Where does the World Bank come in? In the present International Division of Labour, wherein GATT takes care of making rules for trade and the IMF takes care of financing it, there is an unstated prior condition: countries must trade. They must, to that end, agree to devote substantial resources to the sector of what economists call 'tradeables', even though that may be to the detriment of resources for 'non-tradeables' which are more immediately useful to the population. Governments, that is, should be protected from the temptation to concentrate on satisfying the needs of their own people – for food, shelter, transport, and so on. The Bank's particular role is to make sure that all the countries under its tutelage take maximum advantage of market integration opportunities whether they want to or not. The mechanism for forcing potentially reluctant participants to engage in the world market is the set of economic policies called structural adjustment; a vital component of structural adjustment is the insistent implementation of the doctrine of export-led growth.

About five dozen countries, a great many of them in Africa, are now applying structural adjustment programmes under the guidance of the IMF and the Bank. The easy-money decade of the 1970s led many countries to overborrow; in the 1980s they were caught in the squeeze when debts came due at the same time as interest rates soared. As a result, they certainly needed to 'adjust' – their outlays chronically exceeded their incomes – but they were given little choice as to how to go about it. Because the 'seal of approval' granted by the Fund and the Bank can alone give access to credit – not just to loans from the Bank and Fund themselves but from all other sources as well – the Bank can stride into the country on its two legs and set about applying its doctrine. The 'adjustee' has little choice in the matter.

A standard requirement is that the debtor must export at all costs. The ultimate goal of structural adjustment is to restore a positive balance of payments so that the debtor government will have spare cash on hand to service its debts. For a country whose currency is unacceptable in international financial transactions – which means virtually all 'developing' countries – the only option is to earn cash through exports.

In pursuing this objective the Bank and the Fund act as bill-collecting agencies for the creditor countries. The creditors, particularly the United States, take a hard line on debt, no matter how poor and indigent the debtor, insisting on total repayment except in a handful of cases. The social and ecological consequences have been devastating. These consequences are, furthermore, well known and have been documented in any number of books, articles, films etc., some of them by TNI Fellows.[1] They are perhaps best summed up in a single UNICEF figure: an extra half million children die every year as a direct result of the debt crisis.

Neither the Bank nor the Fund has tried to press home to the creditors, their major shareholders, the obvious point that substantial debt relief would be the best – indeed the only – initial step to prevent the total economic and social collapse of sub-Saharan Africa in particular. Greatly reduced debt would imply greatly reduced interest payments which, according to the OECD, in both 1989 and 1990 averaged US$1 billion (100000 million) a month for the miserably poor countries of sub-Saharan Africa. This figure may seem barely credible but it is based on the creditors' reporting systems; it tells us what they themselves declare they have received.[2]

Greatly reduced interest payments would, in turn, mean far less pressure to stress exports. Without debt and the structural adjustment programmes it entails, without the need to invest so heavily in the export sector, Africa could put its resources into building infrastructure; into feeding, educating and caring for its own populations. Such choices would, however, serve only Africans and, even more serious, would violate the doctrine of maximum integration into the world economy.

Sub-Saharan Africa's debt more than doubled between 1982 and 1990, when it reached US$164 billion. In a world where five times that sum can easily be lost on Wall Street in an afternoon without undue stress, where total Third World debt stands at $1,450 billion (nearly nine times as much as sub-Saharan Africa's), it may seem particularly sadistic to have maintained such a burden whose repayment the creditors could easily do without.

One hears Auden's words:

'Every farthing of the cost all the dreaded cards foretell
Shall be paid...'

No one can count the real cost Africans have paid so that, from 1982 through 1990, over US$100 billion could be remitted to their governments' creditors, not least to the World Bank. Did these creditors even register this crystallised sweat and tears as anything more than a blip on their computer screens?

This Transnational Institute (TNI) study examines the consequences of the World Bank's assumption that the more a country can be integrated into the world economy, the better off it will be. TNI Fellows have, over the years and in a variety of research projects, publications, films etc., developed an ongoing general critique of structural adjustment. This is not, however, the goal of this book. More modestly, perhaps, but definitively, the TNI research team proves here that, at least where Africa is concerned, one of the Bank's 'legs' has a serious case of gangrene and should be amputated forthwith.

We set out to explore the export-led growth strategy for Africa, to assess its track record and its effects, and have kept precisely to this focus. This book has a clearly defined, single target; it has no pretensions to being a general treatise on Africa nor on the current phase of Third World 'development'. One consequence of this choice is that, although it is impossible to write about Africa without some reference to the history of colonialism which has shaped present political structures and economic patterns, we nowhere present – even in outline – a systematic economic history of Africa. Any assessment of Africa's predicament, however, and even more so any effort to define ways out of it, must acknowledge the weight of history. Africa has been used as a source of cheap labour during the centuries of the slave trade and, in the past century, as a source of cheap raw materials. The World Bank's economic strategy for Africa fits this latter tradition, emphasising the export of primary commodities such as agricultural products and minerals.

The consequences of the Bank's policy prescriptions have left Africans as impoverished and disempowered as they were by the wave of colonial landgrabbing in the 1880s. Formal independence and aid, however, did to some degree provide a framework which gave the newly independent governments room for manoeuvre and some possibility of generating greater prosperity. Many if not most African leaders squandered this opportunity, but in any case this framework was demolished in the 1980s by the World Bank and the IMF. The debt burden forced African governments to turn to multilateral financial agencies, who would only make new loans or delay repayment of old ones if their economic prescriptions were followed. African governments cannot be exonerated from mismanaging their debts, but they were still defenceless faced with this financial onslaught. The export-led strategy Africans have been obliged to adopt quite simply has not worked, does not work, cannot work. Repeated reports emanating from Washington announcing light at the end of the export tunnel are either lies or illusions and in either case tragic for the countries and the peoples of sub-Saharan Africa.

Normally there should come a time, especially among Bank strategists who pride themselves on their grasp of economic 'science', when even they recognise that their dogged persistence is destined to go unrewarded. All the signs, for anyone willing to examine them impartially, point to failure. The Bank should be willing to reexamine its premises and admit their inadequacy. Instead of trying to fit the poorest of all continents to the Procrustean bed of its theories, it should be seeking genuine ways to help Africa out of its present predicament. This study supplies overwhelming evidence that new approaches are long overdue.

African countries, almost without exception, rely for their foreign exchange on run-of-the-mill commodities – and all too often on just one, two or three of them. These commodities are increasingly produced as well in Latin America and especially Asia. As the traders we quote in these pages explain, in no uncertain terms, these products are often obtainable there with less fuss and bother than in Africa. Prices for these commodities are dire and show no signs of recovery. The 'market' – in the sense of the level playing field or even of the control over any aspect of the earnings from one's own production – is non-existent.

In spite of its efforts, sub-Saharan Africa's trade amounts to less than 2 per cent of total world trade. So long as it is forced to concentrate on 'tradeables' to the detriment of the 'non-tradeables' which alone can cater to people's basic needs – poverty will be compounded.

TNI is immensely grateful to the DDA (the Swiss Development Cooperation Authority) and to ISCOS (the Third World cooperation arm of the Italian trade union, CISL) for generously providing the necessary funds for this enquiry – but our budget, by any standards, was not lavish. TNI is furthermore proud and pleased to contribute this work which we believe will be important to the debate on export-led growth, a debate which should – indeed must – take place. Still, we wonder why TNI should have had to do this work *at all*.

Could not the World Bank, which according to its Annual Report in 1991 had a net income of US$1.2 billion, have devoted some of its resources and its handpicked staff to an examination of export-led growth in sub-Saharan Africa? Could it not have questioned at least partially the success of its prescriptions? Or, if the Bank's attention was otherwise engaged, could not the UN-appointed and well-staffed 'Fraser Expert Group', also charged with examining the future of African exports, have done so? We find it hard to believe that both the Bank and the Fraser Expert Group were somehow unable to obtain the necessary research materials. Had they obtained them, as TNI's team did, we find it hard to believe they would not have been obliged to reach exactly the same conclusions we have reached here. The problem is neither money nor staff. It would seem, rather, to be one of refusal on ideological grounds to confront reality.

The Bank has a ready answer to its critics. The doctrine, it claims, is correct, the principles are inviolable, but the application is faulty. Consequently, export-led growth must be pursued with renewed vigour. There is no alternative.

Before we begin working on alternatives in the next phase of the study, TNI challenges the World Bank's experts to read the following pages and to challenge, if it can, our conclusions, not by simply repeating its doctrines but by marshalling evidence of similar scope and quality. Although our means are puny compared to the Bank's, we have, so to speak, covered the waterfront, not to mention the commodity traders' wharves. The next battle will be to force the Bank and the other structural adjusters who follow its lead to take these conclusions seriously.

This will be a formidable task because we are not dealing with rational argument, dressed though it may be in technical language, but with dogma. If, however, present strategies remain unchallenged, if the Bank persists in its present practice, if it remains deaf not only to its critics but to Africa's suffering, we will know for sure that the continent is in for a painful, forced march into the twenty-first century.

Susan George
August 1992

Notes

1. Among these, Susan George, *A Fate Worse than Debt* (Penguin Books, 1988) and Susan George, *The Debt Boomerang* (London: Pluto Press/Transnational Institute, 1992); Debt Crisis Network Team, *A Journey through the Global Debt Crisis* (Labor Institute, United Methodist Church, Institute for Policy Studies, Washington, New York, 1988).
2. See OECD, *Financing and External Debt of Developing Countries*, 1989 and 1990 Surveys, Paris OECD. 1990, 1991 Tables V.12 'Total Debt Service of Sub-Saharan Africa ...'

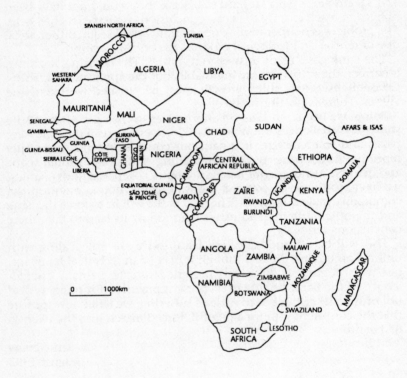

SPANISH NORTH AFRICA

TUNISIA

MOROCCO

ALGERIA

LIBYA

EGYPT

WESTERN
SAHARA

MAURITANIA

MALI

NIGER

CHAD

SUDAN

AFARS & ISAS

SENEGAL

GAMBIA

GUINEA

GUINEA-BISSAU

SIERRA LEONE

LIBERIA

CÔTE
D'IVOIRE

GHANA

TOGO

BENIN

BURKINA
FASO

NIGERIA

CAMEROON

CENTRAL
AFRICAN REPUBLIC

ETHIOPIA

SOMALIA

EQUATORIAL GUINEA

SÃO TOMÉ
& PRÍNCIPE

GABON

CONGO REP.

ZAÏRE

RWANDA

BURUNDI

UGANDA

KENYA

TANZANIA

ANGOLA

ZAMBIA

MALAWI

MOZAMBIQUE

MADAGASCAR

NAMIBIA

ZIMBABWE

BOTSWANA

SWAZILAND

SOUTH
AFRICA

LESOTHO

0   1000km

1. Africa in Crisis

Africa is in crisis and its future depends on the answers to life and death questions – on famine, food aid, the price of oil, irreversible environmental damage, the impact of the AIDS virus, arms sales, democracy. But one further question in particular stands out. Sub-Saharan Africa's total debt is US$175 billion[1] and therefore its dependency on the international financial institutions is unusually strong. The terms on which finance for long-term economic development is provided is the most explosive issue of all. Hope for Africa and Africans depends on this.

The international financial institutions – and especially the International Monetary Fund (IMF) and the World Bank – have told African governments there is only one course to follow: they must build their future on the exploitation for export of the rich mineral and agricultural resources of the continent, a practice begun under colonial rule. Any deviations from this growth path will halt progress. It is acknowledged that the path will be hard and involve suffering, but Africans are assured there is no choice.

This book shows that this path is also a dead end but it espouses no particular alternative. This book merely takes a hard look at Africa's crisis and at the path it is being forced to take. This approach should not lead to despair, but to a much more realistic assessment of what can be done. The core is based on original studies of markets and future prospects for the minerals and agricultural products on which Africa's income presently depends. The book brings together in a single volume information on the prospects for African countries and their strategic commodities. The evidence seriously calls into question the foundations of the policies prescribed for Africa during the 1980s. Africa's economic crisis is, of course, compounded by worsening social conditions, not least the spread of the AIDS virus. However, these aspects are touched on only tangentially. We have limited the focus of the study to sub-Saharan Africa, excluding the Republic of South Africa and North Africa. The book nevertheless reveals one of the underlying causes of the high degree of conflict, up to and including full-scale wars across the continent.

1

Falling Living Standards

The available statistical evidence reveals that living standards in sub-Saharan Africa fell in the 1980s after three decades of modest improvement. Reliable statistics are hard to come by. There are problems in all statistics. They can give a slanted view of reality because even the best statistics hide a host of assumptions which guided the way they were collected and what was counted. These difficulties are worsened in Africa both because much rural production is in the form of subsistence farming and because there is a general lack of sophisticated means for collecting and dealing with basic data.

Table 1.1: *Per Capita* Income in Developed Market-Economy Countries and Developing Countries 1970–88 (in US$ p.a.)

Region	1980 level	1970–80 gain or loss	1988 level	1980–8 gain or loss
Developed countries	10 183	2037	14 124	1904
Developing countries	937	232	1161	-8
of which				
Latin America	2245	561	2617	-189
North Africa	1259	133	1251	-141
Other Africa (including Nigeria)	549	52	505	-96
(excluding Nigeria)	394	-3	360	-25
West Asia (Middle East)	2893	712	2901	-704
South Asia (Indian subcontinent)	232	24	331	75
East Asia	919	388	1658	351

Notes: (1) the figures for *per capita* income are aggregated measures of national GDP of all the countries comprising each region, divided by the total population in each. They inevitably average out what are wide differences in *per capita* incomes among the several countries (see Annexe Table A1); (2) the Middle East and Nigerian losses in the period 1980–8 were a result of falling oil prices which subsequently improved. Source: UNCTAD secretariat calculations, UNCTAD *Trade and Development Report 1990*

Dr Alexander Yeats, a World Bank economist, has challenged World Bank statistics in the following terms: 'Official data appear to be of no utility for determining the level, direction, composition or trends in African trade.'[2] This does not mean that statistics are useless – simply that they should be treated with care. For example, when long-term trends are measured using a methodology and definitions which are consistent over the years, valid conclusions may be drawn. In a 1988 report, the World Bank said that despite 'very important elements of progress, Africa as a whole is poorer today in *per capita* income than it was 30 years ago ... even allowing for statistical and data problems ...'.[3] Four of the five larger African countries,

Nigeria, Ethiopia, Zaïre, Tanzania and Kenya, with adequate statistical services, show what is euphemistically called 'negative growth' over the last decade.

National income figures for the rest of sub-Saharan Africa are unreliable. There are 56 nation states (excluding Eritrea and the Sahrawis) in Africa. The UN defines all but one, South Africa, as 'developing'. Forty-nine are in sub-Saharan Africa. Twenty-eight are in the sub-category of Least Developed Countries (LDCs), because of their low *per capita* income (that is, total income divided by total population), low literacy rates and low contribution of manufacturing industries to their Gross National Product (GNP). Of the 43 LDCs worldwide, 28 are in Africa.

Population growth exerts its own pressure on *per capita* income rates. And while exact figures for population growth in any African country may be unreliable, World Bank technical experts conclude that the sub-Saharan population doubled over the last 25 years and will double again in the next 25 (a growth rate of 3 per cent a year).[4]

World Bank statistics show that:

- Gross Domestic Product (GDP) per head declined in 21 African countries between 1970 and 1989;
- economic growth rates rose by less than 1 per cent in six countries;
- overall GDP actually declined in nine countries between 1980 and 1987;
- there is evidence of a slight recovery after 1987 but only for the oil-producing countries.[5]

United Nations Conference on Trade and Development (UNCTAD) statistics show (Annexe Table A1)[6]:

- among LDCs *per capita* income in 1988 ranged from US$1654 a year in Botswana (on a par with Turkey) to $121 a year in Ethiopia;
- the average *per capita* income in LDCs is $340 a year;
- for all sub-Saharan African developing countries the average is $430.

Prices in world markets for African products have been falling sharply since 1950, with only an exceptional blip for oil and most minerals in the early 1970s. The downward trend is particularly pronounced when falling prices of Africa's exports – mainly of primary commodities – are compared with rising prices for Africa's imports – mainly manufactures. Africa's terms of trade have deteriorated sharply since the late 1970s as Chart 1.1 shows.

Chart 1.1: Export Prices and Terms of Trade

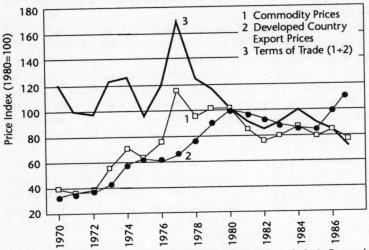

Source: H.L.M Kox, *Export Constraints for Sub-Saharan Growth*, Serie Research Memoranda, Free University of Amsterdam: Statistics for 17 Main Sub-Saharan Non-fuel Commodities, 1971–87

World Bank reports repeatedly shy away from such an obvious explanation of Africa's economic decline. Instead the Bank argues that with such 'external factors (commodity prices, resource flows, interest rates, debt burden etc.) ... econometric analysis generally gives inconclusive results because many of these factors move at the same time.'[7]

This quote comes from a report in which, just two pages earlier, the figures show that between 1970 and 1985 deteriorating terms of trade reduced the total income of sub-Saharan Africa. Taken as a whole (but excluding oil-exporting Nigeria), only 8 out of 34 countries (Gabon, Liberia, Mauritania, Mauritius, Niger, Rwanda, Somalia and Togo) avoided this general trend in incomes (cf. Annexe Table A1).

Debt, Drought and War

Reliable figures exist for the flows of funds into and out of Africa, on loans and investment, and interest and dividends paid on them. The net inward movement of funds ended in the 1980s and a clear outward flow began,[8] much as interest payments on debt. The outward flow was temporarily checked at the end of the 1980s by measures to defer and reschedule debt repayment. But the size of sub-Saharan African debt on the books of Northern industrialised countries' governments and banks rose from US$18 billion in 1976 to $175 billion in 1991. And repayments did not stop. World Bank figures show that debt service payments more than doubled between 1979 and 1987, almost trebling the percentage of export earnings devoted to servicing (that is, paying the interest or repaying capital on) the debt. (Annexe Table A2 shows debts by country.)

Prospects for the 1990s are similarly bleak, unless debt is written off. The UNCTAD *Trade and Development Report* for 1990 envisaged only a small decline in the deficit on the current foreign accounts of all African countries, from the equivalent of 29 per cent to 19 per cent of annual exports, as interest payments were predicted to fall from 17 per cent to 9 per cent of exports. The overall outstanding debt will still be double the annual value of exports. This book is primarily concerned with the prospects for Africa's commodity exports, but it is important to note here that the largest share of African countries' deficit on external account is not caused by the balance on imports and exports of goods at all, but by the balance on services. Table 1.2 shows that the overall deficit is mainly the result of deficits on investment income payments, government borrowing and other debt servicing.

Table 1.2: Africa's External Payments, 1970 and 1989 (all figures in US$ billions)

Items	All developing Africa		Sub-Saharan Africa	
	1970	1989	1970	1989
Export of goods (fob)	+12.9	+62.2	+7.7	+34.6
Import of goods (fob)	-10.8	-68.5	-6.7	-32.4
Balance on goods (fob)	+2.0	-6.3	+1.0	+2.2
Export of services	+2.5	+19.2	+1.7	+7.2
Import of services	-5.8	-38.9	-3.5	-21.8
Balance on services	-3.4	-19.7	-1.8	-14.6
Balance on specific services:				
Transport	-0.9	-6.5	*	*
Travel	-0.1	+4.8		
Other (official)	-0.2	-1.3		
Other (mainly investment income)	-0.5	-3.4		
Non-factor services (debt)	-1.7	-10.1		

Notes: * 1989 figures are not available in the same form for sub-Saharan Africa; fob = free on board (port of origin)
Sources: *UN Monthly Bulletin of Statistics* (May 1990); *UNCTAD Statistical Pocketbook*, Table 2.6 (1989); UNCTAD *Handbook of International Trade and Development Statistics*, *Table 5.1* (1990)

There are also reliable statistics for Africa's rainfall. The documented reduction in rainfall amounts to a significant climatological change. Changing climate has affected the economic situation not only of the Sahel, the region immediately south and east of the Sahara Desert, but of nearly every African country. Rainfall in the Sahel has been below the 1900 to 1960 average for 15 years (Annexe Chart A3). The scale of drought in 1983–5 was unprecedented. The water level in great rivers like the Nile and the Niger dropped to the lowest ever recorded. Thirty million people in 24 countries became dependent on food aid. Millions were forced to leave their homes in search of food. By 1984 more than 80 per cent of Africa's dry lands, with a population of 92 million, were defined as at least 'moderately desertified'. Nomadic peoples have almost ceased to exist. The drought spread into southern and eastern Africa, to Zimbabwe, Botswana and Mozambique. And when the rains came they came in such torrents that floods followed drought. In 1990, after three years of near average rains, the drought returned with the repeated threat of widespread famine. Continuing drought kills trees and the top soil is blown away. The Sahara moves inexorably southward. Wars have erupted in many places as government breaks down and once-peaceful peoples must fight for food.[9]

After reviewing the many-sided nature of Africa's economic decline, the 1988 World Bank technical report comments:

Perhaps the most worrying aspect of the pervasive general decline is the decay of Africa's institutional capacity. Once solid institutions such as well-functioning and efficient bureaucracies, impartial judiciaries, enlightened educational institutions and seats of learning, are now shadows of their former selves.[10]

The report considers that state and para-statal salaries in Africa are high compared with those in other developing countries; a large and widening gap has opened between the formal sector and the much larger informal economy as the absence of a middle layer between the elite and the rest of society leads to widespread graft and fraud.

Equally worrying, is the general political decay in much of Africa. Increasingly, corruption, oppression and nepotism are dominant themes among Africans with regard to the political situation in many African countries. Factors behind this phenomenon need careful assessment.[11]

The Bank's view is that the reason for endemic corruption and widespread repression is that 'the economic ideas that guided development ... put an excessive amount of power in the hands of the government.'[12]

We do not regard this as the whole story. Certainly, African governments have been characterised by the ills which the Bank identifies. Some regimes have been extraordinarily brutal. Some have regarded their dominance of the country simply as the occasion for an extended pillaging of its wealth. They have routinely used torture and massacre to stay in power and, when ejected, their successors have not often been much more respectful of human rights, democratic values or social justice. But Africa's political disaster has to be understood in context. The first element of the context is the brutalisation to which Africa has been subjected from outside since the beginning of the age of colonialism. The second is the artificial nature of the state structure which colonialism first imposed on Africa and then bequeathed to its new rulers; the boundaries drawn by white colonial rulers were for imperial convenience. The attempt to construct nation states within these borders was always destined to cut across the loyalties of tribe and kinship which are both much deeper and more immediate than national loyalties. Thirdly, exploration of Africa first by the colonists and later by the large transnational corporations has been accompanied by corruption; this is the way they operate, the way they find and reward local allies and suborn those who might be inconveniently antagonistic to a new mining concession, a timber contract and so on. To think of bribery in Africa as uniquely or even especially African is simply to forget the tools of the colonial powers and the transnational corporations' trade.

Government by military regimes has been one outcome of economic failure. Most African governments rely on the support of minority ethnic and economic social groups. Few have the possibility, even where the will exists, to deliver either economically or politically to the mass of their populations. The growing violence and instability make the prospects for future recovery much more tenuous. A listing of the main centres of violence and war in Africa gives a fuller perspective for the economic analysis we present. In late 1991 and the first half of 1992 wars were being fought in:

- Ethiopia (although the main conflicts in the multiple civil wars were over);
- Somalia (where rebel forces who overthrew Barre early in 1991 had fallen to fighting among themselves);

- Mozambique (where the Renamo guerrillas originally set up by Ian Smith's Rhodesian government and long funded by the South African apartheid regime continue to attack and terrorise peasants despite peace talks);
- Liberia (where the war spilled over into neighbouring Sierra Leone as the rival insurgents fought for power after their joint overthrow of Doe);
- Mali (where running clashes between the military and civilian demonstrators merged into a confused but violent war, with the government challenged not only by political insurrection but also by widespread banditry);
- Chad (where fighting continued in the latest round of sequential civil wars that have previously often led to armed intervention on opposite sides by French and Libyan forces);
- Uganda (where two decades of warfare continued albeit at a lower level of violence than in former years, as government forces attempted to destroy guerrilla forces in the north of the country);
- Sudan (where the government continued to use famine as a weapon to destroy the southern uprising);
- Burundi (where the minority Tutsi government faces armed insurrection from the majority Hutu) and neighbouring Rwanda (where the Tutsi insurrection against the Hutu government began in October 1990).

War ended in Angola in 1991. There was a ceasefire in Morocco's long war of conquest in Western Sahara in late 1991. In early 1991 economic pressure and ethnic rivalry resulted in bloody clashes and mass displacement of peoples living along the river Senegal valley between Senegal and Mauritania.

Newly intense opposition to dictatorship also led to violent upheavals in 1990–2 in Benin, Burkina Faso, Cameroon, Côte d'Ivoire, Gabon, Ghana, Guinea-Bissau, Kenya, Malawi, Niger, Nigeria, Senegal, Togo and Zaïre – and in Zambia it led to elections in which Kenneth Kaunda was ousted from the premiership.

Although small relative to industrialised nations' military budgets, and even in real terms, the resources spent by African governments on armaments and military strategies appear a fatal diversion of resources away from meeting basic human needs.[13] Moreover, these wars have been provoked and perpetuated by industrialised powers through their direct military support for their political allies. The impact of the Gulf War alone on African economies has been estimated at around 2 per cent of national incomes.[14]

A decline in social expenditure and in quality of life shows clearly from the statistics on infant mortality, life expectancy, numbers of doctors and teachers and proportion of children in full-time education. This contrasts strongly with the advances of the 1960s and 1970s. Between 1970 and 1983 average life expectancy in nine sub-Saharan African countries fell.[15]

The spread of HIV is the final element in the crisis in Africa. World Health Organisation experts estimate that within a decade 25 per cent of the young men of Africa are likely to be infected with the virus.[16] Even were a cure to be discovered before the end of the century, it is unlikely to reverse the death rate which this figure implies. This disaster is on the same scale as the loss of young men from Africa during the two centuries of the Atlantic slave trade.

This profound and multi-faceted crisis demands an honest and thorough examination not just of its causes but of the economic policies which are currently being promoted in Africa to overcome it. For if they cannot work, the crisis can only worsen.

2. The Official Response

Africa has never been short of advice and pressure from outside to go with the loans, grants and other aid for development programmes. For the last ten years African governments have had to accept structural adjustment as a condition for financial support, debt rescheduling or relief from the World Bank, the IMF and other donors. Structural adjustment programmes aim to increase the role of exports in the economy and stimulate the private sector through a combination of wage and price stabilisation policies and austerity measures. A typical IMF/World Bank adjustment package includes at least the following:

- *Currency devaluation* to improve the balance of payments by raising the cost of imported goods and making exports more competitive.
- *Domestic demand management* to cut back government budgets, especially for social expenditure and for subsidies.
- *Freeing of prices* to remove the distortions resulting from subsidies on food, fertiliser and other essentials and from import taxes on luxury items, and to provide an incentive for exports where prices are set in the world market.
- *High interest rates and credit squeeze* to reduce inflationary pressures.
- *Import liberalisation* to open local industry to competition from more industrially developed countries and encourage an expansion of foreign trade exchanges.
- *Privatisation of state and para-statal enterprises* to reduce government protection of inefficient economic activities.

Each of these economic instruments has problems, some more than others:

- *Currency devaluation* increases prices for imported food and hits those who depend on it, mainly the urban poor, while increased prices of imported equipment raise production costs. Devaluation can lead to inflation, but reduces imports of food in competition with local farm production. Devaluation increases commodity exports, unless other producing countries do the same, as they are also under pressure from the World Bank to do.

- *Domestic demand management* reduces public funds available for development, for the local financial component of joint development projects and infrastructure improvements. Incentives through tax concessions for exports are not affected. The impact of *freeing prices* may be nullified if all countries follow suit and world prices are generally falling.
- *High interest rates and a credit squeeze* tend to result in bankruptcies, especially of small local businesses, and may push up costs all round.
- *Import liberalisation* increases dependence on foreign suppliers.
- *Privatisation of state and para-statal enterprises* may not distinguish between fledgling, but strategically important enterprises which add value to raw materials, and the merely inefficient. Local businesses, especially those in export markets, become prone to foreign takeover.

Structural Adjustment Programmes

The central claim of the World Bank is that the countries which have adopted adjustment programmes have fared better than those which have not, and that the longer and more diligently they have 'adjusted' the better the result. The World Bank issued a relatively optimistic updated version of its 1988 report, which in the period 1981–4 shows lower rates of growth in the countries with adjustment programmes than those without, but higher rates from 1985–8.[1] The Bank claims that structural adjustment programmes are working, that corrective operations are on target, notwithstanding external shocks. By taking the medicine a little longer the patient will be cured.

This view provoked outrage among African leaders facing the task and the consequences of introducing structural adjustment programmes. In 1989 they retaliated via the United Nations Economic Commission for Africa (UNECA) with a sharp counter-offensive denying these Bank claims in two UNECA papers, *Statistics and Policies: ECA Preliminary Observations on the World Bank Report, Africa's Adjustment and Growth in the 1980s*,[2] followed by *African Alternative to Structural Adjustment Programmes (AA-SAP): A Framework for Transformation and Recovery*.[3]

Arguments about the failures of structural adjustment programmes have come not only from African leaders and UNECA, but also from the United Nations Conference on Trade and Development (UNCTAD), the United Nations Children's Emergency Fund (UNICEF), the Food and Agricultural Organisation (FAO) and the United Nations

Education and Scientific body (UNESCO) under a coalition called the UN Programme of Action for African Economic Recovery (UNPAAERD). And an IMF study concluded that between 1973 and 1988 'the growth rate is significantly reduced in IMF programme countries relative to the change in non-programme countries.'[4] Eighteen out of 25 countries with adjustment programmes also had IMF programmes.

An independent study by Paul Mosley of pairs of countries in similar conditions, one adjusting and the other not, concluded:

> Despite having a stronger growth record in the latter half of the 1970s, and despite receiving programme aid, the SAL (Structural Adjustment Loan) group of countries have performed significantly worse than their non-SAL counterparts, in terms of the GDP growth criteria during the 1980s ... In addition, for those SAL countries in which compliance ... was high, the performance of GDP ... was even more unfavourable than in the relevant control group.[5]

The forces at the disposal of the World Bank for 'demonstrating' and arguing their case should not be underestimated, however. A vast documentation underpins the five-volume United Nations Development Programme (UNDP)/World Bank Report of 1989.[6] Large numbers of World Bank staff, plus hundreds of African researchers, development specialists, private businessmen and public officials, as well as academics and representatives from OECD countries, were enlisted to prepare the Report. In response to earlier criticisms of neglect of the social dimensions in World Bank and IMF programmes of structural adjustment in Africa, the World Bank ran a large multidisciplinary research project devoted to these gaps in its earlier work.

One can only wish there were a direct link between the weight of official papers and the resolution of Africa's crisis, given the steady barrage of World Bank publications: starting with the Berg Report (1981),[7] long sections on Africa in Annual Reports, *Adjustment Lending* (1988),[8] *Beyond Adjustment* (1988),[9] *Africa's Adjustment and Growth in the 1980s* published jointly with the UNDP (1989)[10] and finally, *Sub-Saharan Africa: From Crisis to Sustainable Growth* (1989).[11]

The arguments between the World Bank and the UNECA in part revolve around technical questions of methodology in computing economic progress and of defining which countries are strong rather than weak 'adjusters', but a real difference lies behind the two entrenched positions. The underlying difference in perceptions and expectations lies in the central assumption of the World Bank's recommendations. This is, that if all the appropriate structural adjustments are made, then African economies will be free to grow through the promotion of their traditional exports of primary products. This most fundamental difference lies at the heart of the analysis of Africa's export performance and possibilities.

Further support for the World Bank's analysis appears in the report by the UN Secretary General's Expert Group, chaired by Australia's former Prime Minister, Malcolm Fraser. This group was established immediately after the World Bank had made its joint report with UNDP in March 1989. Its task was to report on Africa's 'commodity problems' and the UNDP/World Bank's promise of sustainable development. The Expert Group's 1990 report, *Africa's Commodity Problems: Towards a Solution*, acknowledged the 'generous support' of the UNDP and 'the relevant UN agencies and international organisations, in particular the World Bank and the IMF'.[12] The Fraser Group too, told African countries, desperately in need of funds from the World Bank and the IMF, that they must cover their outstanding debts by increasing their commodity exports.

The World Bank report *Sub-Saharan Africa: From Crisis to Sustainable Growth* insists that Africa faces an internal not an external problem. Its view is that Africa must and can find its own resources for its development through external trade.

Declining export volumes, rather than declining export prices account for Africa's poor export revenues. Low income African countries have been worst hit, with substantial income losses in the 1970s and 1980s ...[13] If Africa's economies are to grow, they must earn foreign exchange to pay for essential imports. Thus it is vital that they increase their share of world markets. The prospects for most primary commodities are poor, so higher export earnings must come from increased output, diversification into new commodities and an aggressive export drive into the rapidly growing Asian markets.[14]

Although in the Bank's own reckoning, 'The prospects for most primary commodities are poor', the whole weight of its argument rests on the assumption that Africa's export markets will grow. Structural adjustment measures are all concerned with increasing the role of exports in the economy. They restrict government measures to encourage local processing of raw materials and to protect infant industries, and 'exports' are taken to be the traditional exports of the country concerned – predominantly primary products. The idea that exports are an engine of growth has a long and well-documented history. But we must seriously consider the question of whether and in what circumstances this policy could be repeated. For free trade does not necessarily lead to growth, much less prosperity; it may equally well lead to stagnation, depending on the wider economic context.

Export-led Growth

Successful export-led growth occurs when a country achieves a competitive advantage based upon higher labour productivity and success in concentrating exports on sectors with high rates of growth. At different times, Britain, the US, Germany, Italy, Japan and South Korea have all been able to use exports as the engine of growth.[15] Japan and Korea are instructive cases for Africa. In both cases free trade would have restricted the economy to the export of labour-intensive manufactures – toys, miscellaneous merchandise and low quality textiles. The Vice-President of the Japanese Ministry of Trade and Industry (MITI) explained over two decades ago,

> If the Japanese economy had adopted the simple doctrine of free trade and had chosen to specialise in this kind of industry, it would almost permanently have been unable to break away from the Asian pattern of stagnation and poverty ... The Ministry ... decided to establish in Japan industries which require intensive employment of capital and technology, industries that were from the standpoint of comparative cost most inappropriate for Japan, industries such as steel, oil refining, petrochemicals, automobiles, aircraft, industrial machinery of all sorts, and electronics including electronic computers ... where income elasticity of demand is high, technological progress is rapid, and labour productivity rises fast.[16]

Africa has a different but analogous choice from Japan's: not between labour-intensive manufacturing and advanced technology, but between labour-intensive primary production and the processing of primary products. However, the conditions required if exports are to lead to growth do not lend themselves to exports of primary commodities, namely: concentrating on commodities where technological progress is rapid, where the productivity of labour is rising quickly and which will be increasingly in demand as world income rises (in the jargon, where income elasticity of demand is high).

MITI, according to the World Bank's own reports, intervened with every means at its disposal to shift the Japanese economy towards new technologies: import restrictions, import substitution, selective nationalisation, strict control over access to foreign exchange, positive discrimination towards firms and industries capable of employing advanced technology. The Japanese wage system was designed to offer permanent employment at relatively low wages in proportion to value added, with a high rate of savings and a wide measure of equality; this created a steadily expanding home market but also an increasingly large margin for exports. From the 1960s Japanese exports grew continuously faster than industrial output. Which element led to growth? One simple test is the correlation of export prices and quantities. In the case of Japan, Germany and, earlier, Britain and the US, both the volume of exports and their prices increased over long periods, also rising in relation to the prices of imports.[17]

Korean Paradigm – a Model for Africa?

The most recent examples of successful export-led growth in developing countries are South Korea and Taiwan. Both have exhibited rapid rates of growth in the last three decades. In both countries economic development was indigenous, although much was learnt from the Japanese and some foreign markets were entered by 'piggybacking' – that is, entered via other foreign companies. The annual rate of growth of exports in the 1970s and 1980s was about three times the rate of growth of national income and twice that of manufacturing output.[18]

How was it done? Is there a lesson for Africa's economies? The answer is unexpected. When World Bank staff analysed the success of South Korea's economic development, they felt obliged to reexamine the basic paradigms of neo-classical economics together with its faith in the free working of the market.[19] These World Bank authors concluded their reexamination as follows with a quotation from Paul Streeten:

> [Korea] is used to proclaim export promotion as the key to equitable and rapid growth. And export promotion in turn is often identified with the absence of government intervention and the free play of market forces. But the reasons for the success of Korea are much more complex ... [Korea] promoted labour-intensive import substitution as well as exports; early import substitution led to later exports.[20]

They acknowledge that in the Korean model planners used the 'entire register of policy instruments that economists of a *dirigiste* persuasion had laboured to compile and there was no reluctance at all to intervene in pursuit of industrial, export and growth objectives'.

Korea, far from being a successful example of the logic and benefits of the free enterprise system, is an exemplary 'managed economy in the non-socialist sense of the term'.[21] Direct exposure to the market and economic liberalisation was not the motor of Korean economic advance. The Bank experts contend: 'that the pace of capital accumulation over two decades is a key to Korea's striking economic performance ... This investment was not the outcome of market signalling but to a large extent deliberately contrived by the government.'[22]

Korea's pursuit of export-led growth broke every single one of the commandments prescribed by the World Bank for African governments. For example, several types of selective export incentive operated in Korea between 1950 and 1975[23] (see Annexe Table A4). The Korean economy was not opened outright to free trade and unregulated market forces. The World Bank reports repeatedly explain that many Asian economies have suffered from the same difficulties in the terms of trade for their primary commodities as those in Africa. But, insofar as the Asian economies have overcome these problems, the African experts in the Bank appear to have ignored their colleagues on the East Asian desk and have not reviewed the implications for Africa.

It might be argued that the reason for Africa's economic plight is that Africans have neither the skills nor the experience which could be called on in East Asia. There is not much evidence to support this view and what there is adds up to a serious indictment of European colonial rule. For, whereas Imperial Japan in the first half of this century established processing and refining installations in the territories that were conquered, the Europeans (and especially the British) extracted the raw material in the colonies and processed it at home. Only where colonial settlers became self-governing was this policy modified – at the settlers' insistence.

The scarcity of processing in Africa – oil-refining in Nigeria, copper-smelting in Zambia, alumina production in Guinea, plywood and veneer manufacturing in Côte d'Ivoire, and the sugar factories, breweries and oil mills across the continent – suggest not a lack of technological capability *per se*, but a lack of market openings in Europe and North America for the output of more advanced stages of processing.

There are undoubtedly problems of quality control in African products, but the main issue is lack of investment. One obvious obstacle to progress is the boundaries inherited from the colonial age.

More than half the countries in sub-Saharan Africa have fewer than 5 million people; only six have populations of over 15 million. Like gravity, capital investment relates to mass – the size of the market, range of occupational skills and potential scale of production. The LDCs of sub-Saharan Africa are not only small, but 15 are landlocked and seven are tiny island states. All these 22 are far from a major international port. Yet such countries are being encouraged to embark upon export-led growth!

As well as the problems on the supply side, there are even more overwhelming difficulties on the demand side. Does the world need or want more of Africa's traditional exports? In our reports on demand for Africa's products compiled for this book, we examine each of the main commodities in turn to answer that question. Our examination of one commodity after another reveals the signal weakness of African producers in world markets. Should African countries then withdraw altogether from international trade, cultivate their lands and extract their resources directly to meet their own needs? We think not. Foreign trade is necessary for economic development – no country has ever achieved an improvement in the living standards of its people in total isolation from the rest of the world – but the current structure and terms of trade must be altered to ensure that Africans obtain a larger share in the value of what they produce. Without access to better technology, African development can only stagnate. It is not production for export *per se* that is mistaken but the framework in which production now takes place. It is the conditions of trade which are harmful, not trade itself.

In a bleak comment on the prospects for some 17 African countries in the 1990s, a World Bank official, Mr Kim Jaycox, has concluded that:

> the financial crisis is so deep, the debt burden so heavy that they will not make it. [In these countries the structural adjustment programmes] will not, in fact, work unless there is an increase in the flow of resources from outside. Even on conservative estimates of resource requirements and optimistic estimates of resource availability, a financing gap of at least one billion US dollars remains.[24]

If agricultural commodity prices were to recover to the average levels of 1980–4, it is possible that this gap could be met, but the chance of this happening appears to be slight, as we shall show.

No good can come from attempts to cut Africa off from the rest of the world. African countries need many of the products of the outside world for their economic development, and have much to offer in exchange. The most advanced economies, which have raised not only their industrial productivity but the living standards of their peoples, are those which are most integrated with others in the exchange of goods and services. Autarky is no solution.

3. Africa's Resources

The World Bank's prescription for Africa's crisis is export-led growth based on expanding primary commodity exports. The package of economic reforms to achieve this consists of liberalising imports, freeing exchange rates, reducing subsidies, privatising para-statals, deep cuts in public expenditure and moderating government intervention. These reforms have been and are being implemented swiftly and simultaneously. By contrast, the key elements in South Korea's success were the government's highly interventionist policies of economic management and the careful timing of each step in moving from a closed to an open economy. There was no sudden liberalisation of the South Korean economy. Structural adjustment took place over 30 years. Selective controls on imports were changed as imported goods were replaced from home production. Infant industries were protected until they could stand on their own feet. Export monopolies and subsidised exports were removed and the link between import entitlement and export performance relaxed only as the competitiveness of Korean industry was established. At the same time, food production at home was encouraged by land reform and by high prices protecting farmers from cheap imports. Many controls were still in place in the late 1970s.

Although the objective was the same, and Korea was an open economy by the mid-1980s, the strategy could hardly have been more different from that proposed by the World Bank for sub-Saharan Africa. It is worth considering whether this very different strategy is justified by inherent differences between the two regions.

How then does Africa differ from the Asian 'dragons'? In terms of resources, the two regions contrast sharply. Africa is rich in resources and East Asia has little – rice and soya and fish, some hard coal, gold, silver, lead, zinc, manganese, and tungsten in South Korea. Except for the tungsten, no resources are of major importance in the world economy.[1] Table 3.1 shows that, in contrast, sub-Saharan Africa had 19 non-fuel primary commodities with export values of at least US$100m in 1987, nine of which amounted to more than 10 per cent of total world exports. Africa, in short, is incomparably richer in natural resources.

Table 3.1: Sub-Saharan Africa's Commodity Exports

Commodity	Value (US$m)	Share of World Market (%) 1985–7	1987 price as % of 1982 price
Fuel oil	12 800	14.5	52
Agriculture – Food			
Beverages & tobacco	6754	–	–
of which Coffee	2581	20	93
Cocoa beans	1854	59	115
Fish products	725	4	109
Sugar	580	5	80
Live animals & meat	563	1.5	64 (1)
Tobacco	437	5	86
Tea	336	10	88
Groundnuts & oil	115	21	57
Agriculture – non-food	2113	–	–
of which Timber	670	6	147
Cotton	643	6	121
Hides & skins	190	3	n.a.
Rubber	173	5.5	121
Minerals	3642	–	–
of which Diamonds	1600	40	n.a.
Copper (refined)	983	13	120
Iron ore	380	4	35
Al (2) (primary)	339	2	156
Gold (3)	210	20	118
Phosphates	170	12	78
Manganese	142	35	na

Notes: (1) Earnings not price
(2) Al = Aluminium
(3) Zimbabwe only
Source: UNCTAD, *Commodity Yearbook 1989* and Fraser Report, *Africa's Commodity Problems*, United Nations, 1990, Table 5.

Africa has a larger population: 540 million people – 414 million south of the Sahara – against 175 million in Japan and the Asian dragons. But Africa cannot be thought of as a single entity or even as a single market. There are no established free trade areas; and the various geographical and political groupings (see Annexe Table A1) – the Maghreb in the north, francophone Africa, the UDEAC in the centre and CEAO in the west, the CEPGL around the Great Lakes and the SADCC in the south – have limited economic significance. Africa has in reality 50 separate governments and 50 separate markets. In sub-Saharan Africa only Nigeria and Ethiopia have populations equal to South Korea and only Sudan, Kenya, Tanzania and Zaïre have populations larger than Taiwan. The populations of Ghana, Mozambique and Uganda are roughly equal to that of Taiwan, that is, 16 million. Individually, few African countries have a wider range of resources than South Korea.

Concentration of Africa's Resources

What then is special about Africa's resources? Historically, African territories have been developed for the sake of exploiting a few resources in each, often only one or two mining or agricultural products. Primary commodities account for a large proportion of Africa's total exports, in stark contrast with the cases of South and South-East Asia. For 45 out of 51 African countries (88 per cent of them) primary commodities make up more than half of their total exports. Only eight out of 19 South and South-East Asian countries (42 per cent) show a similar ratio. African countries are highly dependent on a few major exports (taken as more than 10 per cent of the total for any country) as Chart 3.1 shows. The general picture is of a handful of primary products dominating export trade. It is not just the small countries that have high export concentrations. Apart from four of the oil states (Nigeria, Congo, Algeria and Libya), four other countries (Burundi, Guinea, Uganda and Zambia) depend on one commodity for 90 per cent or more of their exports. Export concentration ratios for Africa are much higher than for other economic regions, twice that of other countries which are relatively dependent on agricultural exports like Australia, New Zealand, Denmark or Ireland, or the non-oil producing countries of Asia.[2] There were big fluctuations in the degree of dependency and earnings during the 1970s and 1980s; these ebbs and flows are analysed in later chapters dealing with commodities case-by-case.

Has export concentration been an advantage or a disadvantage? With the exception of the oil states, whose export concentrations are higher as are their *per capita* incomes (except for Nigeria), there appears to be no correlation between the degree of export concentration and the level of income per head.[3] But dependency on only a few primary commodities does open any country to the threat of falling demand for these products. The case of the oil states suggests that it is the demand for the commodity rather than the concentration on its production that matters.

The large share of primary commodity production in national incomes also has a bearing on appropriateness of export-led growth prescriptions for Africa (see Annexe Table A6). Whereas Japan, South Korea and Taiwan all embarked upon the development process with

Chart 3.1: African Exports Concentration Ratios, 1982–6: Countries where 1,2,3 or 4 Products Account for over 75% of Export Earnings

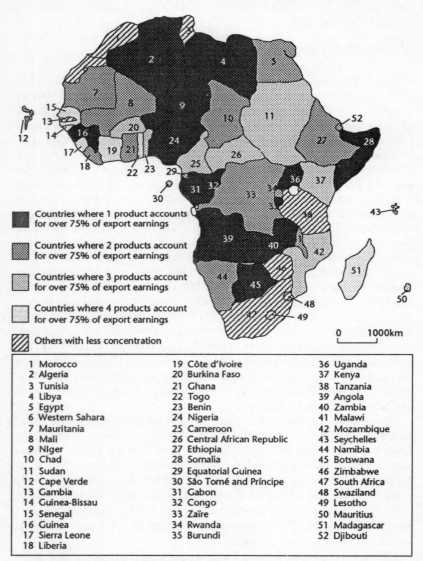

Countries where 1 product accounts for over 75% of export earnings

Countries where 2 products account for over 75% of export earnings

Countries where 3 products account for over 75% of export earnings

Countries where 4 products account for over 75% of export earnings

Others with less concentration

0   1000km

1 Morocco	19 Côte d'Ivoire	36 Uganda
2 Algeria	20 Burkina Faso	37 Kenya
3 Tunisia	21 Ghana	38 Tanzania
4 Libya	22 Togo	39 Angola
5 Egypt	23 Benin	40 Zambia
6 Western Sahara	24 Nigeria	41 Malawi
7 Mauritania	25 Cameroon	42 Mozambique
8 Mali	26 Central African Republic	43 Seychelles
9 Niger	27 Ethiopia	44 Namibia
10 Chad	28 Somalia	45 Botswana
11 Sudan	29 Equatorial Guinea	46 Zimbabwe
12 Cape Verde	30 São Tomé and Príncipe	47 South Africa
13 Gambia	31 Gabon	48 Swaziland
14 Guinea-Bissau	32 Congo	49 Lesotho
15 Senegal	33 Zaïre	50 Mauritius
16 Guinea	34 Rwanda	51 Madagascar
17 Sierra Leone	35 Burundi	52 Djibouti
18 Liberia		

Note: In Cape Verde and the Seychelles 2 products account for over 75% of export earnings. Details of which commodities each country exports are shown in Annexe Table A9.

Source: UN, *Africa's Commodity Problems* 1990 (Fraser Report), Table 2, pp. 103–13; and IMF, *International Financial Statistics Yearbook, 1989.*

very limited external relations, the states of sub-Saharan Africa started with major trading connections. Countries whose exports already exceed one-third of the national income are being instructed by the World Bank to pursue export growth. Although one-third of Korea's GNP is today accounted for by exports, until the 1970s they accounted for only 10 per cent. Japan's exports in 1989 were still only 14 per cent of GNP.[4]

In Africa the picture is quite different. For example, total export earnings from primary commodities as a percentage of GNP in Gabon, Seychelles, Congo, Botswana and Mauritania are all at least 40 per cent. Generally, when a high proportion of national income comes from exports, *per capita* incomes are also high. But Mauritius, with primary commodity export earnings accounting for 36 per cent of GNP, has a *per capita* income more than triple that of Mauritania[5] (Annexe Table A6). Again, it seems that demand for the commodity is more significant in determining income levels. When a country's national income is highly export-dependent this will necessarily have implications for the allocation of resources between domestic consumption and exports, and for the distribution of consumption between domestic or imported products. Export-led growth implies import-intensive growth. Land use will be particularly affected since a country must decide how far cash crops for export should supplant farming for food. If food imports replace a large part of this food production, the local sales price of the imports is crucial for the survival of the remaining farmers.

Land under cultivation in sub-Saharan Africa increased between 1972 and 1989 by 9 per cent, but population increased by 60 per cent.[6] Fortunately, food production rose by 43 per cent. Even so, the drop in production per head was 10 per cent.[7] No major differences exist between the experience of North Africa, South Africa and sub-Saharan Africa (Annexe Table A7). The bad years of drought were widespread, as was the recovery in 1988. Nor was there, in this period, a significant difference between the rise in food and cereals production and the situation of agricultural production in general. Cash crops for export therefore do not seem to have been increased at the expense of food crops, at least not on a continent-wide basis.

Statistics must be used with care in order to track 'food security' because they may include under 'food production' food predominantly for export such as tropical fruits, coffee, tea and cocoa. Production statistics provided by the Food and Agriculture Organisation (FAO) give several sets of indices of growth in individual African countries, one for agricultural production as a whole, one for cereals and several for particular crops, livestock products etc.[8] Since cereals are mostly produced for domestic consumption in Africa, it is important to note what differences appear comparing these particular growth indices. In eleven sub-Saharan countries – Angola, Chad, Côte d'Ivoire, Ethiopia, Gabon, Kenya, Lesotho, Mozambique, Senegal, Somalia, Sudan – food production as a whole rose much faster than the production of cereals. In twice as many cases cereals production outstripped food production as a whole. In a further 20 there was little difference so that the evidence is inconclusive.

Foreign Trade Dependence

Overall, imports of food to Africa have increased since the late 1960s. UNCTAD figures for food imports and exports[9] show that the oil exporters increased their food imports fastest, and actually reduced their food exports (Annexe Table A8). By 1989, 14 food exporters, despite rapid growth in food imports, were still exporting double the level of food imports. In the remaining countries, food imports and exports roughly balanced in the 1980s. Such apparently reassuring trends do not reveal whether food, particularly imported food, is being sold at prices which are affordable to the populace as a whole, nor do they reveal the longer-term impact of structural adjustment on local agriculture and rural society.

What impact has liberalisation and the export-drive had in rural Africa? Much attention has focused on the diversion of land from the growing of staple foods to make way for export crops, but the area devoted to cash crops in sub-Saharan Africa was only increased from 15 million to 18 million hectares between 1960 and 1989. The area under food production by contrast grew from 70 million to 113 million hectares over the same period.[10] The growth in output of export crops has mostly come from the increased use of fertiliser and the extension of irrigation. Large numbers of small farmers have not been able to afford either. But increased foreign trade in agricultural products has had negative effects that have been far more damaging than the diversion of land. Food aid and the liberalisation of food imports have combined to reduce food prices to a point that has actually discouraged African farmers from growing food for the market.

In late 1988 Percy Mistry, a former World Bank senior manager, confessed:

Liberalisation has not worked in Africa ... Unfortunately it has had a much more important effect on export cash crop production than on food crop production. Because the incentives have been to

export to pay debt service, liberalisation has not done much for food
security ... The domestic capacity to switch from imported products
to local products is extremely weak [in Africa].[11]

Why the failure and the weakness? First, and unsurprisingly,
African farmers could not compete with subsidised food imports from
the US and Europe.[12] Second, through the extension of cash cropping,
particularly under the control of foreign agribusiness using plantations or subcontracting, wage labour was introduced into a subsistence agricultural economy with devastating results in certain areas.
Various studies have shown that the subsistence farming systems
of Africa are often based not on a household, which might be
expected to switch fairly easily to a wage system, but on village or
extended family cooperation.[13] This is immediately broken up by the
spread of waged employment and the emigration it entails, especially
for young males. Subsistence farming was not incompatible with a
certain amount of cash cropping. Indeed, this cash was needed to buy
tools and household equipment. Until growth was checked by wars
and drought in 1990, production of food for the market, whether for
home consumption or for export, grew steadily throughout Africa for
30 years.[14] But the cash nexus did not break up the communal
production systems as wage labour has done. For African farmers to
increase their productivity, more and better tools, irrigation and
fertilisers were needed. But they were needed to support and stimulate
the existing production system – not to break it up.
The effect on prices when several African countries all compete to
increase sales in the same market is well summarised by Mistry: 'To
the extent that [Africa] continues to rely on primary commodities to
generate further export earnings, it is cutting its own throat.'[15] But
there is a still worse problem. As Africa relies on export earnings based
on waged work for its economic development, it is destroying its
whole life support system. Relations between men and women in
African villages are also changed by sales of primary commodities on
the world markets where women have fewer rights in the distribution and management of such cash income.
We cannot conclude from this that Africans should withdraw
from foreign trade altogether. Only with trade will they be able to
obtain the tools and machinery necessary for improved productivity. But trade must not be at the cost of the survival of their staple
food production. The import of manufactured goods is of critical
importance for African countries and these have to be paid for with
income from their commodity exports.

Chart 3.2: Developing Africa's Direction and Composition of Imports and Exports, 1989

(A) Source of imports (%): total value = US$70.5 billion

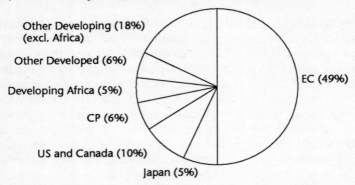

Other Developing (18%)
(excl. Africa)

Other Developed (6%)

Developing Africa (5%)

CP (6%)

US and Canada (10%)

Japan (5%)

EC (49%)

(B) Direction of exports (%): total value = US$56.1 billion

Other Developing (excl. Africa) (8%)

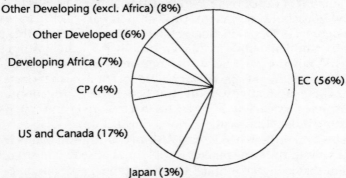

Other Developed (6%)

Developing Africa (7%)

CP (4%)

US and Canada (17%)

Japan (3%)

EC (56%)

(C) Commodity composition of imports and exports

Commodity	% of total imports	% of total exports
Food/beverages	15	14
Crude materials	6	10
Fuel oil	7	55
Chemicals	10	4
Machinery/transport	36	2
Other manufactures	25	15
Total	99	100

Notes: North Africa is included here in Developing Africa; Algeria and Libya account for about half of Developing Africa's exports of oil; CP = formerly Centrally Planned Economies
Source: UN *Monthly Bulletin of Statistics,* May 1991

Currently, Africa's resources are mainly exported in raw material form for processing and refining in other countries. Fuel oil exports are the largest (see Table 3.1). Food products and agricultural materials account for about 24 per cent. Metals and minerals make up 10 per cent. Only 28 per cent of all developing Africa's exports are manufactures, and much of these come from North Africa. Although increasing, food imports still amount to less than one-fifth of total imports. Four-fifths are manufactured goods but too many African imports are destined for tiny urban elites.[16] An often quoted example of this is motor cars, with higher imports to Africa than to other developing regions. Yet most African imports are vitally necessary for economic development – fuel, machines, chemicals, iron and steel. What, then, are the prospects for African countries finding markets for their exportable products and importing these essential supplies?

Three points emerge from an analysis of the current destination of Africa's exports and sources of imports. First, as Chart 3.2 shows, nearly 80 per cent of all the trade is with developed countries, including Eastern Europe and the former Soviet Union. Second, the largest part of this trade is with Europe. Third, trade between Africa and other developing countries comprises less than one-sixth of the total, with intra-African trade at less than 7 per cent.This last figure would be much greater, possibly double, if smuggling were included.

In considering Africa's prospects for expanded trade, we now review the prospects and projections for increased trade with other developing countries as well as with the industrialised countries.

4. What Future for Export Crops?

Africa's wealth has always lain in its agricultural production. The riches of the Nile valley founded the earliest civilisations. North Africa provided the granary of Rome. South of the Sahara most of Europe's African colonies were first developed for their agricultural production. Today, one-third of all Africa's exports is made up of agricultural and forestry products. Excluding the ten predominant oil exporters, the proportion rises to two-thirds. Without the minerals exporters, the remaining 38 countries, with 200 million people, have over 90 per cent of their exports concentrated in agricultural commodities (Annexe Table A9). By order of export earnings, these African export crops and products are: coffee, cocoa, timber, cotton, sugar, live animals and meat, tobacco, tea, fish products, rubber, groundnuts, palm oil, bananas, sisal, spices and fruits.

The list may seem large and varied, but just two – coffee and cocoa – make up nearly half the total of Africa's agricultural export earnings (see Annexe Table A10). The state of world markets for these products is, therefore, of crucial importance for export-dependent African countries. The decline in demand for most of Africa's commodities is the first problem. The second, as the World Bank itself argues, is Africa's falling share of this declining market (see Annexe Chart A5 which shows the decline between 1970 and 1987 for thirteen products). Is it worth trying to increase a share of a declining market? Africa is the dominant supplier of just one product, providing 59 per cent of the world's cocoa, but even here its once near-monopoly position has been eroded in recent years (falling from 75 per cent in the 1970s) by the trebling of Malaysian production in the 1980s.

Declining Markets

Africa still supplies 20 per cent or more of the world's exports of coffee, groundnuts and sisal. But during the 1970s and 1980s Africa's share of the world total has been declining in almost all its major export crops: coffee, cocoa, cotton, timber, live animals and meat. Likewise, the minor ones – groundnuts, rubber, sisal and palm oil – have fared no better. Slight increases have occurred only in sugar, tobacco, tea and fish products.[1] This decline in Africa's share of world markets is repeated with mineral exports. Overall, African exports have done worse than others in the Third World: while the developing countries' combined share of world markets remained at about 20 per cent between 1964 and 1987, Africa's share fell by half, from 4.2 per cent to 2.1 per cent.[2] A declining share of a growing market might simply indicate the arrival of new producers following Africa's original example, but what has happened is more worrying. Many Third World countries have been encouraged by the World Bank to pursue export-led growth, especially those burdened by foreign debts. World trade actually grew more slowly in the 1980s than the 1960s and 1970s,[3] particularly in the case of the European market which takes over 50 per cent of Africa's agricultural exports (see Chart 3.2).

Thus Africa had a declining share of a static, and occasionally even a retracting market. This problem was compounded by a concurrent fall in both prices (unit values) and volumes (Annexe Table A11). The World Bank bases much of its argument for the expansion of African exports on the presumption that *'declining export volumes, rather than declining export prices, account for Africa's poor export revenues'.*[4] The direct implication is that African countries could improve their situation by reducing overvalued exchange rates, by increasing production, becoming more competitive and diversifying their product lines. The Bank claims that

> The expansion of world trade during the past three decades appears to have largely bypassed Africa. If its economies are to grow, they must improve their share in world markets and diversify their exports ... sub-Saharan Africa needs to find new markets.[5]

The World Bank argues that the solution lies in internal changes; the world outside is assumed to be ready and waiting for Africa to re-emerge as a major supplier.

The movement of prices and volumes in African export earnings is greatly influenced by the behaviour of oil prices. The UNDP/World Bank report *Africa's Adjustment and Growth in the 1980s* emphasises that while in this decade 'export earnings fell ... most of the decline came from falling oil prices, which helped oil importers';[6] it insists that 'A longer historical perspective shows that the sharp drop in sub-Saharan Africa's export earnings ... is more a return to the long-term trend (after a period of unprecedented highs) than a persistent decline.'[7]

Falling Terms of Trade

Though this is largely true, the long-term trend for primary commodity prices in relation to prices of manufactured goods – the relationship known as the terms of trade – is one of persistent declines before and since the Second World War. This is shown in Chart 4.1 (note that it refers to all commodity prices, not just Africa's). The upward blip in the early 1970s was not only the result of the hike in oil prices; it was general across most commodities.

Chart 4.1: Real Commodity Prices Deflated by Price of Manufactures: 1870–1986

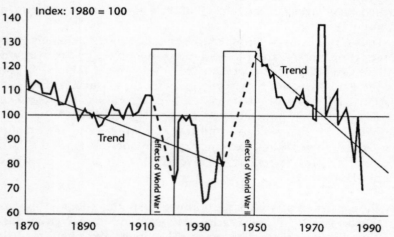

Source: Overseas Development Institute, *Briefing Paper*, March 1988

A comparison of the movements of different regions' commodity exports in the 1960s, 1970s and 1980s (Annexe Table A11) shows that sub-Saharan African primary commodities showed roughly the same movement in export prices as other developing countries, with only slightly worse volumes of exports in the 1960s and 1970s. In the 1980s however, overall African export volumes fell even as they rose elsewhere. Taking agricultural products alone, the prices of the mix or range of African products not only fell faster than others in the 1980s, but while other exporters' volumes had 'boomed' in the 1970s, Africa's had not. Although Africa's agricultural exports did not rise in the 1980s, at least they were maintained, despite falls in other exports.

Although such general figures are inconclusive, Kox's detailed regression analysis of sub-Saharan African export earnings by sub-periods paints a clear picture.[8] His analysis takes five sub-periods of two to three years in the period from 1973 to 1987. In the two sub-periods up to 1980, when earnings were rising, the rise in one is explained by volume changes and in the other by price changes. In the three sub-periods since 1980, when earnings were falling, there are different explanatory variables: in the first sub-period price changes; in the second, changes in volume; and in the latest sub-period neither price nor volume are found to be significant as the explanatory variable.

This analysis of all non-fuel commodity exports from sub-Saharan Africa shows that of the US$12.5 billion fall between 1980 and 1987 in the purchasing power generated, $7.5 billion is accounted for by declining terms of trade. This finding directly contradicts the World Bank's statement that 'declining volumes rather than declining prices account for Africa's poor export revenues.' The regression analysis also shows that just two commodities, coffee and cocoa, were responsible for 74 per cent of the cumulative changes over the five sub-periods.[9]

How do primary commodity producers respond to a fall in price? For two reasons a fall does not necessarily lead to a cut in production. First, state marketing boards continue to sell, even at a loss, because they have to find foreign currency in one way or another, especially when the government must service large foreign debts. The continued heavy indebtedness of most African countries is, therefore, both result and cause of low commodity prices. Second, small-scale producers go on marketing their cash crops as long as the price received covers their outgoings, even if their labour is barely rewarded. As long as cash crops make some contribution, this is a bonus for the household and the community. With no other option open to them, peasant producers go on subsisting on their staple – maize or millet.

The fact that primary commodity output is so unresponsive to changes in price has obvious implications for any predictions about future earnings, particularly predictions made on the basis of economic models in which price is not only the outcome of changes in supply and demand, but also a determinant of such changes. More significant is a detailed appraisal of the target markets for Africa's main agricultural exports. A market's size and strength is primarily determined by people's level of income. Major markets are those with the highest incomes. Consumption patterns relate not only to income levels, but also to fashion and the availability of substitutes, which may be more convenient or cheaper than a traditional product. Most African agri-

cultural exports have suffered directly from competition with substitutes – artificial fibres from timber and oil stocks replacing cotton,
rubber and sisal. Health consciousness has eroded the market for
tobacco and sugar. US and West European demand for the stronger
taste and higher caffeine content of robusta coffee is changing
towards the more subtle, higher quality arabica coffees and new
techniques, such as fast roasting, mean less raw material is needed.

Substitutes from Biotechnology

New discoveries in biotechnology will have the greatest effect on traditional exports of agricultural commodities. Substitutes, new
products, strains and processes are emerging: faster growing coffee
bushes; immunity from disease; micro-propagation of high yielding
cocoa plants; cloning of oil palms to double yields; cell culture and
genetic engineering with enzymes to make high quality cocoa butter
from cheap palm oil and soya bean oil. At first sight, this appears to
be no more than plant breeders have been doing for thousands of
years, ever since men and women selected seeds from the strongest
and most fruitful plants and learned to cross strains within the
limits of sexual compatibility. But biotechnology can widen the
gene pool beyond these limits. Plant materials can be processed by
biological agents, resulting in much faster changes and much more
accurate breeding programmes. Genetic engineering means manip-
ulating cells or molecules to cross or fuse the building blocks of
living organisms. Clones are genetically identical cells or organisms
derived from a common ancestor. Enzymes are proteins which act
as biological catalysts and can stimulate biological reactions. Tissue
culture *in vitro* (literally, in glass, that is, in the laboratory) permits
the rapid regeneration of cells into full-sized plants, and allows for
the monitoring of the effects of intervention in plant growth. Taken
together these techniques amount to a new agricultural revolution.[10]

Biotechnology is extremely expensive and the key research and
experimentation plantations are being funded by transnational corporations. It costs an estimated US$1 million to clone a single gene
and takes the equivalent of 20 years of work to isolate a commercially
useful new enzyme. Biotechnology, moreover, has to be implemented on a large scale – in large nurseries and plantations, with
precisely regulated application of fertiliser and water. Both Nestlé and
General Foods have begun such ventures. Tissue-culture coffee plants
have already been planted in Malaysia, Singapore and Indonesia, with
Japan as the target market. Governments are undertaking research
and development, but are lagging far behind agribusiness. Successful

biotechnology products are patented. How can small-scale farmers in Africa be included? If they are not, how then can they compete? The World Bank wants African farmers and governments to 'get their act together'. It turns out to be not so simple.

Biotechnology is changing the whole nature of the market for commodities. It gives manufacturers much greater flexibility in their choice of primary commodity inputs. The days of relying on one or two sources for primary products are over. For example, cocoa beans, palm oil, beet or cane to manufacture cocoa, margarine or sugar – all these can be switched and substituted whenever the supply of one primary commodity fails and prices rise. Chocolate can be made from palm oil, margarine from rape seed, sweeteners from corn syrup. Inevitably, vegetable oil and sugar prices will fall. Some growers may benefit. But, they will mostly be growing for a few large companies with laboratories and large plantations.[11] Typical small-scale African growers of coffee and cocoa will lose out. Their only hope is that there may be problems ahead for the genetic engineers. The reduction of genetic diversity may increase vulnerability to pests and diseases, unless the breeders have successfully incorporated adequate resistance into the new strains. Plantations need heavy applications of water and fertiliser and cannot rely on the rain and organic mulch of the forests. So, the small-scale farmer may still survive with organic products from dispersed cultivation, but will face the problem of much reduced prices.

Income Demand Elasticities

The chief factor determining the market for any commodity is the income elasticity of demand – that is, how demand changes as incomes rise, what proportion of extra income is spent on that commodity. Consumers in the industrialised countries provide the main markets for primary commodities. Individual consumers do not, however, buy the primary product. They buy a refined, processed, packaged and marketed product. To understand changes in demand we must take into account what goes into making a product. Rising demand for chocolate no longer implies increased demand for cocoa beans. It now may equally well imply a rise in the demand for several vegetable oil ingredients. While demand continues to rise ahead of incomes for most products of modern manufacturing industry, this is not the case for agricultural products. Demand in the developed industrialised countries is failing to rise even as fast as incomes. A 1 per cent rise in incomes in Western Europe leads only to a 0.7 per cent rise in consumption of coffee, to a 0.35 per cent rise in consumption of cocoa, to a 0.2 per cent rise in consumption of sugar and a 0.1 per cent rise in cotton consumption (see Chart 4.2).

Chart 4.2: Income Elasticities of Demand: Percentage Increase in Consumption of Selected Commodities per 1% Rise in Incomes – different regions

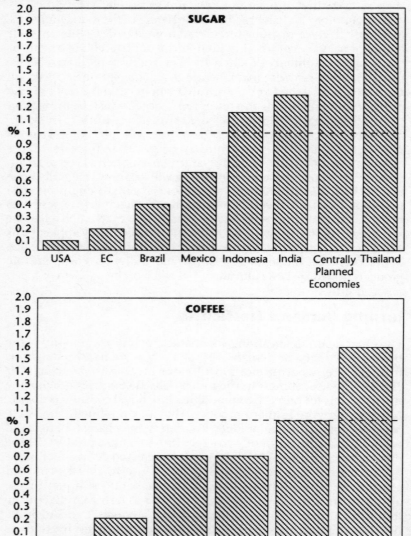

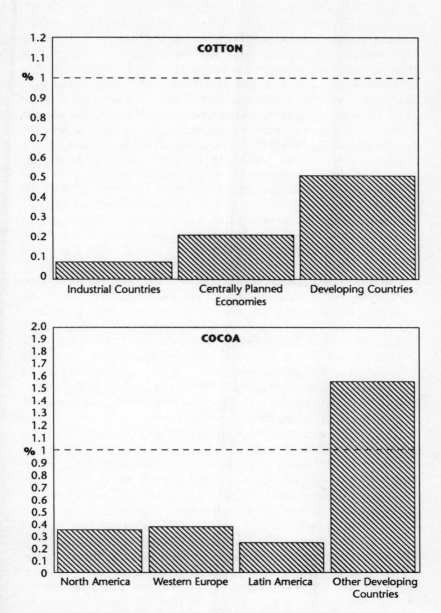

Source: Henk Kox, *Export Constraints for Sub-Saharan Growth*, Table 16

The implication of Chart 4.2 is that the differences in income elasticities of demand in countries at different levels of economic development are very important for assessing prospects for market expansion. Figures for Western Europe and North America are similar, but, taking coffee as an example, Eastern European consumption is rising in line with incomes, and in Japan faster than incomes. The effect of rising incomes on demand is completely different in most developing countries. Consumption of coffee, cocoa and sugar all rise faster than incomes. However, most of Africa's commodity exports go to the developed market economies and mainly to Western Europe, so that the World Bank's view that Africa should look for new markets outside Europe and North America is justified. Asian agricultural producers have raised to 40 per cent the proportion of their exports going to other developing countries. The figure for Africa is around 20 per cent. A further 10 per cent goes to Eastern Europe.[12] New markets for African commodities do exist outside the developed market economies, but they will not equal the developed markets in their scale, since *per capita* incomes are still low and some are in countries with the same products for export as Africa.

Can Africa find markets for expanded and more efficient production of its traditional agricultural exports? The industrialised countries still have most of the purchasing power in the world market. So, what is the future for Africa's main crops – coffee, cocoa, cotton, sugar, tobacco, live animals and timber – in this market? The World Bank published two sets of relatively optimistic estimates for world movements of agricultural commodity prices up to the end of the century, the first in 1988 and the second in a working paper, specifically on sub-Saharan Africa, in December 1989.[13] We have combined these two sets of figures in Annexe Table A12.

World Bank experts estimate that sub-Saharan Africa's mix of products will fall more heavily than all world commodity prices up to 1990, but then rise from this lower base in line with world prices. Based on selected relative prices – that is, price movements for the main agricultural products of sub-Saharan Africa in relation to the prices of manufactured goods – the Bank predicts that prices for African products will stabilise at 1970 levels, after the 1980s boom and the recent slump (see Chart 4.3). This may seem reasonable if, to find a measure of stability, they are looking back to the 1960s. But given the steady falls of these agricultural export prices, by as much as 7.5 per cent a year throughout the 1980s, the Bank's predictions of a complete turnaround and recovery after 1990, with subsequent growth of about 3 per cent a year, appear extraordinarily optimistic.

Everything depends on the performance of just two or three African products.

Chart 4.3: Income Terms of Trade – Aggregate

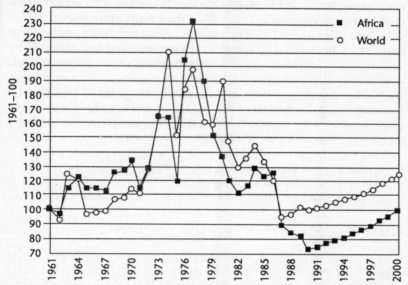

Source: World Bank Paper, *Recent Trends and Prospects for Agricultural Commodity Exports in Sub-Saharan Africa*, December 1989

Future Prospects

What estimates *can* we make, taking into account all the factors which determine demand? The World Bank's projections to the year 2000 tell us what is supposed to happen to selected relative prices. The Bank forecasts:

- a fairly strong recovery beyond the 1986/87 levels for tea, sugar, palm oil, cotton, rubber and logs;
- no return to 1980/81 levels for these commodities;
- some recovery for coffee and cocoa (key African commodities) after 1990 but not to 1986/87, 1970/71 or even 1980/81 levels;
- actual decline for tobacco;
- a price increase for coffee at 3 per cent a year;
- a price increase for cocoa at 7 per cent a year after the all-time lows in 1990.

In fact, 1990 was a bad year and 1991 was dire, witnessing further drops in prices for all but one of the 14 commodities monitored by the UN magazine *African Recovery*. Sugar prices fell by a further 27 per cent, bauxite and groundnuts by nearly 20 per cent. Prices for coffee and cocoa continued their downward slide – the fifth and seventh consecutive declines respectively for these important exports.[14]

In 1989 the World Bank also estimated the future volume of exports of non-fuel commodities from sub-Saharan Africa.[15] Its assumptions for Africa's 'self-sustainable growth' provided for: commodity diversification, GDP *per capita* growth, that is, growth ahead of population growth, and for greater openness to imports. The Bank selected four variants of this central model to judge the outcome of governments' economic policies, depending on whether the Bank proposals were adopted. These four variants were:

- variant 1: no commodity diversification;
- variant 2: no GDP *per capita* growth;
- variant 3: average GDP growth 0.5 per cent above population growth;
- variant 4: less openness than in the central case.

Kox has analysed these models to assess the implications for export earnings for each of sub-Saharan Africa's main commodities up to the year 2000 (see Annexe Table A13). The calculations cover the main non-fuel commodity exports making up 75 per cent of the total. His analysis suggests some unexplained underlying assumptions on the part of the World Bank:

- no large diversification from traditional exports;
- an export earnings growth rate of around 5 per cent a year;
- price rises of just over 3 per cent a year;
- export volume growth rate of 1.5 per cent.

In short, the World Bank believes that export volumes of sub-Saharan Africa's commodities to the year 2000 will grow by some 16 per cent on average for all products. The World Bank's working paper forecasts increased volumes from 1988 to 2000 for seven specific agricultural commodities exports:

- coffee up by 2%;
- cotton by 41%;
- tobacco by 11%;
- groundnut oil by 7%;
- cocoa up by 18%;
- sugar by 39%;
- tea by 63%.

Only palm oil volume is forecast to fall, by 50 per cent.

We see that the Bank forecasts a 5 per cent annual growth rate in export earnings, which assumes a growth in market demand of the same rate. As their overall forecast stands, such a growth in demand means that consumers must be prepared to buy more of the commodity at the higher price. Our analysis of key products in the following chapters shows that such an outcome can be seen as highly unlikely.

The Bank's December 1989 working paper offers a different calculation of earnings growth from that in the UNDP/World Bank Report (see Annexe Table A14). The working paper shows the value of exports at 1985 dollar values and purchasing power. Calculations are both for sub-Saharan Africa and the world. It shows a 16 per cent rise in the value of African export earnings between 1988 and the year 2000, set against a 28 per cent rise in worldwide exports of the same commodities.

The World Bank expected Africa to experience worse than average price falls from 1988 to 1990, but then to see prices rising on average in line with world prices. Here its assumption is that even if governments apply the World Bank policies, sub-Saharan African countries will fail to raise the volumes of their agricultural or non-fuel exports anywhere near in line with world volumes. Once again, the World Bank experts imply that the fault will lie with Africa's internal economies and not with external constraints. A further implication is, however, that worldwide export sales of these crops will increase over the next decade at a faster rate than sub-Saharan Africa's.

The past movements of prices and volumes of exports and future developments in biotechnology provide reasons enough to question the World Bank's optimistic forecasts of rising demand for sub-Saharan African products. And indeed at the end of 1989 the World Bank revised downward its overall price forecasts for primary commodities to the end of the century. This was after the mid-1989 collapse in commodity prices, ending a gradual recovery between 1985 and 1989. The revision reduced forecast price increases over the decade from 2.9 per cent to 2.1 per cent per year. How many more changes will the Bank be obliged to make? Such changes in its forecasts suggest we should be wary of accepting any long-term predictions of price movements, particularly when they run so strongly counter to past trends.

Even assuming the viability of long-term predictions, we still question whether they are comparing like with like, when they show the movements of prices and volumes of particular commodities exported from sub-Saharan Africa and the rest of the world. Both the different mix of products and the different varieties need to be considered. The future of African coffees and cocoa perfectly illustrate this, given the changes in consumer taste, expenditure patterns and the threat from alternative sources and substitutes. A clearer picture of this issue follows as we take each of Africa's main agricultural export commodities and look at trends in demand.

5. Which Cash Crops?

If Africa's economies are to grow, they must earn foreign exchange to pay for essential imports. Thus it is vital that they increase their share of world markets. The prospects for most primary commodities are poor, so higher export earnings must come from increased output, diversification into new commodities and an aggressive export drive into the rapidly growing Asian markets.[1]

World Bank, 1989

Coffee

Coffee is sub-Saharan Africa's largest single non-fuel export, with 18 per cent of all non-fuel export earnings in the 1980s. Twenty-five sub-Saharan African countries export coffee, but only eight are major producers, with 750 000 or more bags (60 kg each) a year.[2] Of the two main varieties of coffee, the *arabica* grows in the highlands, and gives high quality mild coffee for filtering, the *robusta* from the tropical lowlands gives the stronger tasting coffee for manufacturing the soluble, so-called 'instant' beverages. Arabica coffees fetch higher market prices than robustas, on average 50 per cent more. About two-thirds of African production is robusta coffee.[3] Kenya, Tanzania, Ethiopia and Rwanda-Burundi grow arabica coffee and Madagascar is now introducing these plants. The chief African robusta producers are Côte d'Ivoire Uganda, Zaïre, Cameroon, the Central African Republic, Togo and Zimbabwe. Angola and Nigeria were once important producers, but ageing trees and little replanting have reduced production. Production has also declined in Côte d'Ivoire, Cameroon, Ethiopia and Madagascar[4] as a result of falling prices. Exports of higher value coffee from Africa have increased but, overall, there has been a fall in both the quantity and quality of African coffee. As a London coffee trader reported in 1990, 'African coffee is more or less sold on its merits. It has gone down in quality in the last 10 to 15 years, particularly the robusta quality. Aggressive selling by the newest sources, [like] Indonesia hasn't helped.'[5]

Volumes of exports as well as prices declined sharply after 1980/82 (Annexe Table A11). The decline in the market share of Africa's coffee exports has been persistent from 1985/87 to 1990/91.[6] African exportable production was 33 per cent of the world total in 1970, 24 per cent by 1980 and 20 per cent by 1990/91. One significant cause of this is a steady change in demand from robustas to arabicas. All the traders interviewed for this book emphasised this trend. Worldwide exports of arabicas almost doubled between the 1960s and 1980s. Exports of robusta rose by one-third in this period but Africa's share fell from 85 per cent to 62 per cent.[7]

While demand for African coffee fell, demand for South-East Asian and Central American coffees grew steadily. In the 20 years to 1988/89, the output of Indonesian robusta alone more than doubled.[8] This is how a member of a London coffee trading house described the situation:

Everyone's talking about Africa losing its share of the market. It's going to continue because the research has been done and the trees are planted [in South-East Asia]. And despite these low price levels Indonesia is finding it profitable to produce coffee. They couldn't produce coffee at these prices in Africa.

From 1976 to 1978, world coffee prices were artificially high because Brazil's crops were hit by frost. After that, a fall in prices was only to be expected, but the fall has taken prices below the average in the 1960s and early 1970s because the increase in supply has so far outstripped the growth in demand. As prices fell, output temporarily increased. Producers desperately attempted to compensate by selling bigger volumes.

What then is the future for African coffee? At the end of 1989 the World Bank forecast generally rising volumes and falling prices until 1991. For the rest of the 1990s it predicted a steady 20 per cent rise in the volume of sales and a 30 per cent rise in prices. But as Chart 5.1 shows, no such growth is forecast for Africa, in fact a 10 per cent fall in volumes is foreseen for the 1990s.[9] (Detailed figures are shown in Annexe Table A14.) This fall in volume is barely compensated by slightly rising world prices. This means that although Africa used to do as well, if not better, than the rest of the world in its coffee exports, it is now going to do significantly worse and its earnings from coffee exports will be slightly lower in real terms in the year 2000 than they were in 1988.

Traders see reasonably buoyant prospects for coffee in general because of the rising demand for arabica: more consumption of roast and ground coffee and higher proportions of arabica – up to

Chart 5.1: Income Terms of Trade – Coffee

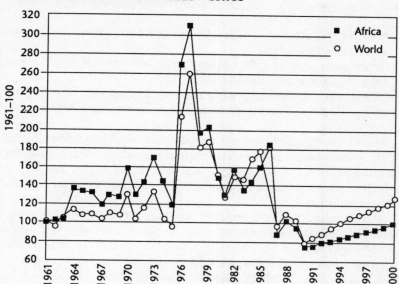

Source: World Bank Paper, *Recent Trends and Prospects for Agricultural Commodity Exports in Sub-Saharan Africa*, December 1989

30 per cent – in soluble coffee. From 1976/77 to 1986/87 world consumption of arabicas rose from 35 to 50 million bags (35 million washed). By contrast, consumption of robusta coffees – Africa's predominant coffee product – has stagnated at 12.5 million bags.[10] The prospects for African coffees in the 1990s are less good, not only because of the high proportion of robusta, but also because of its generally poor quality. As a London coffee trader put it in 1990:

> You can't generalise, of course. You have to look at individual coffees: Ugandan robustas by and large have a good reputation, a slightly better flavour than Indonesian and they have managed to ship reliably and maintain quality despite everything. Kenya as well. West Africa has a lot more problems. So has Tanzania. No price incentives and their coffee is dreadful. Robusta's pretty foul-tasting anyway … its days are numbered.

Major buyers expect overall demand to stay flat. Good quality coffee will continue to have a selling edge. On this basis alone, interviews with traders revealed an all too common reluctance to 'bother' with African coffees:

> 'I won't buy African coffee – except possibly Ugandan.' (Coffee buyer, London, 1990)
> 'Only Kenyan is of first quality... ' (Trader on the Futures and Options Exchange, London, 1990)
> 'We would not use Zaïrean, Madagascan or even Ugandan because of the quality.' (Buyer for transnational corporation, UK, 1990)

The reputed dishonesty and unreliability of all but a few African trading counterparts were also commonly cited as a reason for steering clear. A London coffee buyer said, for example, 'We do not buy direct from Africa. It means having to take double cover because of delays and unreliability.'

A further traders' gripe about African coffee is that high exchange rates lead to relatively high prices. As prices crashed after 1989, many large trading companies, operating on ever-tighter margins and with an increasing credit squeeze from their own financial creditors, lost money as a result of their past investment and cooperation with Africa. Several went bankrupt.

With the run of the market and ample choice of supply, even coffee traders admit that, from a producer's perspective, 'One of the problems is that coffee buying is concentrated in such few hands – Suchards and General Foods, the largest roasters', not to mention Nestlé with half of the world's soluble coffee market.

Perhaps, given a financial incentive, African coffee producers, especially arabica producers, could improve the quality and reliability of the product, but what chance would they have of selling it? The answer is, unfortunately, not much. From 1980 to 1989 the coffee market was stabilised by an export quota system. This was negotiated by the International Coffee Organisation (ICO), which has members from both consumer and producer countries but is in practice dominated by the largest consumer, the US, and the largest producer, Brazil. This quota system acted as a strategic support to African coffees and smaller producing countries in Latin America. However, US and worldwide demand has been falling since 1988, particularly for soluble and, therefore, robustas.[11] Surplus supply, especially from Brazil and Indonesia, made a new agreement impossible and prices collapsed in 1989. According to a member of the US National Coffee Association, 'When export quotas were suspended in July 1989, coffee became a non-administered world market and a pent-up demand for higher quality Central American and Colombian milds was released.'

By 1990/91 stocks had risen to 36 million bags, equal to nearly half of annual exports. How, then, could the World Bank expect demand and therefore prices to start rising thereafter? First, because the Bank expected low prices to knock 'high cost' producers out of the market, reducing supply. Second, it argued that the 1980s decline in US coffee consumption – when Americans were switching to soft drinks – was now ending. Third, it predicted increased demand as incomes rose in Japan and Eastern Europe. Traders and manufacturers in the US and UK interviewed in late 1990 all assumed the East European market would expand, especially for robusta. This is an area of potential growth for African producers. But surviving the price and market squeeze of the early 1990s is the first priority. Although firm growth in demand is predicted for arabicas, that market is not open to penetration by African robustas.

There are two further problems with the World Bank's predictions. New manufacturing techniques will gradually result in more end product for less raw material – for example; 'fast roasting' saves around 3 oz/lb. And agribusiness development of biotechnology will continue to have a substantial effect on coffee supply and demand.[12] Nestlé's Malaysian subsidiary, EASTRACO, is developing tissue cloning from the world's best quality and fastest growing coffee trees. Philip Morris/General Foods – with, like Nestlé, nearly half of the world market – is doing the same. Large tissue culture coffee plantations are already established in Malaysia, Singapore and Indonesia. Indonesian coffee is in direct competition with African coffee. The African Centre for Technological Studies predicts that by 1995 South-East Asian coffee will undercut even Brazil, the largest single producing country with a third of world production.[13]

African countries failing to match this upgrading process will not be able to meet market conditions for quality or price. African production already compares unfavourably with Latin American and South-East Asian producers in a number of key indicators:

- average yields (measured in kgs/hectare) are already lower in sub-Saharan Africa than elsewhere with three exceptions: Kenya, Rwanda and Cameroon;
- since 1970 all African yields except Cameroon's have fallen while Latin American and South-East Asian yields have risen;
- prices paid to African producers fell in the 1980s (except in Kenya) while they rose in Brazil and South-East Asia;
- falling prices have meant little replanting and scant resources for new technology.[14]

Africa's predominantly small-scale farmers do not have the resources of large agribusiness investors in Asia and large farms in Brazil to apply new technology. Even if it takes as much as five to ten years for this superior technology to become widespread, it will exert downwards pressure on world prices far sooner. In the light of all this, the World Bank's forecasts strike us as hopelessly optimistic. Nothing seems likely to redress an emerging imbalance in direct investment and trade flows unless there is appropriate financial support for African farmers to compete and a quite unexpected upturn in world demand.

Cocoa

Cocoa is Africa's second or third largest non-fuel export earning commodity (ranking just before or just after copper in most years), with about 13 per cent of non-fuel export earnings in the 1980s. Unlike coffee, which originated in Africa and was later 'exported', cocoa originated in Brazil and was later introduced to West Africa. The name of the typical African cocoa variety, *forastero amazon*, reflects this. In Africa it thrives in lowland forests, growing under the shade of larger trees. For almost a century Africa was the world's major cocoa producer; as late as 1970 it provided three-quarters of world production.[14] Ghanaian cocoa was the favourite, with the nicest taste and best butter quality. Cocoa melts at body temperature – the phenomenon of cocoa melting in your mouth is what makes it so delicious. Ghanaian cocoa prices set the standard for all others. At its peak, cocoa accounted for 60 per cent of Ghana's export earnings.[15]

During the 1970s Ghana's output steadily fell. After the 1981/82 season it fell by one-fifth. This crash in output was repeated in all the other main African cocoa producers – Cameroon, Nigeria and Côte d'Ivoire. Africa's total share of world production dropped from 60 per cent to 55 per cent (Annexe Table A15). The chief cause was that world prices fell sharply, not just from the 1977 peak of more than four times the 1960s average, but also from the second peak in 1985 of three times the 1960 levels. By 1987 cocoa prices were only 50 per cent above the 1960s average.[16]

By then world output was outstripping demand. African producers' shares of this tougher market declined and they reduced their output, even while output was flourishing in Central and South America and in South-East Asia. As in the case of African coffee, worsening terms of trade hit all producers, but why was Africa particularly affected? Traders also cited political instability and general economic deterioration as a factor. According to a cocoa trader in London: 'In [Côte d'Ivoire] we might see a reduction of market share because it's so in debt – they're not even keeping up the roads – everything's falling apart. The civilian government has let things go to pot!'

But an equally important factor was the way production and sales are organised with large numbers of small-scale farmers – 2 million in Ghana alone – selling to government marketing boards.

The World Bank view is that African governments generally take too high a share or 'rent' out of export earnings.[17] In countries where the dominant economic activity is export-oriented, the marketing boards are the chief source of income for governments: to pay for government employees, roads, schools, hospitals and other public services. Buyers from the state marketing boards purchase cocoa in the regions and pay farmers by the 'head-load' (20 kg) with cash or credit notes. If the local currency is devalued, the farmers should get more cash for the beans. They frequently do not.

The serious problems with marketing boards reflect the general condition of many African states. To take an example, the payroll of the Ghanaian Cocoa Marketing Board rose from 22 000 in 1964 to 100 000 in 1985 with no increase in output. In 1986, an investigation showed that 15 000 were 'ghost' workers – non-existent or dead – and the staff was trimmed to 44 000.[18] In addition to issues of fiscal probity – the price paid, promptness, validity of credit notes, settling accounts with shippers – if the farmers do not generally trust the government or its agents, they will not pick or sell, unless forced to by hunger. Ghana's marketing board has paid perennially low prices to cocoa farmers; Cameroon and Côte d'Ivoire have slashed farmers' prices. As a result there is little incentive for long-term actions of replanting and investment. As a member of a London brokerage house remarked, 'Except Nigeria, governments control the cocoa industry in Africa and it's not worth their while investing in cocoa.' This stores up trouble for the future: after 50 years cocoa trees are past their peak; it takes ten years for a new tree to mature, although the new hybrids do so more quickly.

In the past cocoa producing countries have tried to protect themselves against competitive overproduction and price falls by membership of the International Cocoa Organisation (ICCO). The ICCO includes Central and South American as well as African producing countries and meets with consuming countries to take action through the International Cocoa Agreement (ICA). In the 1980s producing countries agreed to withhold supplies and build up stocks to stabilise prices. But stocks grew, storage costs rose and they ran up debts. The consuming countries, especially the European Community, refused to meet the debts and abandoned the ICCO, anxious to get free of the restrictions of the ICA and to be able to buy cocoa where it was cheapest – in Malaysia. A New York buyer put it this way: 'Five years of overproduction, the prospect of record closing stocks and the likelihood of another sizeable production surplus in 1990/91 – Malaysia and Indonesia are breaking all records – suggest pessimism for cocoa prices.'

Malaysia only began growing cocoa in the 1970s, as part of a policy of diversification because natural rubber sales were falling. It seized its chance in the world market in 1988, when the Côte d'Ivoire, then the world's biggest cocoa producer, withheld supplies in a bid to raise prices.[19] Manufacturers do not like Malaysian cocoa. 'Malaysian cocoa is not desirable', commented one trader. 'It melts at a higher temperature, the butter quality isn't as high [as African] and it's more bitter. The colour's not right. It's a problem if you get a cocoa powder that's red!' Since prices reflect 'buyer desirability', Malaysian cocoa trades with a discount against contract prices. Nigerian and Ghanaian cocoa generally trades 'at par', and in the second-hand market (outside the terminal markets) 'above par'.

But Malaysian cocoa can be blended. Buyers retooled their factories and soon got used to it, especially because it was cheaper than the African or Brazilian sources. By 1989 Malaysia accounted for over 10 per cent of the world's total cocoa production.[20]

Malaysian cocoa arrived on the world market just when demand was slack, sending the price on its sharp downward trajectory. By 1989 cocoa stocks amounted to over 1 million tonnes – more than half a year's consumption. The ICA could no longer guarantee prices. The ICCO collapsed as Malaysia sold outside the agreement to non-ICA members, especially the US, the largest single buyer.[21] Traders see it clearly: 'Without Malaysia we wouldn't have a low price now.' Prices recovered slightly in 1990 as stocks were run down, but attempts to renew the agreement in mid-1991 were unsuccessful as cocoa bean prices reached all time lows.[22]

In the words of a New York commodity buyer, 'The good news is that the world wants African cocoa; the bad news is that their price is lousy.' Africa's cocoa, although preferred as the 'best basic cocoa, worldwide' according to the same buyer, cannot match Malaysian prices, which are the result of high yields. These high yields have been achieved through heavy investment in biotechnology. Pest-resistant, fast-growing hybrids were developed to suit the local soil conditions. Plants reach maturity far more quickly than the norm. High density planting on big estates worked by wage labour replaced the more typical interspersed forest planting by small-scale farmers, each with no more than one hectare under cocoa, and often much less.[23] Brazil and Malaysia have higher proportions of large size plantations in which advanced technologies can be applied more easily than with the interspersed forest planting.[24]

From beans to chocolate, cocoa goes through several stages of processing (Annexe Chart A16). The first stage is cleaning, roasting, shelling and tanning. It is a dirty, smelly business, traditionally done by hand on the farm. On the big estates, machines do it and eliminate much contamination and infestation which small farmers' family labour leaves behind. The second stage is to blend the shelled and dried bean – the nib – with other nibs for grinding. Nibs are ground into cocoa liquor – called liquor because the fat melts with the heat of the grinding. The liquor is then hydraulically pressed to make cocoa cake, which is milled into cocoa powder, and cocoa butter which is added to cocoa liquor, sugar, milk and other ingredients to make chocolate.

Each of these stages adds value to the raw bean. Between 1977 and 1990, the total weight of nibs ground worldwide rose by more than 50 per cent – from 1 389 000 tonnes to 2 137 000. But while African exports of beans rose nearly in line with the world total – sustaining its two-thirds share – Africa's share of grindings stayed at around 8 per cent or 9 per cent (Annexe Table A15). By contrast South-East Asia's share of grindings rose from 0.06 per cent to 6.5 per cent of the total in the same period. Malaysia's grindings rose nearly eightfold in the second half of the 1980s – from 9000 tonnes in 1984 to 70 000 in 1990.[25] World exports of cocoa butter and cocoa powder also rose in the 1970s and 1980s, but Africa's share of the total declined while exports from Singapore multiplied ten times.[26] Processing not only means value added, but, in the case of cake, the price did not fall over the period whereas bean prices did. In 1990 the price ratio between beans and butter was at an historical high but producers' share of the value of the final product is always small (Annexe Table A16).

Attempts have been made to expand African processing. In 1989 Nigeria banned the export of raw beans. Exports of beans had already been reduced from 223 000 tonnes in 1976 to 70 000 tonnes in 1986/87, with an increase of exports of cocoa butter from 6000 to 10 000 tonnes. But the ban failed in the face of low prices and the high cost of the processing machinery.[27] Biotechnology is even more expensive and, without backing from government institutions, beyond the reach of small farmers.

Even if the product and the marketing systems could be improved, that would still not guarantee prosperity. The stark reality is that world demand for cocoa has been growing at 2 per cent a year, while output has been rising at 4 per cent. Stocks at the end of 1990 were equal to one-quarter of world annual exports. Yet the World Bank expects demand to rise in the future at 3 to 4.5 per cent a year, with prices rising 5 to 6 per cent; it expects sub-Saharan Africa's exports to increase at 1.6 per cent with Côte d'Ivoire, Ghana and Nigeria holding their place at the top of the world table.[28] In the light of past experience and our knowledge of future technological developments, such forecasts are implausible, not to say irresponsible. The new applications of biotechnology to cocoa production are not only resulting in large-scale plantations, processing plants and mass production of chocolate, with which small countries and small family farms cannot compete; they are also leading to the substitution of cheap palm oil for expensive cocoa butter by a process using enzymes to upgrade the lower grade oils and fats. Genencor of San Francisco has filed patents and achieved successful results in small-scale trials.[29] Although the prices of substitutes for cocoa butter – shea, vegetable and other oils – are not yet competitive, it is only a matter of time before that changes. Then the prospects for Africa's small-scale cocoa-producers will be dismal.

Palm Oil and Groundnut Oil

Africa's palm oil production contributes less than 1 per cent to sub-Saharan Africa's export earnings and groundnut oil even less than palm oil. Until the 1960s Nigeria was the world's largest producer, generating half the world's supply.[30] Cheap palm oil no longer comes from Africa. Africa's share of the total is now 2 to 3 per cent[31]. Cameroon, Congo, Côte d'Ivoire and Zaïre have increased output recently, but transport costs and lack of rainfall have made competition with South-East Asia virtually impossible. In Malaysia and Indonesia tropical forest has been felled to grow palms in virgin soil. Over 20 tonnes of fruit bunches per hectare can be produced there compared with 16 tonnes in Côte d'Ivoire, 14 in Nigeria and 9 in Ghana.[32] The World Bank expects the terms of trade for palm oil to double worldwide between 1990 and 2000.[33] Africa's terms of trade for palm oil are set to stay at 10 per cent of 1960s levels. Again, small-scale African production cannot compete with large-scale Asian plantations.

Palm oil and many sources of vegetable oils – groundnut, soya, cotton seed and rape and sunflower seed – are now coming into direct market competition because of the increasing flexibility offered to manufacturers by biotechnology. The increased production of many of these oils is being subsidised in the US, Canada and the EC. The cost to EC taxpayers of turning Europe's fields yellow with rape seed is estimated at some £2 billion.[34] The prospect for Southern producing countries is of lower future demand – affecting both volumes and prices. In Europe margarine and cattle cake once consisted mainly of imported oils. Today, in the UK for example, 50–80 per cent is made from home grown rape seed.[35]

Groundnut oil is now the chief African vegetable oil product. Together with groundnut cake and groundnuts themselves, this is an important African export, making up slightly over 1 per cent of sub-Saharan non-fuel foreign currency earnings. Groundnuts from Africa, like palm products, used to sell mainly in Europe and have been equally heavily hit by competition with subsidised Northern vegetable oils.

Groundnut prices have fallen steadily since the 1960s, with a brief blip in the early 1970s, to a level which is only 10 per cent of the terms of trade in 1961. Ever hopeful, the World Bank foresees no further decline in the 1990s, but shows Africa's terms of trade quite flat to the end of the century, with world prices rising slightly.[36] There is still a market for high quality groundnuts and room for local processing. But consuming country health regulations are becoming increasingly strict. Achieving quality control, particularly over aflatoxin – a carcinogenic mould – implies added costs for laboratory and testing equipment in the context of what is, overall, a low-value product. A nut merchant in London has this to say about the hygiene-conscious Swiss: 'It is virtually impossible these days to import a nut into Switzerland [currently the most stringent]. Fortunately, new liability regulations and 'due diligence'[37] procedures generally mean that the buck stops with the exporters.'

Not surprisingly, groundnut growers are moving into vegetables and flowers for the European market. Africa's hopes cannot be based on a growth in exports of vegetable oils.

Sugar and Sweeteners

The World Bank views sugar as 'a commodity that is projected to do better in the 1990s compared with its very poor performance in the 1980s ... However, prices are likely to remain extremely variable.'[38] The Bank forecasts a slight fall after 1991 followed by some recovery in the last years of the 1990s, with sub-Saharan Africa faring better than the rest of the world's sugar producers. Sub-Saharan Africa (excluding South Africa) produces only 5 per cent of the world's sugar. Its relative advantage is due to its privileged access to the European market. Mauritius has done particularly well under the Lomé

Convention quotas (agreed between the EC and African countries) for cane sugar, with about half the annual quota of 1.3 million tonnes.

One sugar trader regarded Mauritius's success as essentially unrepeatable: 'They've capitalised their access to the European market. I couldn't advise this for other countries. It's a whole marketing strategy based on government. It demands luck and skill and doesn't happen overnight. Mauritius found the right formula.'

After 1992 the 'special access' for African, Caribbean and Pacific ex-colonies (ACP countries) may not be maintained. The EC has enormously increased its own beet sugar production – up to 15 per cent of world output of beet and cane – and regularly builds up annual surpluses amounting to 3 or 4 million tonnes.[39] These surpluses are about equivalent to sub-Saharan Africa's entire output. Furthermore, African sugar is not a purely export-oriented crop. Sub-Saharan Africa consumes more sugar than it produces and has to import refined sugar from South Africa and Europe.[40] And according to a sugar trader, 'There has never been a sugar mountain in the EC – they export their sugar mountain at subsidised prices.'

Dealers in London and New York expect rapid growth in demand for sugar in Africa; it is a cheap source of calories. Sugar production in Africa may well expand to meet this, but there is a problem: sugar refining remains in the hands of European companies. A single company, Tate & Lyle, refines nearly all the cane sugar imported into Britain. Investing in sugar factories is costly and not financially attractive given the generally low and fluctuating world price. An executive in the sugar industry stated:

> There's no major investment because of the state of the world market. It's not a commodity to put a lot of money into, perhaps just for import substitution. If the GATT [General Agreement on Tariffs and Trade] round agrees to reduced protectionism then yes, but not at present.

Interviews with sugar traders also revealed a deep distaste and suspicion for such projects without expatriate management. 'The sugar industry has fallen apart when run by emerging nations. Fundamentally they lose all discipline. If it breaks down it becomes shambolic and no amount of [higher] world prices will help', one trader said.

Bookers, for example, installed and managed sugar factories in Guyana, Kenya and elsewhere and then handed them over to local management with varying results. Examples of well-run factories cited by traders were all under the control of expatriates or foreign companies. There is actually little place for increased exports from sub-Saharan Africa, whether raw or refined; put at its most brutal, 'African sugar is irrelevant. African countries can do nothing to control sugar prices. It's not even a place with large sugar plantations – availability is a problem. They can't produce enough let alone export.'

International Sugar Organisation quotas no longer operate. While Mauritius and Swaziland will probably hold on to their European markets, other sugar producers will turn to the internal market. Considering the potential expansion of the East European market as Cuba's production falls and its economic links are sundered, traders all pointed to the proximity of other major suppliers: the former Soviet Union produces 9 million tonnes a year, Poland 2 million. These tonnages could certainly be expanded to meet rising demand, if it were not met by subsidised exports to the East from the EC. Nonetheless, because of uncertainties in the East, traders were expecting prices to rise again in 1992 as stocks were cut back.[41]

Biotechnology is now having the greatest influence on demand and prices for sugar through the supply of sweeteners. Maize starch is transformed by enzymes into a sugar replacement – High Fructose Corn Syrup (HFCS). This has ousted sugar from most US soft drinks, including Coca Cola and Pepsi. As a direct result US imports of sugar fell by more than half between 1970 and 1987, from 5.3 to 2.2 million tonnes. Japan is also switching from sugar to HFCS. Its HFCS production increased almost eightfold between 1978 and 1988, from 84 000 to 650 000 tonnes. Japan does not grow maize and this level may be its peak.[42] But Japan has never traditionally bought from sub-Saharan Africa; its main sources are South Africa and Thailand. Politics as much as economics influence the choice between sugar and HFCS depending on pressures for the protection of the local farm lobby, but fructose is sometimes promoted as having some health advantages over sucrose in order to reinforce demand for HFCS.

A further substitute for sugar may become available through the development of single cell proteins (SCP) which use fuel oil as their base and could mount a challenge in the markets for both sweeteners and protein animal feed. Some oil companies, including British Petroleum, began SCP production in the early 1970s, but the sharp oil price rises of that decade caused them to have second thoughts. SCP is not a clear and present danger as a substitute and, indeed, sugar itself is a major source of fuel. Nine-tenths of Brazil's cane produces fuel alcohol (ethanol) for domestic use. Cuba is likewise converting much of its sugar into fuel and will doubtless have to pursue this path even further.

Unfortunately for sub-Saharan Africa's sugar producers, whose costs are not among the lowest, sugar must be exceedingly cheap (or subsidised, as with Brazil's troubled ethanol programme) to be used economically for non-food products.[43] All the traders we interviewed stressed the importance of low-cost production. Africans are at a disadvantage because of poor transport and inefficient plant operation. How can investment in overcoming these problems be viable against subsidised competitors, especially when prices for sugar are so uncertain?

Timber

Africa has long been famed for its hardwoods – mahogany, makore, obeche, sapele – and the price of timber has been steadily rising on world markets. Timber exactly fits the World Bank's critique: despite these improved prices the volume of Africa's sales and export earnings has been falling. Africa's share of world exports of non-coniferous timber has fallen from around 8 per cent of the world total to 6 per cent. Meanwhile, the Bank points to Malaysia and Indonesia as sterling examples for increasing their shares to a combined 42 per cent.[44] The Bank is congratulating the South-East Asians for cutting down their tropical forest at a faster rate than the Africans. Roads have been built and the infrastructure improved to remove the timber as fast and efficiently as possible with the result that in Malaysia 16 per cent of the forest cover has been obliterated since 1972, 50 per cent in the Philippines. 'Only' 6 per cent of Africa's forests have been lost since 1972.

Individual countries' stories are more alarming: in Côte d'Ivoire, the leading exporter of African hardwoods with one-third of total African exports, forest that once covered 45 per cent of the land area was reduced to just over 20 per cent between 1972 and 1987.[45] The results of logging are in fact much worse than these figures imply, because land is still recorded as forest even after the loggers have extracted the trees they want. One need hardly point out the dangers of such unsustainable felling in soil loss, flooding, climatic disturbance, the disappearance of plant and animal species and the destruction of human forest dwellers' communities.

We are not arguing that there should be no timber exports from the Third World – only that they should be sustainable and the producing countries should get the maximum added value by exporting wood products rather than logs. Tragically two-thirds of the beautiful hardwoods from Côte d'Ivoire and Malaysia have been exported as logs.[46] From the early 1970s to the mid-1980s African countries made progress in increasing the proportion of wood products in timber exports: from 16 per cent to 33 per cent in Côte d'Ivoire, 45 per cent to 59 per cent in Ghana and 24 per cent to 46 per cent in the Congo. But for Gabon and Cameroon, 80 per cent to 90 per cent of timber exports were still unsawn logs. Even the term 'wood products' generally means sawn planks.

As one US trader saw it, 'Ghana has the most manufacturing capacity and timber. If they don't try and dictate the market there will be plenty of demand in the US.' But if instead of 'dictating' the market, Ghana and other countries simply bow to it, they will waste their forests and not even gain the added value of making more valuable wooden products than mere planks. Africa's exports of timber products with more local value added, like veneer sheets, plywood and block board have barely risen (see Annexe Table A17). Once again, Asian producers are moving faster and obtaining better prices; they are increasing the proportion of wood products in their timber exports. Where African producers are doing the same the advantage is considerable. For example, Cameroon earns around US$200 per square metre for logs or $400 for sawn timber but $500–$600 for veneer (mid-1989 prices).[47]

Timber trade analysts have suggested that Africa could take over the role of supplier of raw logs, mainly to Japan.[48] In the late 1980s the market for tropical hardwoods was divided about equally between the US, Europe and Japan, with South American timber going to the US, African timber going mainly to Europe, and Asian timber to Japan. But as Malaysia increased its sawn and planed exports and Brazil consumed more of its sawn wood, all industrialised countries began to turn to Africa for raw logs. The implications for Africa's forests are ominous because tropical logging is wasteful. In 1980 a US Task Force on Tropical Forests reported that in one typical South-East Asian concession, only 3.3 per cent of the trees were removed for commercial purposes but in the process 57 per cent of the residual forest was destroyed or seriously damaged.[49]

To be fair, the World Bank is fully aware of the devastating results of commercial logging, fuelled by the need to step up export earnings for debt repayment. One Bank study states that, 'rough estimates show that the economic costs of unsustainable forest depletion in major hardwood exporting countries range from 4 per cent to 6 per cent of GNP, offsetting any economic growth that may otherwise have been achieved.'[50] The Bank has even estimated that fewer than ten of the 33 developing countries which are now net exporters of tropical timber will still be able to export timber products by the end of the century. The total value of the export trade will have dropped by $2 billion to US$10 billion. The Bank has begun to insert clauses into its loans provisions, especially in Africa, which require sustainable levels of logging, leaving the rest of the forest undisturbed. Donors to the Bank's soft lending arm, the International Development Association (IDA), have insisted on environmental criteria as a condition for continued contributions. According to one study, sustainable uses of the forest – such as rubber tapping, fruit and nut collection, the extraction of pharmaceutical ingredients and tourism – can give as good an economic return as logging.[51]

The European Community has gone further than the World Bank in making environmental agreements with its ACP (Africa, Caribbean and Pacific) partners under the Lomé Convention. It has already agreed to reduce tariffs on ACP processed timber imports. The International Tropical Timber Organisation (ITTO), with 40 major producers and consumers, aims to deal not only with trade but with the developmental and environmental aspects of the world's forest resources. Its work is being monitored by environmental watchdogs like Greenpeace, which has, so far, found it wanting. Largely catering to the immediate interests of the timber industry, success will depend on the contributions traders are prepared to put into its Special Projects Fund for sustainable forest management; British and Dutch importers have agreed to impose a surcharge on tropical timber imports for this purpose.[52] Timber exports can only continue to provide an important contribution to Africa's export earnings if related to appropriate programmes for conservation, reforestation and the development of a local manufacturing capability. Africa needs to add value at source because higher transport costs from Africa to the US (US$75 a cube in 1990) than from Malaysia and the Philippines ($55 a cube) act as an insuperable price disadvantage in the markets with growth potential.[53]

Fishery Products

The fishing industry is often excluded from studies of agricultural products. But it contributes 5 per cent of sub-Saharan Africa's non-fuel export earnings, as much as timber and sugar (Table 3.1). The main exporters are Senegal, Mauritania and Côte d'Ivoire. Ghana, Madagascar, Cape Verde and Mozambique also have fishing industries. In the 1980s world exports more than doubled in value and prices rose by over 10 per cent. African countries benefited along with other producing countries. Somewhat surprisingly, Africa is actually a major importer of fish and spent some US$400 millions in 1985–7 for these imports, against exports of about $725 millions.[54] Fish processing (plus preservation and freezing) has to be carried out where the fish are caught; this means value is added where the primary commodity comes from, which is advantageous compared with many African exports. However, considering the protein deficiency in average sub-Saharan diets, the net export of fish from Africa is not desirable, at least from the nutritional standpoint. The danger, too, of over-fishing many of the main fishing grounds is real. Far more fishing is done in coastal waters than in the vast expanse of the Atlantic or Indian oceans and African countries cannot always easily protect their coastlines against Japanese and European fishing vessels.

Live Animals, Meat, Hides and Skins

When we see the pictures on our TV screens of dying animals in the African droughts it is hard to imagine that both live animals and meat are major African exports. They usually appear in the statistics, alongside fish products, under the heading of 'other non-fuel commodities'. A closer look shows that African export earnings from this source exceed those from tobacco, tea or bauxite (Table 3.1).

Yet, export-led growth based on meat products seems both unlikely and undesirable. First, because Africa contributes a mere 1.5 per cent to the total world exports (Table 3.1) and its animals are exported on the hoof or dead, not tinned or otherwise processed, which means no value is added locally. Second, meat-exporting countries are among Africa's poorest and most drought-stricken: Chad, Sudan, Niger, Somalia, Mali, Botswana and Namibia. Exports have fallen sharply since the severe drought of 1985, and higher prices have not offset the drop in export earnings.

Sub-Saharan Africa's undressed hides and skins account for a little over 1 per cent of its total exports. The two main suppliers are Namibia and Ethiopia, with a much smaller contribution from Kenya. All told, exports of some US$200 million of the undressed skins do not presage export-led growth in this sector, unless Namibia and Ethiopia can increase their leather manufacturing industries.

Tobacco

A World Bank Working Party document states:

Tobacco is one of the few agricultural commodities in which sub-Saharan Africa's performance has been better than that of other regions. But because of consumer health concerns, world demand has been slowing down over the last 15 years and should slow further in the future.[55]

African tobacco producers have not only retained but even increased their share of world exports, but tobacco's share in sub-Saharan Africa's export earnings has declined to just over 3 per cent of non-fuel export earnings. It is still an important export crop for Zimbabwe and is Malawi's major source of export earnings. World prices have dropped sharply since the peaks of the early 1980s and are not expected to rise. The World Bank forecasts a further fall in the 1990s.[56] Again, there is little hope of export-led growth here and most African tobacco is exported unprocessed. Sub-Saharan Africa consumes 80 000 tonnes and exports 180 000 tonnes but markets elsewhere are not growing. The largest and fastest growing market is China, where cigarette consumption is 1.5 trillion (million million) a year, over 1000 per head per person, but China has been reducing imports and increasing exports.[57]

Tea

Tea's only rivals as a stimulant are coffee and the cola drinks, the latter arguably a youth market and both under the critical scrutiny of health experts. World tea consumption has grown fast and steadily – doubling in 20 years – and Africa's production has a proven track record of providing quality teas. Africa earned more than 10 per cent of the value of worldwide tea receipts in 1985–7, though it sold only 4 per cent of the volume.[58] Prices were low in the late 1980s, but the World Bank expects them to rise rapidly for the rest of the century, with African teas leading the way.[59] However, according to a former tea taster in London, 'Over the last twelve years ex-garden prices (that is, the price received by tea gardens) have been declining even as the market price has nearly doubled – the equivalent now of £1.40/kg ex-garden winds up as £3.00/kg.' Nearly all of the processing of tea takes place in the tea-producing countries because this work must be done on the estate in case the leaves are damaged or ferment before being dried and rolled. Breaking, sieving, drying and packing for export can all be done by Africans, so value is added locally. It is one cash crop that could be encouraged. Currently tea contributes only 2.5 per cent to sub-Saharan Africa's non-fuel export earnings, and at this level will not replace projected falls in income from other commodities.

The constraints on an expansion of African tea production are, first, that US imports of tea are mainly from Latin American sources, supplying cheap tea for tea bags and instant powdered tea. Lipton (Unilever) holds 45 per cent of the US market. Growth areas in the market – for example for iced tea – are being filled by imports from China and Argentina. A US buyer reported that 'the African proportion of the US tea market is not likely to change in the coming years.'

African teas go mainly to Europe and the UK in particular. Tea consumption trends are strongly related to historical and cultural preferences. This is the second constraint: African producers are unlikely, even with increased production, to establish their teas as strong, single-origin market brands in the way that many of the Indian, Sri Lankan and Chinese sources have done. A British importer and blender explained the problem: 'There are few origins that will actually suit the British taste without blending, especially African. It just tastes wrong. Companies are trying it, for example African organic tea, but the product is failing in the marketplace.'

There are two further constraints. First, land shortage: in Kenya and Malawi, the two main African producing countries, there is a shortage of suitable land for much expansion of production.[60] And second, traders distrust tea that comes from small growers. In Asia, tea is grown on large estates owned by a handful of companies. They pay low wages and offer poor conditions to the pickers, who are mainly women, but quality is carefully controlled. In Kenya and Malawi, tea is produced by small-scale growers. Their associations have been establishing rigorous quality control to enable them to compete successfully in the world market.[61]

Cotton and Textiles

Cotton is the third largest non-fuel export earning commodity for the African continent. Although Egypt produces nearly half of this total, cotton still provides 5 per cent of sub-Saharan African non-fuel export earnings, slightly less than timber (Table 3.1). Sudan is the major producer, but Zimbabwe, Mali, Côte d'Ivoire, Burkina Faso and Benin are also exporters.

In the early 1970s prices fell and cotton production was cut back. Since the mid-1980s, better prices, improved varieties and greater use of fertilisers and pesticides have raised exports again, particularly in the West African francophone countries.[62] Anxieties about the effects of monoculture remain, and agronomists are studying appropriate rotation systems in West Africa. Where cotton is inter-cropped with food crops, yields are low and the use of 'modern imports', as the World Bank describes chemical fertilisers, herbicides and pesticides, is not generally practised. The Bank evidently regards increased cotton exports, under what it calls 'supportive macro-economic policies ... [with] assured input supply and efficient marketing structures', as one of its success stories. It predicts healthy growth for Africa's cotton exports in the future[63] – a steady rise in both volumes and prices to the end of the century, with particular advantage accruing to African growers, because of their low cost structures.[64] However, the Bank simultaneously recognises that cotton faces a long-term decline because of competition with the growing range of artificial fibres. Demand for cotton goods unfortunately does not rise as fast as incomes either in the industrialised countries, or in developing countries (see Chart 4.2). Synthetic fibres tend to be substituted for cotton as incomes grow and technology allows. A slight, discernible preference for cotton in industrialised countries is not significant in the long term because of low overall population growth.

The most obvious market for cotton goods is Africa itself where cotton and yarn exports in 1985–7 of approximately US$1600 million compare with textile, yarn and fabric imports of approximately $2900 million. Less than half of these exports came from sub-Saharan Africa, which is a net importer of yarn and clothing (see Annexe Table A18). Yet, textile manufacture is one of the first industries that all developing countries seek to establish and there is no reason why Africa should not follow suit so as to substitute imports with home production.

During the 1980s cotton textiles featured strongly in export successes of the Less Developed Countries. But the prospects are not as rosy for Africa now, unless the importing countries undergo some 'structural adjustment' of their own within their textile industries. The Multi-Fibre Arrangement (MFA), first introduced in 1974, is what requires the 'structural adjustment'. Pressure from exporting countries has finally elicited a commitment from the US and EC to phase the MFA out, but it is difficult to predict what, if any, opportunities might open up to African producers as a result.[65]

Rubber

The last of the agricultural products under review, with over 1 per cent of Africa's export earnings, is rubber. Natural rubber is mainly exported from Liberia, but Cameroon, Côte d'Ivoire and Nigeria have increased exports in recent years. While world output has been rising, Africa's share has remained fairly steady and prices have recovered from the low levels of the early 1980s. The world rubber market is rather less volatile than others we have looked at in this chapter. As one industry executive said,

> Rubber prices do not fluctuate as much as some other commodities. Its movements generally reflect the welfare or otherwise of the industrialised economies. It doesn't make you rich necessarily. If you're starting out on rubber, you could put your money in a building society and get more return in six years.

Tyre production absorbs 70 per cent of natural rubber production and 80 per cent of the production of all rubber. Artificial and natural rubber are not perfect substitutes; they are used together to make tyres. Recession in the early 1990s has reduced sales of cars and thus demand for rubber, but demand in this industry is cyclical and is expected to pick up slowly. The International Rubber Agreement (INRA), the only surviving commodity agreement, raised its support price by 8 per cent at the end of 1990.

In 1987, Africa's share of the slowly expanding world rubber market was just over 5 per cent – small compared to major producers like Malaysia with 41 per cent, Indonesia with 25 per cent, or Thailand with 21 per cent. Brazil is now a net rubber importer, although the tree (*Hevea Braziliensis*) grew there naturally; it was brought to Kew Gardens, England, germinated and then taken to South-East Asia. Firestone Tire Company established rubber plantations in Liberia in 1914, owned half the country and ran it as a virtual private colony. Most of the large rubber companies own estates in South-East Asia: Goodrich and Goodyear (US owned), Bridgestone (of Japan, which now owns Firestone), Sumitomo (of Japan) which now owns Dunlop, Michelin (of France), Pirelli (of Italy) and Continental (of Germany).

These companies also buy in the open market and sell rubber latex for uses other than tyres. Increasingly, Malaysian and Indonesian estates have long-term direct contracts with manufacturers; not all estates are owned by the tyre companies, which do not want to be troubled with the vagaries of agriculture.

So African producers, even small-scale ones, could get into the market. The premium market is for high quality latex which is tapped and taken to the estate factory to coagulate or, in the case of smallholders, simply coagulated into a slab and sold by weight to a middleman, who sells to a re-miller. Production on smallholdings accounts for 70 per cent of world rubber production. However, smallholders cannot necessarily satisfy the strict technical specifications for rubber sold on the international markets. Moreover, bad quality and infrastructure problems mean that African producing countries continue to lose potential earnings from rubber. There are others who get hold of those lost earnings for themselves, as one dealer explained:

> African rubber, although there's a lot of it and quite high grade, is generally discounted – about 6 per cent – because of uncertainties of shipment and irregular quality and condition. Because of this West African rubber is sometimes traded very cheaply, brought to Europe and inspected and repackaged. It's perfectly silly logistically, but there are big margins for the traders doing this.

There are several distinct stages in rubber processing and some must be carried out in the producing country. Manufacturing of tyres and rubber goods, however, takes place in the industrialised countries and producing countries get only a small part of the value added, particularly where the estates and factories are owned by foreign companies. The worst news for Africa in this respect is that manufacturers and traders have deep seated prejudices and scepticism about African society and production; take the views of this buyer – not necessarily the product of pure prejudice, but hard for any African exporter to break through:

> The difficulties come in the way that the factories are run – carelessness, leaving rubber in the rain, slabs not put in polythene bags on the pallets, so that wood splinters get into the rubber ... It's not that the trees aren't happy in West Africa, it is largely the chaos that makes up West Africa's politics that makes things so difficult ... Very crudely, West African governments don't care. For example Nigeria used to be the biggest producer. It's gone down hill in 20 years or more ... Estates no longer offer direct to brokers but via politicians getting their cut ... the one-time French colonies are better. They have maintained a strong presence and bequeathed something rather useful – a reasonable respect for education.

There are real difficulties for importers from Africa. Africa's civil wars – for example in Liberia since late 1990 – cause economic havoc and human tragedy. If and when the country recovers and if problems of corruption, inefficiency and quality are then solved the market may no longer be there. Rubber faces a declining market because of advances in new technology as is the case for other traditional primary commodities. A US company executive interviewed signalled increased demand for polymer and plastics as a big threat to African exports to the US. Even without this, experts forecast slow growth in world rubber demand.

Other Agricultural Products

Many other agricultural products contribute smaller amounts to Africa's export earnings – spices, sisal, bananas and other fruits, vegetables, flowers and honey. For some of these products the markets are growing. The volume of world sales of spices, for example, increased by 22 per cent between 1982 and 1987 while actual earnings leapt by 75 per cent. Unfortunately, Africa's market share of spice exports dropped in these same years from 12 per cent to only 8 per cent.[66] Madagascar is the chief African spice exporter, but African exporters are all forfeiting their share to South-East Asian producers.

Demand for hard fibres like sisal has stagnated or fallen throughout the 1970s and 1980s in face of competition from synthetics. Prices for sisal halved between 1982 and 1987, reducing African earnings from US$55 million to $15 million. Madagascar and Tanzania were the main suppliers of sisal.[67]

In spite of an expanding market for bananas over the last decade and modest improvements in price since 1983, Africa's output has dwindled. Earnings in the 1980s rose only from US$36 million to $55 million.[68] The two main banana exporters, Côte d'Ivoire and Somalia, are both EC partners under the Lomé Convention. As such they have enjoyed some protection in the European markets but this may well end in 1992. Future prospects for an expansion in this field against strong competition from Central America are poor.

On the other hand, non-traditional fresh fruit exports alongside honey, vegetables and flowers, do show some expansion. By 1990 fully 10 per cent of Kenya's export earnings were derived from air-exports of fresh vegetables and flowers.[69] Zimbabwe and Senegal are following suit, but their exports still represent less than 1 per cent of their foreign earnings. It is also hard to say how far this market can be expanded. Speciality foods and flowers have a high income demand elasticity – demand rises ahead of incomes in consuming countries. There are drawbacks however. The market has strict quality requirements which can only be achieved through high production costs, including intensive use of labour and heavy use of pesticides. In practice this means production on large farms, often as part of a diversification on European-run farms, and a large proportion of the crop being dumped on the local market – one that may effectively not exist – at a fraction of the cost.

Finally, as with so many products, the control of fresh fruit and flower markets is in the consuming countries and concentrated among a very few companies. Barring the establishment of European-style fruit and vegetable marketing cooperatives, it is unlikely that small-scale producers or farm labourers will gain much from expanded exports of fruit and vegetables.[70]

By the end of the 1980s, Africa's agricultural exports had become even more concentrated, nearly 60 per cent in just two commodities and the range, or basket of commodities, has narrowed (see Table 5.1). This means that Africa's agricultural exports as a whole are over-dependent on the vagaries of a few international market and trading systems. For nearly all primary commodities the market has been declining. Some African products face other intrinsic problems, including market resistance and the preference of international traders for other sources or varieties. Significant new markets for African commodities are simply not there.

Table 5.1: Composition of Africa's Agricultural Export Package: Shares in Sub-Saharan African Total

	1973/75	1985/87	1988/89
GROWING SHARE			
Coffee	18.1	24.8	19.0
Cocoa beans	14.6	17.8	15.2
Cotton	7.2	6.2	9.2
Fish products	2.3	6.3	9.4
Sugar	5.8	5.4	6.5
Tobacco	2.7	4.0	4.6
Tea	1.8	3.2	3.3
Rubber	1.7	1.7	2.8
Hides and skins	1.9	1.9	2.1
Subtotal	56.1	71.3	72.1
DECLINING SHARE			
Vegetable oils	9.9	2.5	3.3
Timber	9.2	7.6	7.7
Live animals and meat	5.6	5.1	4.7
Cotton yarn	6.5	6.2	3.8
Cocoa products	3.0	3.0	2.2
Cereals	1.9	1.2	1.3
Hard fibres, sisals, etc.	1.6	0.3	0.3
Bananas	0.6	0.5	0.5
Other	5.6	2.3	4.1
Subtotal	43.9	28.7	27.9
TOTAL	100.0	100.0	100.0
In US$m	6917	10 362	10 470

Note: Vegetable oil includes groundnuts
Sources: Henk Kox, *Export Constraints for sub-Saharan Africa*, Serie Research Memoranda, Free University of Amsterdam, 1990, Table 1; UNCTAD, *Commodity Yearbook, 1991*

6. Africa's Mineral Wealth

The geological formation of southern Africa bears a wide range of minerals and is legendary for its mineral wealth. In Britain, at least, southern Africa was the land of Cecil Rhodes, and famed for its immense South African gold and diamond mines and the great mineral companies – Anglo American, de Beers and Consolidated Goldfields. One history recounts that:

> Between 1867 and 1935 more than £1,200 million was invested in Africa ... most of this ... directly or indirectly in the development and exploitation of Africa's mineral resources. Mineral production multiplied six-fold in 40 years, while mineral exports rose from a value of £15.5 million in 1897 to one of £102.72 million in 1935, as the mining companies expanded their operations in South and Central Africa and began to invest in West Africa.[1]

Although historically African mining was opened up by British capital, with African mines accounting for 7 per cent of all British overseas investment worldwide by 1913,[2] today these companies are mostly South African owned with some American and British shareholders. Britain's predominance in African mining withstood two world wars, despite disinvestment following both of them.[3] In the 1960s South African and Rhodesian mines were extremely lucrative and the output exported from these mines alone was the equivalent of one-eighth of all UK imports.[4] Shareholders received some £80 million annually in dividends and royalties from British companies in Africa, and throughout the 1950s and 1960s returns on mining investments remained well above the returns on capital in home industrial companies.[5] The bonanza began to fade after the 1970s as competition grew and the long post-war boom subsided.

South Africa, with its treasures of gold and diamonds, has always received the lion's share of this investment (see Annexe Table A19). Besides South Africa, the main exporters of gold are Ghana, Ethiopia and Zimbabwe, while diamonds come principally from Botswana, Sierra Leone, Zaïre and the Central African Republic. Until recently Namibia's considerable production of diamonds was included in

South Africa's figures. South African capital has not only supplanted British and American investment, in giants like Anglo American, but now has a large stake in the production and marketing of gold, diamonds and other minerals throughout the whole of southern Africa (see Chapter 8).

Chart 6.1: The Minerals and Metals Market – Sub-Saharan Africa's Share (excluding the former Soviet bloc)

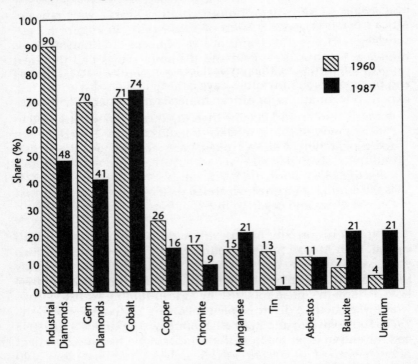

Source: USBM *Mining Annual Review*, World Bureau of Metallurgical Statistics, World Bank from *Mining Development in Sub-Saharan Africa*, Peter M. Fozzard, paper presented at the MEP Conference, Madrid, November 1989

Sub-Saharan Africa exports gold and diamonds, but also large quantities of copper, bauxite, iron ore, uranium, phosphate rock and manganese; smaller quantities of asbestos, beryllium, cadmium, chromite, cobalt, germanium, lead, lithium, nickel, platinum, tantalite, tin, tungsten, nickel, vanadium, zinc. The differing importance in world markets of the main minerals and metals is shown in Chart 6.1.

Southern Africa has long dominated two markets – diamonds and cobalt – with 74 per cent of exports from 'non-communist' countries. In the 1960s copper accounted for 26 per cent of world production but by the 1980s this share had shrunk to 16 per cent. In absolute terms African output had only dropped slightly, but output from Chile, Mexico, Peru, Poland and China had greatly increased. Largely because of its declining share of the world copper market, sub-Saharan Africa's contribution to world mineral supplies in general has been declining. Only in bauxite, uranium and manganese ore have Africa's shares more than marginally increased.

Relative prices, compared with those of other developing regions, have not been the main cause of Africa's falling share of mineral exports. But civil wars, the physical location of the mineral deposits and transportation difficulties have contributed directly to the fall. Export concentrations for African minerals are greater than for agricultural commodities: copper accounts for 98 per cent of Zambia's exports and, until the beginning of the 1990s, 58 per cent of Zaïre's. The economic importance of Northern Rhodesia (now Zambia) and the Belgian Congo (now Zaïre) as colonies was based on that one mineral. Excluding oil from the exports of Angola, Cameroon, Congo, Gabon, Nigeria and Seychelles, there are other almost equally large concentrations on one export commodity. Diamonds account for nearly 78 per cent of Botswana's exports, one-third of the Central African Republic's and Sierra Leone's. Bauxite constitutes 89 per cent of Guinea's exports and 24 per cent of Ghana's. Iron ore provides 64 per cent of Liberia's and 45 per cent of Mauritania's exports. Uranium and thorium make up 85 per cent of Niger's exports and a large part of Namibia's. Phosphate rock supplies 47 per cent of Togo's and 12 per cent of Senegal's exports. In the case of most of these minerals, the two or three supplying countries are the only African suppliers.

Such export concentrations imply that small countries must find their resources for development – building and maintaining roads and port facilities, the education and health-care of the labour force – from just one or two commodities, a very narrow economic base. If that base collapses, the country faces disaster, but even if it does not, there are problems for government taxation policy when just one or two industries must carry the whole burden. Nearly 50 per cent of the GNP of Zambia is based on mineral exports. Over the last 20 years, Zambia's national income (GNP) moved almost exactly in line with the international movements in the copper price (Chart 6.2).

In Botswana, Mauritania, Liberia and Zaïre the situation is similar. Mineral exports account for more than 25 per cent of GNP. This

Chart 6.2: Zambian Gross National Income and the International Copper Price

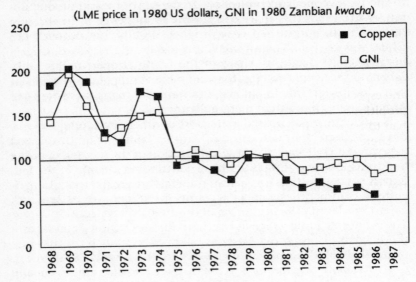

(LME price in 1980 US dollars, GNI in 1980 Zambian *kwacha*)

Key:
1. London Metal Exchange price in 1980 US dollars
2. Gross National Income in 1980 Zambian *kwacha*
3. 1980 = 100

Source: Henk Kox, *Export Constraints for Sub-Saharan Africa*, Serie Research Memoranda, Free University of Amsterdam, 1990

dependence is similar to that of agricultural exporter countries like the Gambia, Ghana, Côte d'Ivoire and Mauritius. The fact that countries with a wide range of products and least export concentration – for example, Cameroon, Côte d'Ivoire and Zimbabwe – have high or above average *per capita* incomes cannot be ignored in any attempt to understand Africa's economic crisis (see Annexe Table A1).

Countries blessed with plentiful supplies of oil and diamonds may be able to live with high export concentrations, but those without either must diversify. Agricultural commodities are threatened by natural problems like crop failure or ageing plants, while mineral exports rely on constant economic strength to sustain investment. This depends on the decisions of outside investors and Africa has not been a favoured region for direct foreign investment in recent years. Indeed, during the 1980s the tendency was towards disinvestment, notwithstanding the aim of World Bank structural adjustment policies to attract foreign investment back by improving Africa's image and export performance.[6]

The 1988 World Bank projections to the end of the century for sub-Saharan African non-fuel export earnings assumed that the proportion of mineral and agricultural earnings would stay the same – at 3:7. The Bank forecast an average annual 5–6 per cent increase[7] for both, and did so in spite of the actual decline in the last decade of Africa's non-fuel export earnings by 3.4 per cent a year. The Bank's projections and especially the over-optimistic estimates were based on seemingly propitious conditions in 1987/88 which did not last. The Bank later had to revise its figures downwards (see Annexe Table A20).

There were fundamental weaknesses in recommending export growth based on Africa's mineral prospects. From 1960 to 1987 Africa's share of the world market for minerals fell (Chart 6.1); and the World Bank itself expects this to continue with Africa falling behind Latin America and Asia for the rest of this century. Analysis of African mineral production raises several general problems which are not dealt with in the World Bank's export-led growth proposition and so we list them here:

1. Value Added in the Producing Country
The mineral producing countries retain a very small proportion of the overall value of the finished product. Negligible value is added in the mineral producing countries.

2. Declining Inputs in Modern Industry
Mineral use – that is, inputs of minerals in modern industrial production per unit of output – is declining.[8] Although worldwide demand for minerals has increased over the last three decades, it has not increased as much as industrial growth itself. General reasons for this include better design, a switch to synthetic materials, changes in demand for goods and services, recycling of used materials, and biotechnology-led savings. Many goods now contain smaller quantities of metals than a decade ago. Specifically, there is a shift away from heavy mechanical engineering industries where sales have been falling (by 3 per cent a year in the UK between 1978 and 1985) to electrical engineering and electronics (where sales have been growing by 3 per cent a year over the same period).[9] New recycling technologies have increased the use of scrap metal in steel and other metal production. Plastics and ceramics are replacing metals in many uses from car bodies and containers to nuts and bolts and paperclips. Optical fibres are replacing copper in telecommuni-

cations (a 45 kg length of fibre cable can transmit as much information as a tonne of copper wire).[10]

3. Instability in the Former Soviet Bloc

The entry of the former republics of the Soviet Union and Eastern European countries into the world commodity market is already affecting prices, although possibly only in the short term. The former Soviet Union is the largest world producer of iron ore, lead, zinc and manganese, the second largest producer of gold, chrome, platinum, magnesium and phosphate and among the largest producers of silver, bauxite, copper and diamonds. Of note also are Polish coal and copper, Albanian chrome and Czechoslovakian gold.[11] The overall trend in exports is down, especially in manganese, chromium, copper and magnesium. To meet debts in the West and increase imports of essentials and of new technology to upgrade their economies, these countries are taking all the minerals they can produce onto the world market.[12] In the longer term, increased consumption in these countries and in China could add significantly to world mineral demand.[13]

4. Foreign Investment

Mineral deposits in former Soviet Republics and Eastern European countries may attract Western capital at the expense of Africa. Already, there are joint ventures between large mineral companies from the West and Eastern European companies.[14]

5. Biotechnology

Biotechnology is being applied to the exploitation of low grade ores. Bacterial leaching can extract normally insoluble mineral compounds containing copper, zinc, nickel and lead among others. Over 15 per cent of all copper produced in the US is extracted in this way, making new use of mining waste and low grade ores. US reports indicate that strategic materials like cobalt and platinum could soon be recovered by leaching. Biological treatment of toxic and other waste has been one of the first large-scale applications of biotechnology. The process not only produces heat and power, but recovers valuable materials from what was previously refuse.[15] Biotechnology can also make different inputs for industrial products interchangeable. Prices will fall as manufacturers turn to the cheapest inputs.

6. Demand in the Industrialised Countries

Part of the 1980s' failure of world demand for minerals to keep pace with production and supply resulted from the generally reduced demand in the industrialised countries' economies. The rate of growth of industrial production slowed from 3.4 per cent over 1970–9 to 1.8 per cent over 1980–7. Within the general decline in consumption of metals and minerals in the 1980s compared with the 1970s, there are some differences among the different markets (see Annexe Table A21). Behind the ups and downs of boom and slump, however, there is a long-term trend, sometimes described as 'the end of the era of materials'. Income elasticities of demand for almost all materials are low since, as incomes rise, people spend more on services and relatively less on goods. Of Africa's minerals, only aluminium, nickel and chromium (for stainless steel) have retained their share of consumption in industrial countries. Consumption per unit of output of iron ore, copper and tin in world industry has nearly halved since 1965 (see Chart 6.3).

Chart 6.3: World Consumption of Commodities per unit of GNP

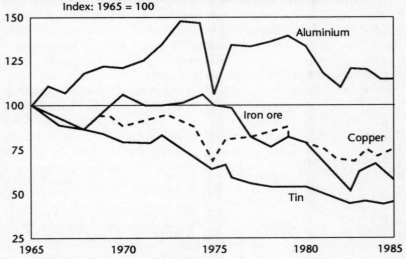

Source: ODI Briefing Paper, March 1988

Copper

Copper is found in metamorphic rock formations worldwide, but mainly in the US, Canada, Chile, Papua New Guinea, Australia and southern Africa. It generally occurs along with other minerals, such as silver, gold, lead, zinc and cobalt. Most of the known massed deposits have been worked out and copper ore has today to be extracted from rock in which the metal may comprise as little as 0.5 per cent. The rock is dug out, crushed and placed in flotation chambers. It is then concentrated, roughly 30 per cent copper, with other elements in it such as gold and silver, ready for further processing. Very little African copper is exported as concentrate. The copper salts may be extracted by leaching, especially of low grade ore or mine waste. Most ore is roasted to extract the sulphur and then smelted to produce blister copper, so called because of the bubbly appearance of its surface. This is still an impure form of metal, but it can be cast into large flat ingots and exported as such. Zaïre exports about half of its output as blister for refining elsewhere. The refining is done by electrolysis, using a pure copper cathode and the blister ingots as anodes. The remainder of Zaïre's and all of Zambia's output is exported in refined form. Small amounts – 1 or 2 per cent of the ore produced – remain in the producing countries for local fabrication into copper products. Botswana exports its copper as ore, Zimbabwe and Namibia as blister, and Zimbabwe refines about one-third of its output for local manufactures (see Annexe Table A22).

Africa supplies somewhat less than one-fifth of the world's total exports: about 3 per cent of ore exports, one-third of blister and one-fifth of refined. But this share has been declining. African output has fallen while output elsewhere, especially in Chile, has increased.[16] There are still considerable reserves of copper-bearing ore in both Zambia and Zaïre, but investment in mining and refining plant has been reduced in recent years while investment in Chile and the US has been expanded.[17] In Chile, debt for equity swaps have enabled US companies to buy very cheaply into Chilean operations and open up new, large-scale mines.[18]

Exploration investment – at 1 per cent of the value of mineral production – is particularly low in Zaïre. This contrasts with 6 per cent in Canada and 13 per cent in the US and Australia.[19] The World Bank and Fraser Reports emphasise the need for African governments to take action to encourage direct foreign investment in new exploration and in expanded mineral production through joint ventures and other means.[20] But nearly all African mining is already at least partly operated and owned by private companies, generally a South African company in the de Beers, Anglo American, Chartered group; management is nearly always in the hands of the expatriate company, for example, in Zambia Anglo American, in Zaïre the successors to the Belgian Union Minière. The practices of these companies are considered in Chapter 8.

Maintaining copper output in both Zambia and Zaïre is proving extremely difficult. Zambia reduced its output from 700 000 tonnes in 1976 to 500 000 tonnes in 1989. The Nchanga mine produces about one-third of Zambia's total output and will be worked out before the end of the century.[21] In 1989 the World Bank demanded reforms including a 50 per cent currency devaluation and reduction in state food subsidies as a condition for rescheduling Zambia's US$7 billion debt. The aim was to make Zambia more attractive for foreign investors. But the primary objective of the mining rehabilitation programme, financed by the World Bank, the African Development Bank and EC loans, is greater efficiency – not increased production. Costs including storage costs are to be reduced and power supplies improved.[22] Landlocked Zambia has a grave transport problem. A single-track railway line, out of action for years, leads west to Benguela; and the Tanzam line running east to Dar-es-Salaam in Tanzania (at least 1500 miles) is slow and already operating at full capacity.[23] Zaïre has similar problems and has had to cut back its previously stable level of production of 500 000 tonnes a year, to 440 000 tonnes in 1989.[24] By contrast, Chile, producing 1.5 million tonnes a year in the late 1980s, was planning expansion.[25] Zaïre has debts of more than $8 billion, like Zambia, and also adopted the programme of structural adjustment required by the World Bank, but profits of the Gecamines have not been reinvested by the government in the copper industry.[26]

While a more efficient African copper mining industry might indeed provide an important base for African development, it is the state of the markets and potential earnings which will determine investment decisions. World demand for copper grew much more slowly – just over 1.5 per cent a year – from mid-1970 to mid-1980 than in the previous decade when annual growth was just over 4 per cent. Rates of growth below 1 per cent in Europe and North America pulled the average down, despite growth of around 4 per cent in Japan, China and East Asia. A recovery after 1985 to a worldwide average of 3.5 per cent fuelled estimates of demand for copper growing at 3–4 per cent a year.[27] This was shortlived: a price collapse in 1989 led to downward revisions of about 2 per cent. Always volatile, prices fluctuated exceptionally at the turn of the decade; 1990–1 saw a high of almost £1800 a tonne and a low of under £1200. Political instability in producing countries has been one obvious cause of rising prices. In recent years rebel forces respectively attacked mines in Zaïre and closed down the giant mine in Bougainville (Papua New Guinea) for some time to come. The attack on Zaïre sent the price of cobalt – essential for aeroplane engines – rocketing up from US$4 to $40 per lb because Zaïre supplies 69 per cent of the world's cobalt, but the market soon settled.[28]

African copper producers are being challenged by the construction of much larger and more efficient smelters in America, but the price they can get is not high enough to encourage new investment.[29] The Fraser Report advises African governments to invest in new plant, but these governments do not have the funds even to pay their outstanding debts. Outside finance is far more attracted to Chile and Eastern Europe or into new technology in the US. Future prospects for copper have been so varyingly described by the press and traders interviewed that it is hard to develop a clear picture. Comments range from the euphoric: 'era of prosperity forecast for copper' at the start of 1990,[30] to 'a very sober period ahead for the copper mining industry', according to a mineral analyst interviewed at the end of the same year.[31]

The world market for copper is dominated by the large US copper companies. The US is the largest single consumer – almost twice as much as Japan – using one-fifth of the refined total. It is also the largest producer of refined copper (16 per cent of the total) and is now second only to Chile as a producer of ore and blister. The US is also the largest copper importer – buying 800 000 tonnes from abroad (about 40 per cent of its total consumption of over 2 million tonnes).[32] The state of the US economy is thus the main determinant of demand and prices.

In the 1920s, US producers Copper Exporters Inc., which then accounted for 75 per cent of world output, used their dominant position to get monopolistic profits which had the effect ironically of stimulating copper mining in Northern Rhodesia. In the wake of the 1929 Wall Street crash, the US imposed a prohibitive tariff in 1932 on copper imports. Faced with these barriers other producing countries formed a cartel to regulate the market.[33] Today, in the presence or absence of an international copper agreement, the market rules but the US rules the market. The US copper companies are quite prepared to use their stocks to discipline any producing country that gets out of line.

The US imports copper principally from Canada and South America; Western Europe imports from Africa; Japan from Australia; and Eastern Europe from the former Soviet Union and Poland. The US now barely imports any copper from Africa, Japan a little.[34] These trade flows are determined partly by transport costs, but also by the historic and continuing patterns of capital investment. Fast growing markets for copper exist in both Eastern Europe and East Asia, but the former Soviet Union, Poland, Mongolia and China are all copper producers with expanding output, although China still imports.

The key to demand is the absence of substitutes for copper. In the US, 40 per cent of copper goes into the building industry, mainly for plumbing, 15 per cent into industrial machinery, 23 per cent into electrical and electronics applications, 12 per cent into power generation, and 10 per cent for motor vehicles. The amount of copper in cars is increasing because of a growing demand for auto-accessories that require it. In Europe, Japan and South Korea, more than 50 per cent of copper goes into electrical engineering. Less goes into construction than in the US,[35] but copper is beginning to replace cast iron, steel and lead in the European construction industry. Future demand for virgin copper will depend on the speed with which recycling is taken up. Recycled scrap now supplies 40 per cent of US copper needs.[36] In developing countries house building and machine manufacture will continue to require copper, but whether new electronics or car producing centres will emerge is uncertain. Recycling technologies will also be used.

The large number and complexity of variables determining demand for copper prevent confident predictions about demand and price over the next decade. But the developing countries of South and South-East Asia are now major consumers of copper, taking 680 000 tonnes a year. Eastern European countries, not including the former Soviet Union, consume a similar quantity. Brazil and Mexico combined consume about half as much. Africa's total consumption is just 28 000 tonnes.[37] In sub-Saharan Africa there is practically no fabrication of copper goods from refined copper, despite the wide range of applications and diverse demand.

Diamonds and Gold

Before Namibia became independent, its diamond exports were part of South Africa's and did not figure in discussions of sub-Saharan Africa's economic performance and prospects. Now, however, Namibian diamonds are included in sub-Saharan export earnings and this makes them the second most important mineral export. It is still difficult to estimate exactly how much Namibia contributed to South African production and profits. Figures for the 1970s from the United Nations Centre for Transnational Corporations (UNCTC) show that Namibia's share of South African exports of gems was nearly 40 per cent, while its share of South Africa's exports of gems and industrial diamonds combined was nearly 20 per cent.[38] Output in the 1980s was half 1970s' levels. Working from these estimates and allowing for different ways of presenting the figures – UN statistics are in carats, the IMF's in monetary values – diamonds appear to have contributed almost as much as copper to sub-Saharan Africa's export earnings in 1985–7 – a total value of somewhere between US$1000 millions and US$1600 millions (Annexe Table A23). This was almost 45 per cent of the world diamond market, excluding the former Soviet bloc.

The future of this market remains in the hands of de Beers (part of the Anglo American group). In 1991 de Beers took marketing control of both Angolan output and a part of Soviet production. The company continues to control the release of diamonds onto the market through the Central Selling Organisation, maintaining prices at levels it believes are sustainable. How long de Beers can continue to do this is hard to predict. Its success in recent years is attributable to increases in gems sold to make jewellery, demand having risen as personal incomes have risen (especially in the Middle East). Between 1980 and 1985 the value of diamonds grew by 20 per cent in real terms – well ahead of any other mineral.[39] As an investment, they may continue to attract rich elites everywhere.

While diamonds are a valuable export resource for African producing countries, only three sub-Saharan countries are recorded as major producers: Botswana, Namibia and Zaïre. Diamonds are important for Sierra Leone and Angola too, but the estimate of one minerals expert is that 75 per cent are smuggled out of the country – diamonds are ideal as contraband – and do not appear in the merchandise statistics.

Africa produces nearly two-thirds of the world's gold, 45 per cent from South Africa and 20 per cent from sub-Saharan Africa.[40] Gold is a precious metal, rarely found near the earth's surface and only in certain geological formations. Its rarity combined with its glitter and its softness has made it the almost universal currency throughout the ages. Apart from Africa, other sources, in order of importance are: the former Soviet Union, the US, Canada, China, Australia, Papua New Guinea, Colombia and the Philippines. Mexico and Peru, formerly major producers, now produce modest quantities. In sub-Saharan Africa the gold producing countries include Zimbabwe, Ghana and Zaïre; to a lesser extent, Mali, Ethiopia, Zambia, Namibia and the Central African Republic; and, with the advent of small-scale alluvial projects, Botswana, Burkina Faso, Congo, Gabon, Liberia, Sierra Leone, Sudan and Tanzania.

The value of the gold that is mined or panned depends on factors that make its price even harder to predict than that of other minerals. Apart from its use in industry and in jewellery, gold is held by governments as a reserve currency and by rich individuals as a hedge against inflation. Demand for gold, therefore, depends on government decisions to hold or sell reserves and on expectations about general levels of trade and movements of prices, all of which defy firm prediction.

During the 1980s demand for gold rose more slowly than world supply (which includes mined gold, re-use of scrap and government sales). Sales for fabrication doubled, but gold as an investment fluctuated with the uncertain economic climate, generally on a downward trend. Since the peak in 1980, the price of gold has moved on between US$350 and $450 a fine ounce, except for 1985 (Annexe Table A24). The World Gold Council estimates that at a price of $350 per ounce, about one-tenth of the gold mined each year (currently over 1800 tonnes) becomes unviable; at over $450 per ounce the re-use of scrap becomes profitable.[41] The price range is reinforced by the behaviour of investors who calculate along these lines. Stability would seem to be assured, but there are some contrary indications. Demand is expected to grow at about 5 per cent a year to reach 2500 tonnes in the mid-1990s. New investment in US, Canadian and other mines means that supplies from the West will probably rise to 1900 tonnes a year. A fall in the output of around 300 tonnes in the former Soviet Union will be offset by predicted large-scale increases from the Philippines and Colombia. With high levels of recycled scrap, as much as 400 tonnes available, and some central bank sales expected, the supply side is set to soar to 2800 tonnes – that is, 300 tonnes above demand.[42] This explains why the World Bank forecasts declining real prices for gold to the end of the century (Annexe Table A20). Gold remains a valuable foreign exchange resource for many developing country governments short of hard currency, but not necessarily an important export commodity because the market for gold responds precipitously and negatively to competitive selling. To recommend new investment would thus seem mistaken in this case. African governments, and particularly Ghana, have been criticised – by the Fraser Committee, for example – for not undertaking more exploration of their natural resources. But caution in proceeding with highly capital intensive investment in mineral extraction – especially of gold – seems prudent in the circumstances. Analysts are generally unenthusiastic about investment in gold mining, not because it is Africa in question, but because the investment has already been made in the US, Canada and Australia.

Aluminium from Bauxite

Aluminium derived from bauxite is the most widely distributed metallic element in the earth's crust and is the most widely used of all non-ferrous metals. Alumina (aluminium oxide) must first be extracted from the bauxite ore. The alumina content is only about one-fifth of the total. Aluminium is produced by electrolysis with a carbon anode which combines with the oxygen in the alumina when the current is passed through and sufficient heat is generated to reduce the alumina to metal. The process requires plentiful, cheap electric energy. Africa supplies about 20 per cent of world bauxite production, almost all of it from Guinea, but aluminium production in Africa is negligible.[43] The Volta Dam in Ghana and Sanaga Dam in Cameroon were designed to make it possible to refine African bauxite (though neither country produces much bauxite),[44] but the quantities produced have been disappointingly small. Practically no aluminium is consumed in sub-Saharan Africa (Annexe Table A25). Africa's trade in bauxite is entirely in the raw material.

The largest consumers of bauxite are the US and the EC. Roughly a third of US imports comes from Guinea; they hit a peak in 1982–4, followed by decline.[45] Demand for Guinea's bauxite slackened after 1985 because production from new non-African sites was steadily rising. Until the 1970s nearly all bauxite production was controlled by a small number of transnational companies, which owned the processing and smelting capacity. Then a number of independent non-integrated or government producers entered the trade, attracted by the then high prices. But between 1980 and 1982 the price of aluminium was halved, to US$0.40/lb, and only slowly recovered to half the 1970s' level in real terms by 1987. Prices rose because of a shortage of aluminium in 1989.[46] Analysts expected consumption to rise ahead of production, but investors delayed, discouraged by the cost of building new smelters when aluminium prices were still below $0.90/lb. This level was reached briefly in 1990, but the price subsequently dropped again.[47]

Increased demand for bauxite is not envisaged because plastics are a useful replacement and more aluminium is being recovered by recycling. This has two advantages: it re-uses the metal and needs less energy than processing bauxite into aluminium. In 1989 the US recycled some 850 000 tonnes (47 million cans), a recycling rate of 62 per cent. Currently the European rate is 16 per cent, but the target is 35 per cent.[48] As these recycling rates increase and the practice spreads to Eastern Europe and beyond, the trend to recycle combined with the use of plastics means that demand may fall in the long term. In mid-1991 aluminium stocks were at an all time high of 540 million tonnes and were expected to grow further because of increased supplies from the former Soviet Union.[49]

The example of South Korea reveals that developing countries may have expanding needs for alumunium. Between 1982 and 1987 South Korea's imports of aluminium doubled and imports of refined copper rose from 30 000 tonnes to 107 000 tonnes. But between 1976 and 1987 South Korea also increased its own smelter production of copper from 30 000 tonnes to 163 000.[50] Moreover, building aluminium smelters is a capital investment that even the richest countries are balking at and this means that Africa must continue to export the unrefined raw material.

Iron and Steel

Iron ore passes through several processes before use as mild steel for construction or special hardened steels for engineering and manufacturing. Most steel works integrate the process in a continuous line, to avoid the cost of reheating and to re-use the heat generated. Sub-Saharan Africa exports about 25 million tonnes of iron ore each year.[51] Zimbabwe has the only sizeable sub-Saharan African steel works. Even the combined output of the Zimbabwean plant and of those in Egypt, Algeria and South Africa make up barely 0.5 of 1 per cent of the world's total. Even the first stage of processing the ore into pellets or sinter in Africa is rare (see Annexe Table A26). When African diggers have done their work and the iron mountain has gone, there will be nothing left but a hole in the ground and an abandoned railway line to a decaying port. So much for export-led development.

Demand for iron ore depends on demand for steel. Iron ore is bought by steel makers in bulk long-term contracts. Consumption worldwide grew steadily until 1988, but since then demand has stagnated. Iron ore demand has been falling in the US and Western Europe for two decades. In the 1980s even Japan showed falling demand despite a strong growth in the economy. Several tendencies lie behind this. Steel is being replaced by plastics and aluminium, particularly in the manufacture of containers and in the motor vehicle industry (the overall weight of cars is falling); a rise in incomes and spending power does not increase consumption of steel-based goods; re-use of scrap is increasing, and much smaller stocks of steel are being held. In the future, demand for scrap is likely to increase further because of expanded production of steel in small-scale electric converters. Once scrap from Eastern European countries and the former Soviet Republics has been disposed of, a scrap 'shortage' may make iron ore once more competitive, especially where Direct Reduction of Iron (DRI) processing is in place.[52]

To be ready for this, the biggest iron producing countries – the former Soviet Union, Australia and Brazil – with highly capitalised, low cost mines are planning a large expansion of output. This will put smaller, high cost mines out of business. World Bank forecasts to the end of the century suggest continuing price erosion (Annexe Table A20).

In sub-Saharan Africa, there are just two major producers of iron ore – Liberia and Mauritania – and one minor producer in Zimbabwe, contributing a little over 3 per cent of the world total with a combined value in 1987 of US$350 million. In 1970 their market share was twice this. Only Liberia has a plant for producing iron pellets, which fetch a better price, but this plant can cope with only 25 per cent of its ore output (Annexe Table A26) and present political conditions render its viability doubtful. Progress has been slow in a World Bank and European financed scheme in Mauritania for a new mine and rail and port facilities for the production and export of concentrates.[53] In the interim, Mauritania's foreign debt has risen to over US$2 billion, or four times the country's annual export revenue. Exports are a large share of both Mauritania's and Liberia's national income. In each of these two countries the economy is dominated by just two commodity exports: in addition to iron ore, Liberia has rubber and Mauritania has fish (Annexe Table A9). These commodities' combined export earnings provide over 75 per cent of each countries' national income. Both have small populations, a little over 2 million, and low living standards, especially Mauritania. Neither offer appropriate conditions for building steel works.

One sub-Saharan African country, Zimbabwe, has developed an iron and steel making capacity, albeit on a small scale, prompted into this course of action when, as Southern Rhodesia, the country was cut off from its normal imports by international trade sanctions. Zimbabwe exports no iron ore. Its annual production of 2 million tonnes is all converted into pig iron and sinter, producing just over half a million tonnes of crude steel. Output doubled between 1976 and 1986 but has since fallen slightly.[54]

A modern steel works may have a capacity of anything from 2 million to 10 million tonnes a year. Building one is a major capital investment. In South Korea annual steel output is now 18 million tonnes, based almost entirely on imported iron ore. Indonesia, Turkey, Brazil and Venezuela have all expanded or even doubled their steel output in the last decade.[55] If they can do it, we may wonder why sub-Saharan Africa cannot. In the case of iron ore and steel the answer does not lie wholly with the uncertainties of future markets or prices. The other factors are dealt with in the final chapters.

'Exotic' Minerals

Paradoxically perhaps, Africa is so rich in mineral resources that it has not needed to industrialise. African elites have lived very well by exporting agricultural products and minerals and importing machinery and manufactured goods. Each country has been fortunate in having one or two products to export. There are many valuable minerals not yet covered in this chapter. The list of ten minerals (reproduced in Annexe Table A27) gives a total value to sub-Saharan exports of US$910 million at the end of the 1980s. Even this list excludes some 'exotic' minerals:

• The platinum group – especially platinum, palladium and rhodium – which are in strong demand for catalytic converters in cars and in the petro-chemical industry. A new deposit is being mined in Zimbabwe.
• Vanadium, an important steel hardener, is found in South Africa and Zimbabwe.

Africa has a large share of known world reserves of chromium ore (in South Africa and Zimbabwe), manganese ore (Gabon) and cobalt (Zaïre and Zambia). These three minerals are used in making specialised steels. Demand has declined because of the cutback in aircraft production and the use of alternative hardeners.

These rare or 'minor' metals often play a strategic role in the manufacture of advanced industrial products. Their prices, however, do not reflect this. Apart from an upward turn in metal prices slightly ahead of industrial prices in 1988–9 (Chart 6.4), the trend has been downwards. A large proportion of exotic metals is traded by specialist traders. Many, like bauxite and iron ore, are not traded in markets at all, but transferred directly, from mine to finished product, within the operations of single transnational companies. Even where African countries are by far the largest producers – as they are, for example, of diamonds, platinum, cobalt and chromium – they can rarely influence the market performance of these minerals and the returns for them.

Finally, exports of phosphate rock were worth US$139 million in 1987 (Annexe Table A27). The exporting countries, Senegal and Togo, have 3 per cent of world output and 10 per cent of exports. They export their total production. Zimbabwe also produces phosphate rock, much less than either Togo or Senegal, but none is exported.[56] Phosphate (not an exotic mineral) is a key component in fertilisers; exporting it in large quantities is not consistent with Africa's need for fertilisers to stimulate agricultural yields. There are negligible imports into Africa. Asian demand, especially in India and Indonesia, for phosphate rock is growing, but in the US and in Europe previous use was excessive and resulted in severe pollution; its use is now being cut back. World market prices are steady, but lower than 1980 levels in real terms (Annexe Table A20).

Chart 6.4: Commodity Price Indices, 1991

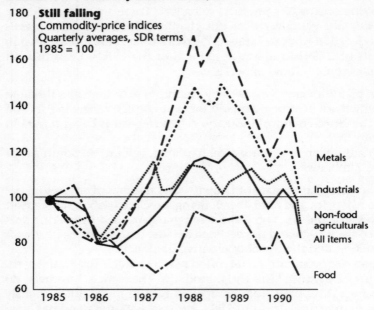

Still falling
Commodity-price indices
Quarterly averages, SDR terms
1985 = 100

Metals
Industrials
Non-food agriculturals
All items
Food

1985   1986   1987   1988   1989   1990

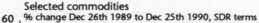

Selected commodities
% change Dec 26th 1989 to Dec 25th 1990, SDR terms

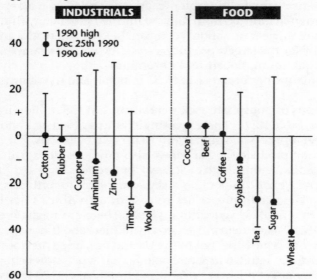

INDUSTRIALS   FOOD

1990 high
Dec 25th 1990
1990 low

Cotton   Rubber   Copper   Aluminium   Zinc   Timber   Wool   Cocoa   Beef   Coffee   Soyabeans   Tea   Sugar   Wheat

Source: *The Economist*, January 1991

Revised World Bank figures envisage firm future demand for most exotic minerals (with the exception of uranium, demand for which is being affected by changed attitudes to nuclear power plants) but even the Bank does not expect a return to the price levels of the 1960s and 1970s in constant, that is, real, terms (Annexe Table A20).

Mineral consumption in the industrialised or industrialising countries will continue to grow, despite the different trends identified in the use of substitutes and recycling. However, the structure of ownership of sub-Saharan African mining companies and their domination over markets mean that little benefit is accruing to African producing countries. Expansion of markets is unlikely except for the 'metal hardeners' or exotic minerals; for the remainder, oversupply is keeping prices low even though Africa's minerals are a non-renewable resource.

7. Africa's Fuel and Energy Resources

Most sub-Saharan African countries rely primarily on wood to satisfy their fuel and energy needs. Coal is found in parts of southern Africa[1] and there is oil and natural gas in North and West Africa (Annexe Table A28). Oil is by far the largest single African export commodity, earning five times as much as coffee, and more than all agricultural commodities taken together; it accounts for 40 per cent of sub-Saharan Africa's export earnings (over 50 per cent for the entire continent) and much more in years of high oil prices. Sub-Saharan African countries produce less than 4 per cent of the world's fuel oil, but supply almost twice that proportion of oil exports (Annexe Table A28). Most of the oil is exported as crude, and refined elsewhere. When oil prices fell in the 1980s, the African exporters were hard hit and, as the World Bank says, the oil price cut accounted for about half of the fall in prices of African primary products.[2]

For those African countries fortunate enough to have it, oil wealth should have provided a foundation for economic growth; as the World Bank points out, it has done so quite spectacularly elsewhere.[3] However, oil reserves are not evenly distributed. Only three sub-Saharan African countries have significant reserves – Nigeria, Angola and Gabon. Their reserves are much smaller than those in North Africa, yet they account for 90 per cent of total known sub-Saharan African reserves – Nigeria alone has 80 per cent (Annexe Table A28). New discoveries may cause these figures to be substantially revised. (For example, in 1986 estimates of Gabon's reserves trebled[4].) Nigeria's output is just over 60 per cent of total annual sub-Saharan production; Angola's is about 18 per cent and Gabon's is around 7 per cent. Other sizeable producers are Cameroon and Congo, although their reserves are small. Except for Cameroon, oil represents more than 90 per cent of the export earnings of all of these countries. Zaïre, Côte d'Ivoire and Benin are also oil producers (Annexe Table A28). Ghana exported oil between 1978 and 1981, but stopped in 1986 because production – 1250 barrels a day (b/d) – was unprofitable.[5] Prospecting continues, particularly offshore, and there are many so-called 'oil-hopefuls' in Africa: Gabon, Senegal, Ghana and the Gambia, for example. Prospecting was restarted in the wake of the 1990–1 Gulf crisis and war.

Exploratory drilling in Angola and Namibia was taken up when their civil wars finished; if oil prices rise, exploration will be more actively pursued.[6] Today, however, oil wealth in Africa is concentrated in a handful of countries.

One reason why oil has not notably contributed to those countries' economic growth lies in the relations between the international oil companies and the local governments. Nearly all the major international oil companies – Mobil, Texaco, Chevron, Amoco from the US; and Shell, BP, Agip-Phillips and Elf from Europe – maintain operations and exploration in West Africa. Exxon, the world's largest, does not, except for the small 'Espoir' field in Côte d'Ivoire.[7] Shell has a dominant position in the English speaking countries; Elf is the leading operator in the former French colonies; Amoco, BP, Chevron and Conoco all have concessions in the Congo; US companies work mainly in Angola, where fields are operated by Chevron, Texaco and Elf. Amoco is exploring inland from Zaïre, Burundi and Tanzania in the vicinity of Lake Tanganyika.[8] In most countries, the government issues a licence for prospecting and production and receives a royalty in return, but a state-owned oil company may also take a participating share in the venture. In Nigeria five foreign oil companies operate under licence – Shell, Chevron, Mobil, Agip-Phillips and Elf – and produce most of the oil.[9] Each of these companies has a joint venture arrangement with the state-owned Nigerian National Petroleum Company (NNPC). The distribution of shares varies in each case.[10] At the prospecting stage it is usual for a consortium of foreign companies to join with the state-owned enterprise in exploration. In Gabon, for example, Shell and Elf have shares in the venture through their own companies, Shell Gabon and Elf Gabon, while the government has both a direct stake in the venture and shares in Shell Gabon and Elf Gabon.[11]

African governments which want to drill for oil must turn to foreign companies for assistance with the first stages of exploration. At least 30 large and small companies are involved in oil reserve exploration in sub-Saharan African countries; most have links with major companies (Annexe Table A29). These companies base their investment decisions on the geological prospects, the likely demand and the potential return on their capital. Prospectors are very sensitive to the level of 'rents' or income that African governments take from oil production and they are easily scared off by governments which want to take high rents from the oil.[12] Both royalties and taxes have been higher than average in the Congo, Gabon and Ghana (Annexe Table A30). Oil companies withdrew from Ghana because operations became unprofitable. In Nigeria rates were higher still, and in 1986 the government had to guarantee oil companies a minimum profit of US$2 per barrel and to introduce the concept of a 'realisable price'. This was taken as the average of published product prices in the calendar month of pumping.[13] This price was then used to calculate taxation and royalties. The agreement between the Nigerian government and the oil companies also provided for some flexibility in profit levels when prices rise and fall sharply, set fees for pumping government oil and provided for some tax exemptions.[14]

Nigeria's military leaders sought to justify the *coup d'etat* in 1989 as a response to what they called the desertion by major oil companies.[15] They were just not lifting the oil. But a variety of factors were both cause and effect of this flight: low after-tax profits, political unrest and economic uncertainty. Some individual company shares in oil production had been dropping anyway: Shell from 75 per cent in 1970 to under 50 per cent in 1987, Gulf from 20 per cent to 16 per cent over the same period. But this was because Mobil, Agip, Elf and Texaco shares rose to a combined level of 32 per cent, and newcomers Ashland, Pan Ocean, Tenneco and Phillips established small shares in the 1980s.[16] The Nigerian government, although anxious to increase oil output, does not actually control the process. The NNPC regulates licences, distribution and refining of oil but does not produce it.[17]

Finally, Nigeria and Gabon, both OPEC members, have to bargain for their quota of oil output. Nigeria's share of the OPEC world production total reached 10 per cent in 1985. Since 1972 it had averaged 7 per cent, but each figure is a quota of a changing output total. In 1979 OPEC output was 30 million b/d; just half that in 1986 (see Chart 7.1). After steady growth until 1979, world oil production then fell, and OPEC producers' output fell faster. Exports declined even more sharply than production, with OPEC's share of world exports dropping from over 80 per cent before 1979 to only just over 50 per cent after 1985. Nigeria's share of world exports fell from nearly 7 per cent to just over 5 per cent. As sub-Saharan Africa's oil is mostly exported, the region has suffered heavily from the collapse, not just of world oil prices but of world oil consumption. Both recovered somewhat after 1984 but had not reestablished 1977 levels by 1992. In short, though oil is wealth, few countries have it. And because of the power of the oil companies, those that do can only use a small part of the 'wealth' to finance their development programmes.

Whereas South Africa consumes over 16 million tonnes of oil products a year (most of which came from the Middle East under special and often clandestine arrangements to avoid the anti-apartheid trade embargoes), only four other sub-Saharan countries – Nigeria,

Chart 7.1: Oil Production and Export, 1962–86

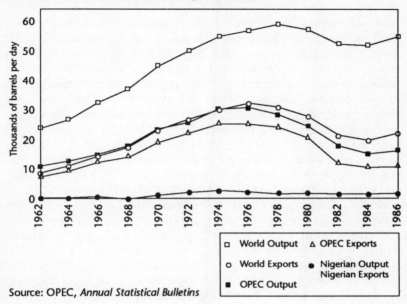

Source: OPEC, *Annual Statistical Bulletins*

Côte d'Ivoire, Ghana and Kenya – consume more than 1 million tonnes a year. Annual energy consumption *per capita* in the UK is equivalent to over 3000 kilos of oil;[18] even making a very generous estimate for use of wood in Africa, that figure is 15 times the African average and 5 times as high as that of Gabon which has the highest level of commercial consumption in Africa. Other developing countries also use more energy than African countries; commercial fuel consumption *per capita* in India is twice as great as in sub-Saharan Africa, Malaysia's is 6 times as great.[19] These levels depend, of course, on the degree of industrialisation.

With overall annual output of more than 100 million tonnes of fuel oil, sub-Saharan Africa could meet its imports of 14 million tonnes of oil a year and its total recorded commercial energy consumption of 29 million tonnes. Use of wood from non-commercial sources, estimated at 75 million tonnes,[20] could probably be reduced quite sharply, providing incalculable benefits to the environment, if some of the oil exported to destinations outside Africa were instead traded within Africa.

Oil Refining

High production costs and conflicts of interest between foreign and local oil companies have meant a minor role for oil as a basis for African economic development. Sub-Saharan Africa's oil has been largely exported as crude fuel for refining elsewhere: less than a quarter of the oil produced in Africa is refined there. Refineries do exist in Nigeria, Congo, Gabon, and Côte d'Ivoire producing for export markets; and in Angola, Kenya and Ghana producing mainly for home markets.[21] The Kenyan refinery in Mombasa has an annual capacity of about 4.7 million tonnes, but Kenya, not an oil producer, imports only about half that volume, and consumes even less, so that the plant operates at half capacity. Per barrel refinery costs are high and exports fell from 1.6 million tonnes to 500 000 tonnes in 1987.[22] A major refinery in Côte d'Ivoire, established in the 1980s, has operated at well below full capacity because of declining oil production and competition with the new Port Harcourt refinery in Nigeria, which, with a capacity of 7.5 million tonnes, could meet Nigerian and neighbouring non-oil producing countries' demand.[23] Gabon and Congo have adequate productive capacity to meet their domestic needs and still export, but lack markets for the refined products (Annexe Table A31). Angola's case is similar, but foreign oil companies operating there are not even developing refined products.[24]

Nigeria is the only sub-Saharan African country with a major programme of refining, as well as oil-based industries. It can refine up to 15 million tonnes of its annual production of 65 million tonnes.[25] A basic petro-chemical industry is developing, producing a range of oil-based products: polyesters for plastics, carbon black for tyres and other rubber products, benzene for solvents and detergents, and butane gas for heating.[26] While Nigerian oil production is dominated by transnational oil companies, investment in petro-chemicals has been principally financed and operated by the state company.[27] Since 1989, private foreign and domestic investment in a second stage of petro-chemical industrial development has been encouraged.[28] This should give a boost to local construction and engineering industries, but the emergence of entrepreneurs with industrial rather than merchanting inclinations is slow. Managerial skills are at a premium.[29]

The very strength of state-controlled, oil-based petro-chemical industry has held back the development of natural gas in Nigeria. While this may be an all too typical example of government developing sectional interests without regard for the long-term common national interest, the World Bank's solutions to this 'syndrome' are no better. The Bank insists that governments withdraw from direct involvement in production and privatise their holdings, thus ruling out selective state intervention. In fact state intervention can successfully contribute to industrialisation, as in South Korea, where the state has protected infant industries, coordinated the activities of competing private companies, and enabled local and necessarily weaker companies to develop without the competition of foreign transnationals.[30] Nor is it true that state enterprise, even if it runs a deficit, is necessarily badly managed or inefficient. The Paris Metro, for example, runs at a deficit and is well managed; its *other* contributions to the economy more than make up for the publicly-financed deficit. Indiscriminate privatisation often represents a narrow and crude approach to the notion of 'cost'.

Predicting Future Demand

Sub-Saharan Africa's demand for oil to use as energy or in the petro-chemical industry is not likely to grow rapidly in the short to medium term. The markets remain outside Africa. The major oil companies have traditionally been interested in maintaining a worldwide range of oil sources to provide security against interruption to any one source.[31] The 1990–1 Gulf War demonstrated the political commitment of oil importers to prevent disruptions in overall oil supply and oil profits, but it also showed that expanded Saudi oil production could immediately make up for any shortfall in supplies to meet world demand. Future oil exploration and production of Africa's large untapped reserves will continue where reserves are proven, but not to guarantee diversity of supply at any cost. Hopefuls like Senegal and the Gambia are likely to be left aside.

In the early 1990s, the world is awash with oil. Major producing countries – Saudi Arabia, Kuwait, Iraq and Iran – all need cash. None can afford to hold down its production to keep up prices, which would permit the upgrading or exploitation of less profitable fields.[32] Although hard to predict with any certainty, several trends in future demand can still be discerned. The first is the decline of US and European reserves; the second is a rise in Chinese production, counterbalancing stagnation in production in the former Soviet Union; the third is the rise of demand among the newly industrialising nations – South Korea, Taiwan, Hong Kong and Singapore.[33] The least clear of all trends is movement in demand in the West, representing half the world market. The rate of recovery from the economic recession and the effectiveness of energy conservation measures will determine Western demand.

In the late 1980s developing countries and former Soviet bloc countries as a whole were net exporters of oil while developed countries were net importers (Annexe Table A32). A geographically based pattern of trade in oil is clearly apparent: North America imports mainly from the Americas, followed by the Middle East; Western European countries import largely from each other but also from the Middle East, Africa and the former Soviet Union; Japan's oil comes from the Middle East but also from China. Western Europe is now more energy self-sufficient than North America.

The US has great influence both as an oil producer and the largest single consumer of oil. It imports 15 per cent of internationally traded oil. Production has fallen from a peak in 1970, and the decline accelerated in the late 1980s (Chart 7.2). US consumption, after a sharp drop in 1978, has been rising steadily since 1982. Imports were temporarily affected by the 1979 cut in consumption, but reached similar levels – 44 per cent of total demand – by 1989. Dependence on imported oil rose to 60 per cent in 1990, even though in 1989 the US Department of Energy projections forecast that degree of dependency being reached only by the year 2000. That estimate was based on a price of US$20 per barrel; at US$28 per barrel, the projection was for a 55 per cent dependence by 2000.[34] Prices in 1991 were below their baseline estimates, which implies that low-cost Middle Eastern oil will continue to replace the high-cost US product. If Africa is to expand its share of the US market its oil must be low-cost.

Oil experts have developed an indicator of the production capacity of a particular deposit or oil reserve, called the reserve/production ratio (R/P). A ratio of 20 would mean the deposit would last for 20 years at the current rate of production. When applied to US production it reveals a crucial factor that will influence access to US markets in the future. The rule of thumb is that 'if the R/P falls to 9 or 10, then the deposit is being destroyed in much the same way that sucking too hard on an ice cream soda, or driving an automobile too fast may cause excessive depreciation.'[35] The overall US R/P is now less than 9, making the US the only major oil producer with a ratio of less than 10 – that is, at current rates of extraction, US oil reserves will last less than a decade.

Increasing US dependence on imports will affect the world oil market. This may be good news for sub-Saharan African oil producers. Nigeria's oil exports to the US have begun to rise after a period of decline. In the 1970s about 40 per cent of Nigeria's oil exports went

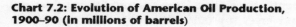

Chart 7.2: Evolution of American Oil Production, 1900–90 (in millions of barrels)

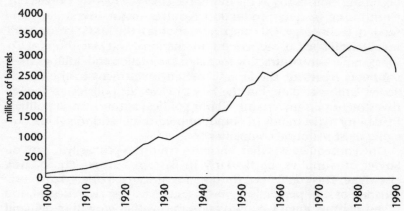

Sources: H. Landsberg, S.H. Schurr, *Energy in the US: Souces, Uses and Policy Issues*, 1967; Energy Information Administration, *Annual Energy Review*, 1987

to the US. In 1984 this fell to 14 per cent, when Nigeria was forced by world prices to seek markets in Europe – in Germany, the UK, Spain and Portugal. The proportion going to the US has recovered steadily, reaching nearly 50 per cent in 1987.[36] But the bad news is that the increased US demand for foreign oil has not resulted in a rise in price. Therefore, while low world prices increase US imports, this demand is not conducive to investment in new fields and expanded production, except where production costs are expected to be low. If prices do rise, bringing opportunities for higher cost production and investment in Africa, they also make US production viable, with a resulting cutback in US demand for imported oil.

African oil exporters' prospects depend not only on the degree of demand but on the strength of the competition. US oilfields are not the only ones which are running down. Britain's output of oil and natural gas, the largest in Europe, peaked in 1985 at 123 million tonnes, of which 83 million tonnes were being exported as crude petroleum. In 1985 UK imports were 27 million tonnes, resulting in a balance of payments surplus of roughly US$11 billion.[37] The UK is now becoming a net importer of oil, with North Sea crude oil production down from 2.6 million barrels a day in 1986 to 1.8 million a day in 1992.[38] Norwegian North Sea production (48 million tonnes in 1987) is less than half the current UK output, but is expected to remain at current levels longer.[39] The former Soviet

Union was until recently the world's largest oil producer and second largest exporter, but faces myriad difficulties. Oil extraction is becoming more costly as the more accessible reserves are worked out. Continuing or new production requires major investment and modern technology. Oil company consortia – the MMM group made up of Mitsui and Co, McDermott International and Marathon Oil Co, for example – are contracting for major exploration and drilling. These contracts represent the largest foreign investment in the former Soviet Union to date, but the lack of clear-cut policies on foreign investment plus uncertainty about political authority and political instability make trends in output unpredictable and this is discouraging most major oil companies.[40]

One consequence is that European countries primarily reliant on Soviet oil supplies, particularly in Eastern Europe, are looking elsewhere. This could open the door for African exporters, but a combination of slow population growth and increasing awareness of, and investment in, energy conservation means that growth in demand for oil is likely to stabilise. Declining reserves in North America and Europe may not have much effect on the African oil industry.

In marked contrast, populations in developing countries are growing, which may in the long term affect oil demand. In the short term, industrialisation is the key factor. It is estimated that by the year 2000, 27 per cent of the world's population will live in South and South-East Asia and 35 per cent by 2020. The population of sub-Saharan Africa will be 10 per cent of the world's total.[41] In Latin America the rate of growth is lower.[42] China's population is predicted to stabilise over the next decade, but growing Chinese demand for fuel may be met by its own considerable reserves. Short-term, local reserves are sufficient to meet projected needs in Africa and Latin America but long-term they are not.[43]

Longer-term projections of consumption raise fundamental issues about fuel and energy policy. The problem is not so much that oil reserves are finite and therefore exhaustible, but that the profligate use of oil and petroleum is a major cause of global warming. Thus the long-term solution is likely to involve energy efficiency and the use of renewable energy resources, including solar, wind and wave power. It is the high-consumption economies of the rich North which are the main markets but the design of fuel and energy policies for Third World countries is likely to incorporate these concerns as far as possible. There is no case for simply imitating the earlier irresponsibility of others.

Thus, although fuel oil and natural gas are convenient and easy to distribute and though they currently represent the main source of fuel for transport, heating and electricity generation, energy policy in Africa should not depend on them alone. Africa cannot rely on wood for its fuel needs without inflicting serious, perhaps irremediable, damage on the environment and ensuring continued desertification. Even a balanced policy of forest utilisation will not supply enough wood for future fuel needs. World coal reserves are large but Africa's are not. Coal-fired electricity generation is not a better option than wood burning from the environmental perspective, even with tougher controls on sulphur emissions. The claims of the nuclear power industry to offer a new economical energy source do not survive scrutiny in the wake of the Three Mile Island and Chernobyl accidents and the growing evidence of the health risks for populations living in the vicinity of nuclear power stations. Public concern is likely to impede the development of nuclear power in countries where governments are accountable through elections. For other countries, international pressure arising from fears of nuclear weapons proliferation may equally well obstruct nuclear power.

In the medium to longer term we can expect a likely expansion in demand for oil accompanied by investment in ecologically responsible energy sources. In the short term, industrialisation is increasing demand for oil more quickly than national incomes are rising. In 1990 a commentator in *Energy International* observed of ASEAN countries:

The fall in the price of oil since 1986 and sustained economic growth have strongly stimulated the demand for oil – 5 per cent in 1987, 12 per cent in 1988 – from the ASEAN and newly industrialising countries. In some countries the growth in oil consumption is astronomical: in South Korea in 1988 19 per cent, in Thailand and Taiwan 15 per cent. Estimates for 1989 were put at 12 per cent in Taiwan, 14 per cent in South Korea and 18 per cent in Thailand.[44]

To date this increased demand has not pushed up oil prices. The question then is how soon rising demand may begin to catch up with current productive capacity. Oil output from existing capacity can easily be increased. During the Gulf War Saudi Arabia alone produced 10 million b/d, a fifth of OPEC's total, and even Nigeria achieved its full capacity of 2.3 million b/d.[45] Few analysts predict that any of the existing producers, even those inside OPEC, will be inclined to accept restrictions on production to boost oil prices in the short term.[46] Middle East production costs are likely to remain lower than those of most other producers. Existing fields in sub-Saharan Africa will also continue to produce oil and to export, but only at current levels of output and export earnings. New exploration in Africa will be slow and hesitant until prices rise – and that will also bring US production in Texas and Alaska back into the picture.

8. What does Africa get out of its Trade?

Sub-Saharan Africans produce raw materials for export whereas processing is undertaken elsewhere. This is the motif of every commodity story in this book. With very few exceptions, Africans consume hardly any of their own production – mainly staple foods, sugar and some fuel oil, timber and fertiliser. Africa's production is so oriented towards export markets that its share of world production is much smaller than its share of world exports of many commodities. Africans exercise little or no control over their exports because the markets for these commodities are in others' hands. Any attempts at direct control over the production and export process is limited by the trading involvement and investment power of foreign companies. Export trade in both agricultural commodities and minerals is dominated by foreign companies, which either own the plantations and mines, or control most of the links in the chain of commercialisation. State marketing boards may act as trading intermediaries between the many small-scale producers of cocoa, coffee, tobacco, cotton or vegetable oils, and the foreign buyer; but the real power, the heritage of a century of colonial rule, remains in the hands of outsiders. The basic structure which forces most African governments to exchange their exports of primary products for imports of manufactures is unchanged and provides little or no room for manoeuvre.[1]

One factor limiting access to better markets and preventing more value-adding activities in Africa is the nature of the markets themselves. Free and open markets are not the norm for the commodities they have for export. Nearly all of these markets are to some degree controlled, distorted, manipulated, dominated or simply 'closed' by the large buyers.

In *closed markets*, companies move the raw materials from their own mines or plantations within their own organisation and accounting structures, costing them at each stage of their commercialisation at prices which do not necessarily relate directly to outside market prices. In closed markets it is seldom possible to tell at what price the

95

commodity is transferred. Where the commodity is traded within large companies, only the supply and demand for that proportion of the world's production which is offered on the market is recorded. Cases of closed market commodities are fuel oil, diamonds, bauxite and iron ore; and partly closed markets include those for copper, aluminium and other minerals.

In *controlled markets*, companies may buy from a variety of suppliers, including their own mines and plantations; yet the sheer volume of their trade as a percentage of world production means they can influence markets significantly. Markets for African commodities like coffee, tea, cocoa, tobacco and vegetable oils can all be termed 'controlled'.[2]

When African production comes into direct competition with products from the industrialised countries, markets for these products tend to be distorted by the political and economic power of governments of these countries to restrict imports and to subsidise their exports. Sugar, wheat, maize and rice are examples of *distorted markets*. Even in relatively free markets, for example, for cotton, rubber, hard fibres and hides and skins, the market is often dominated and subject to manipulation by only a few companies. For example, in 1983, 85–90 per cent of world exports were marketed by between three and six of the largest transnational corporations.[3]

African producing countries face three separate problems in the face of controlled or dominated markets. First, they can seldom add value to the raw product through processing and refining. Foreign-owned companies may specifically prevent this if they also own processing factories outside Africa. Furthermore, the industrialised countries' tariff barriers escalate with each additional stage of processing for most primary commodities. These barriers naturally act as a commercial and economic disincentive. Second, producing countries have no way of knowing whether the prices they are paid accurately reflect the value of their products to a vertically integrated transnational company (TNC). The actual route of the transaction is likely to be concealed, often via subsidiaries registered in countries like Switzerland or the Bahamas, where local regulations do not require companies to make their accounts public. Third, as trading companies merge, producing countries have fewer and fewer alternatives. There may be only one buyer in their country. While access to market information to check the going prices would definitely improve their bargaining power, no real leverage can be gained if there is no alternative outlet. The seller in this position has to accept whatever price is offered, especially if the product offered is in direct competition with other comparable sources.

According to a UN study, producing countries retain an average 15 per cent share of the final retail value of products made from the main primary agricultural commodities. This means that for non-industrialised countries, 85 per cent of the value is added outside.[4] By contrast, the same study found that the industrialised countries received as much as 94 per cent of the retail value for their exports of 12 of the same 19 commodities. The producing country share for cocoa, tobacco and cotton – commodities which require extensive working up or processing – is as low as 6–8 per cent. Tea, coffee and bananas need less working up, so the share may be 15 per cent. Tea is an exception because processing must be done after picking to avoid spoilage, and only blending and packaging are done elsewhere (Annexe Table A33).

One justification frequently invoked for the low proportions of value added to primary products in producing countries is logistics. Transport of the raw material to the final market for refining, processing and fabricating may be cheaper. The final market for the finished product is likely to be in the industrialised countries. But this constitutes a vicious circle for producing countries, which remain unindustrialised because they remain a poor market. Historically, the first countries to industrialise established their overseas colonies as suppliers of raw materials and maintained their dominant position by putting up tariff and other barriers against imports of processed goods with the aim of protecting their industries.[5] Only a few countries – Japan and South Korea are the latest – have succeeded in breaking through these barriers to set up their own industries.[6]

The transnational corporations which dominate world markets operate by taking optimum advantage of different conditions for the various stages of processing; their scale and scope of operations give them global production synergies. Production synergy might dictate that research, development and design take place at a company's Northern home base, cheap labour be used in a second place, hydro-electric power in a third, tax concessions in a fourth, market proximity in a fifth.[7] There is no special reason, to take a typical example, why garment manufacturing should take place where the cotton is grown. Many other considerations also enter into such decisions: availability of cheap, semi-skilled labour, proximity to a port, tax concessions from the host government, political and economic stability and so on.

Even though a country producing a primary product may retain an average 15 per cent of its final value, that average includes many direct and indirect costs; so the individual producer receives a far smaller proportion. The grower gets only 3.5 per cent for cotton and no more than 1–2 per cent for unprocessed coffee 'cherries'.[8] Slightly more of the value added will accrue to the farmer, the more processing is undertaken – hulling and washing coffee, cleaning and fermenting cocoa – but at this micro-economic scale farmers face the same narrow range of options which their countries do at macro-economic levels. Sales are usually made to a local merchant or to the agent of a marketing board for whatever price can be got at harvest time. Farmers sell in direct competition with each other. To store the product requires access to credit; to process and export requires organisational capacity and infrastructure. Direct exports can give farmers a better deal, even when export taxes or commissions to the government marketing board have been paid. But alternative market outlets are few and, as the interviews with traders in Chapters 5 and 6 make clear, African exporters have a bad reputation to overcome in the marketplace.[9]

One African strategy to strengthen bargaining power with foreign buyers, and especially with TNCs, has been to nationalise production facilities – for example, tea estates and cotton plantations – and to bring internal purchasing operations under government control through marketing boards. There is some evidence that shares of retail value retained can be increased to around 40 per cent in the case of soluble coffee (see Annexe Chart A34), but this still leaves more than half of the value added outside the producing country and such benefits often reach only the government bureaucracies at the expense of the farmers.[10]

Achieving influence in markets does not necessarily require total vertical integration – ownership and control of each stage of the trading process from plantation to retail outlet – although some TNCs do operate from a dominant position in production, trading and processing, like Unilever in the case of tea.[11] Companies may equally well contract out production and the first stage of processing, while retaining their role in product selection, quality control, transport, shipping and insurance and supply of the finished product to the marketplace. In this way companies can avoid responsibility for the vagaries of production, producers' complaints about pay and working conditions and can monitor the product and switch suppliers if they are not satisfied. While production-to-market trading chains are often long and complex, TNCs have generally established control over the key stages of international marketing. Chart 8.1 shows who controls the chain from production to consumption. TNCs predominate, which means that the cocoa smallholder receives no

Chart 8.1: Who Controls What in the African Agricultural Export Chain?

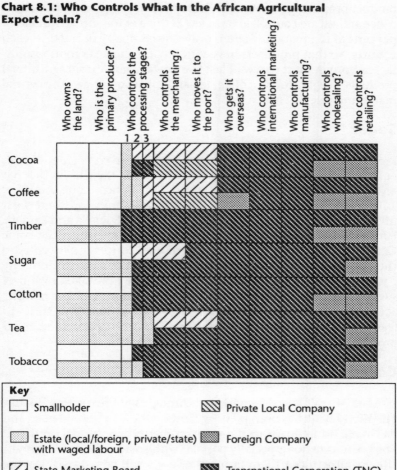

Key

☐ Smallholder

▨ Private Local Company

▦ Estate (local/foreign, private/state) with waged labour

▧ Foreign Company

▨ State Marketing Board

▨ Transnational Corporation (TNC)

Source: UN Centre on Transnational Corporations, *Transnational Corporations and Non-fuel Primary Commodities in Developing Countries* (New York, 1987); and F. Clairmonte and J. Cavanagh, *Merchants of Drink* (Third World Network, 1988)

further income after handing over the product at the first stage of processing.

It is in their dominant and controlling position in international marketing that the small number of TNCs – large trading companies like Czarnikov, Cargill, E.D. & F. Man, or Philip Morris – exercise their power, although these companies may not be involved in primary product processing (see Annexe Table A35). The markets for bananas, coffee and tea are controlled by as few as three or four firms with 85–90 per cent of the market.[12] Often only one company operates in each country, so that producers have virtually no choice (a monopsonistic position). A short review of just five sub-Saharan African agricultural products – sugar, cocoa, coffee, tea and tobacco – shows the central marketing role of TNCs.

Sugar

Most sub-Saharan African sugar is processed by two companies – Sucres et Denrée (SucDen) in France and Tate & Lyle in the UK. SucDen has a virtual monopoly of sugar exports from the francophone countries; Tate & Lyle has sugar estates in Ethiopia and Zimbabwe, and sugar mills in Kenya, Mauritius, Mozambique, Nigeria, Somalia and Zambia. Furthermore, cane sugar export quotas, negotiated under the Lomé Convention, gave former European colonies concessionary entry to the EC market on condition that 90 per cent of exports from any country went to Tate & Lyle. Tate & Lyle have now taken over beet sugar processing in the UK. If they phase out cane sugar refining activities in favour of subsidised sugar beet production, this will leave the African, Caribbean and Pacific Lomé Convention sugar producers without their concessionary market.[13]

Cocoa

Most of Africa's cocoa is marketed through state marketing boards. The World Bank has been pressing hard for these to be disbanded and has made future loans to some governments conditional on this.[14] The boards are not especially popular with small-scale cocoa farmers either, but without them farmers' options will be reduced, leaving them no alternative but to sell directly to foreign companies in the trading chain: the big TNCs – E.D. & F. Man (formerly Gill & Duffus), Philip Bros, Mercuria and SucDen; the cocoa processors – W.R. Grace-Berisford, SucDen and Cargill; or the chocolate makers – Mars, Hershey, Cadbury/Suchard and Nestlé/Rowntree.[15] These companies have been setting up their own subsidiaries in West Africa to purchase cocoa direct from the farmers. In 1988 the complete harvest in Côte d'Ivoire was bought by SucDen, with French government assistance to save the local marketing board from bankruptcy.[16] But these same transnationals are investing heavily in biotechnology to increase their purchasing leverage and manufacturing flexibility, further restricting the room for manoeuvre of small-scale African cocoa producers.

Coffee

Coffee production in Africa is also largely carried out by small-scale producers who often sell via state marketing boards. World Bank reforms will have a similar effect on coffee as on cocoa. A large share of sub-Saharan Africa's coffee exports is already handled by international trading companies like E.D. & F. Man, Rothfoss and Berisford. In 1989, for example, half of Cameroon's coffee was sold to just two international trading houses.[17] The robusta coffee, which is used for instant soluble coffee products, mainly goes direct to processing companies like Nestlé, Jacobs Suchard and Sara Lee. High tariffs for processed coffee entering Europe and North America mean that Africa will continue to export the primary product (see Annexe Table A40).

Tea

Tea production in Kenya has grown as a result of the strategy of one of the dominant traders in tea. Thus Unilever, which now incorporates Brooke Bond and Liptons, is the world's largest tea packer supplying roughly 30 per cent of tea consumed in the industrialised countries. Unilever aimed to reduce the concentration of tea production in India and Sri Lanka and to this end it has worked directly with the Kenya Tea Development Authority which controls about half of all Kenya's tea production.[18] Of 25 tea estates in Malawi, 21 are controlled by large companies – Unilever, Lonrho and Eastern Produce.[19] In Uganda the British company, Mitchell Cotts, has a large stake in production on estates held 49:51 with the government.[20] Since a significant share of the value added to tea necessarily takes place in the producing country it is not surprising to see the involvement of TNCs – via investment and ownership – in production.

Tobacco

TNC buyers take about two-thirds of the annual sub-Saharan crop and export 95 per cent of this in unmanufactured, leaf form. African cigarette manufacture is wholly for domestic consumption and is almost entirely controlled by the British American Tobacco Company (UK), Rothmans (South Africa) and Philip Morris (US). These three companies together with SEITA (France), Casalee (Belgium), Gallaher

(UK), Universal Leaf Tobacco (US), A.L. Van Beek (Netherlands) and Andrew Chalmers International (UK) dominate the market for African tobacco.[21] These companies, or their subsidiaries, have concentrated their activities on one or other of the several tobacco growing countries, leaving little competitive opportunity for independent or individual growers. Several companies have interests in the related shipping lines.[22] Nearly all operate as part of the international cigarette oligopoly – a limited number of competitors controlling the bulk of cigarette production and sales outside Eastern Europe and China.

In the case of a number of new African agricultural exports like fruits and vegetables, rarely more than 25 per cent of the final retail price is retained in the producing country, even when further processing in the consuming country is negligible.[23] This is because of high transport costs, especially for air freight, of import duties, of the mark-ups of wholesalers and of high average retail margins, generally not less than double the wholesale price.[24] Exporters are in a weak position because freight companies, wholesalers and retailers account for the larger share of value in this product chain. In this case also, a few companies from the importing country operate in a vertically integrated way, for example, Dalgety in the UK.[25]

Minerals and Transnational Control

TNCs also dominate the international marketing of Africa's minerals. But their involvement in the producing countries is more extensive than for agricultural products because of the high cost of the equipment involved and the importance of integrating production processes with marketing operations (see Chart 8.2).

Most mineral extraction and processing in Africa is undertaken by a small number of very large TNCs with subsidiaries all over the world. As with agricultural products, total vertical integration is not necessary, but TNCs control the central marketing stages. Just three or four companies control the smelting, refining and recycling of copper and dominate international marketing; just six companies own half the world aluminium producing capacity as well as half the bauxite production. A few steel-making companies control iron ore production and the scrap market and seven oil companies dominate Africa's oil reserves. Gold mining and refining are also controlled by just a few companies, and diamonds by just one company, de Beers, which manages virtually the whole international market.

The complexity of the interlocking relationships between a few companies means that nobody except the 'spider' at the centre of the

Chart 8.2: Who Controls Mineral Production and Processing?

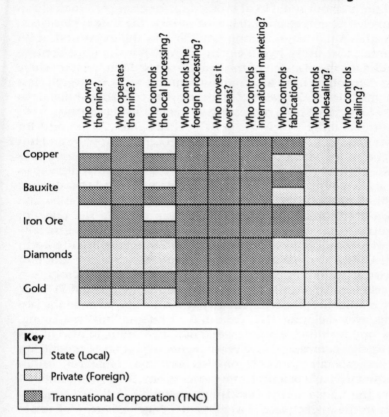

Source: UN Centre on Transnational Corporations, *Transnational Corporations and Non-fuel Primary Commodities in Developing Countries* (New York, 1987)

'web' has any control over what is happening, or can easily establish what is going on. Even where the government has majority ownership of a local mining company, as, for example, in the case of Zambian copper, the mines are operated by Anglo American. Even after independence, Namibia's copper exports are managed by a subsidiary of the South African Goldfields group and its uranium exports are in the hands of the British transnational, Rio Tinto-Zinc.[26] One consequence of this is a loss of national decision-making power, particularly over how much refining is done inside the country, and, therefore, how much value is added (see Annexe Table A36). The foreign company decides this, though there are cases where local conditions favour some local processing, for example, when cheap hydro-electric energy is available. In Guinea, the state is participating with all the major aluminium TNCs in the expansion of an alumina plant using hydro-electric power. But the joint venture provides for the dispatch of the bauxite to southern Ireland, where these companies have a secondary refining plant.[27] Overall, less than one-third of the value of all developing countries' minerals in the 1970s derived from processing in the producing country,[28] but proportions differ widely for individual minerals: 78 per cent for copper and tin, 42 per cent for zinc, 25 per cent for iron ore and just 10 per cent for bauxite.

TNC control over processing creates a serious impediment to Africa's long-term development. If exports are to lead to economic growth those exports must have as much value added as possible and market access must be improved. The gap between the price for unprocessed raw materials and for the final product is generally very wide. To take one example only, 4 to 5 tonnes of bauxite worth about US$37 a tonne at the point of shipment yield 1 tonne of primary aluminium metal worth as much as $1300, which in turn can yield semi-fabricated products worth between $1500 and $1700.[29] There is little that producing country governments can do in the face of this overwhelming TNC control over international marketing. Those options which exist are weak: nationalisation, joint ventures with foreign companies, royalty payments, export taxes, production levies or corporate profit taxes on TNC operations. Moreover, African governments have practically no power to enforce any conditionality on the transnational companies operating in their countries. Power in the marketplace is what counts. Much of Africa's bauxite is refined into alumina in Jamaica because of the proximity of both the sources of fuel oil and the North American market. In the 1970s the Jamaican government tried, by increasing taxes and levies, to raise its share of the final price of the alumina produced. The share rose from 10.6 per cent in 1973 to 34.5 per cent in 1977, but sales declined sharply, and the government was forced to cut its share back to 27.3 per cent. After the Manley government was defeated in 1981, the share was cut still further as a condition for continued operation.[30]

The weak position of governments of producing countries is reinforced by the difficulty in determining whether or not they are receiving the full market value for their primary commodities. Here difficulty arises from the system of transfer pricing operated by TNCs. An international company moves products at different stages of production between different parts of its organisation, putting a price on each transaction which does not necessarily reflect market prices. The company may opt for 'arm's length' relations between its several parts so that products are transferred at market prices. Sometimes, however, it may be advantageous for the company to fix prices artificially in order to increase its overall profit. It will choose this strategy in several situations.[31] For example, when a company operating in several countries intends to run down one operation and expand another without moving capital between countries it might fall foul of exchange controls. The operation to be run down pays more for its inputs from other parts of the company than the market price and gets a poorer price for its output, while the operation to be developed gets a cheap input or a specially good price for its output.

Mineral production is particularly affected by the form of transfer pricing in which a TNC avoids paying taxes on its profits in a country where taxes are high. Avoidance is simple: profits are kept low by assigning artificially low prices for the output in that country. This is an especially valuable device where the profit can be made in a 'tax haven', as countries with very low or zero taxes on company profits are called. A subsidiary company registered in the tax haven may be, in effect, a 'dummy' company, doing nothing, but nominally receiving products into its books at a low price and transferring them elsewhere at a high price. No tax is paid on the profit thus obtained and in countries where taxes are high, there indeed appears to be no profit. The third use of transfer pricing by TNCs is an extension of the second. Tax havens generally have no laws requiring the divulging of profits or indeed of any accounts of company operations.[32] Not only does the parent company avoid paying tax, but the original producer of the commodities cannot learn at what price his products were sold. The ups and downs of the market and the many grades and qualities of the product are such that it is very difficult for a government in a primary commodity producing country in Africa or elsewhere to know whether the export prices it is receiving from a TNC operating in its territory are the prices at which its products were actually disposed of on the world market, or would have cost on the open market at that time. By deliberately under-pricing commodities in its returns to a host government or over-pricing the equipment imported, a TNC can avoid a part of the taxes or levies which the government may be seeking to impose on TNC profits or export values.

The industrialised countries generally have sophisticated tax inspection and collection systems for investigating and detecting tax evasion and enforcing the law; but even they find it hard to detect determined abuse of transfer pricing. Most African countries and especially the smaller ones are, by contrast, poorly equipped both for detection and prosecution of transfer pricing abuses. The desperate need for foreign investment may force governments to ignore their own laws and allow the practice to continue. Government officials are poorly paid and susceptible to bribes to ignore abuses.

Even without corruption, African governments experience great difficulties in controlling TNCs' operations. All transnational mining companies practise transfer pricing. Detection of small-scale abuses – 'small' is considered to be a maximum of 5 per cent of the current market value of services and 2 per cent of the spot (that is, current) price of goods – is nearly impossible; even full disclosure of financial records of both the local subsidiary and other subsidiaries would not provide evidence. Therefore prices that justify such discrepancies are generally quoted, which reduces the recorded value of the company's operations in the country where the commodities are produced and therefore the company's tax liability. Even these minor downward adjustments to sales values have disproportionate effects on the local subsidiary's tax liability, because taxes in the mining industry are generally based on profits and not on turnover or fixed assets and because profits at the margin may be considerably reduced by small reductions in recorded sales values.[33]

Prima facie evidence for large-scale transfer pricing abuse is often quite easily obtained. Motivation, opportunity and means are obvious enough. The tell-tale sign is always the long-term, very low profitability of the mining subsidiary of a TNC in a Third World country. These signs are visible in many African subsidiaries of transnational mining companies, with the notable exception of certain South African companies. Questions can be deflected easily about differences between recorded export values of minerals or the profits made from their export and the general level of world prices in the commodity markets, because fluctuations in market prices often render comparisons meaningless. Sales of minerals by 'hedging' on the market – forward buying and selling – also make it difficult to determine sales values at any given time. Profits from these legal trading operations are naturally claimed by the company that makes them. Similarly, checking the accuracy of prices charged for imported equipment against specific origins, suppliers and exchange rates would require an army of government inspectors.

The UN Centre on Transnational Corporations (UNCTC) analyses of the bargaining positions of Third World governments relative to transnational corporations show that, once access is obtained to financial statements on exports made by companies to host governments, one can make meaningful comparisons with the accounts of similar operations in industrialised countries. This is especially useful where arm's length trading takes the place of transfer pricing. Even when detected and documented, however, transfer pricing abuses are seldom made public. They usually result in a non-legal form of redress, with the transnational company agreeing to discontinue the practice and to compensate the country concerned by taking future action to increase investment or purchase more inputs from local sources.[34] In return, the government of the country agrees not to disclose details of the findings of its investigations; it wants neither to reveal its own inadequacy and corruption, nor to lose the business of the transnational involved. We present four examples of transfer pricing abuses by TNCs that have affected mineral exports from sub-Saharan Africa. The names of the countries, the companies and the minerals involved have had to be omitted, since no legal case has been prosecuted.

Case 1

A TNC with its parent company based in a tax haven, formed a wholly owned subsidiary in an African country to mine a particular mineral and was offered a five year 'tax holiday' at the start of its operations. When the 'tax holiday' ended, the African subsidiary sold all of the products that were mined to its parent company at roughly two-thirds of their market values, and continued to do this for 20 years. No profits were recorded, so no taxes were paid. This was against existing legislation and constituted an abuse. Local Customs and Excise were supposed to allow exports only at market prices; the Central Bank and the Ministry of Mines had the responsibility for approving sales prices, and the Inland Revenue Department was supposed to collect taxes based on true profitability. Government officials made public statements during this period about this transfer pricing abuse, but no investigation was ever mounted. There was evidence of bribery involving government officials.

In this case, there was little or no cooperation between the several government agencies and each blamed the other for the lack of proper control overall. None of them had access to information about the international market for the mineral concerned or knew the identity of the final customer for the product. The country's radio, TV stations, and its one weekly newspaper reported only the local news. Government agencies had no telex or fax machines and almost no access to international telephone systems. The postal service was poor and unreliable, there was no photocopying equipment and very few typewriters in government offices. All the brightest people worked for TNCs or had left the country; the level of skills in government agencies was basic.

The country had been a member of a producers' association, but the government could not afford to keep up its membership fees, although mining of the mineral represented a large proportion of the country's entire economy and taxation of the company's operations could have supplied the major part of the government's revenue. The situation changed with the overthrow of the government. A new government official decided to ask outside consultants to investigate the case. They found *prima facie* evidence of substantial transfer pricing abuse and attempted to prove it. First, the local subsidiary was asked to provide the government with information on the prices paid to the parent company for the mineral by end-users. The transnational parent company refused, pointing out that under prevailing tax laws where the company was registered this was a criminal offence and the chief executive of the company would be jailed. Second, comparisons were made of the prices paid at the ports of origin and destination against other shipments of similar materials from Africa. But it was found that the transnational parent company also had a controlling interest in the shipping company transporting the mineral. Finally, sources within the trade were questioned on the sales prices of the exported minerals.

Calculations of lost earnings over the 20-year period show that the extra earnings would have wiped out the total national debt and increased government revenue by many millions of dollars. The consequences of the investigation are not clear as yet, but it seems likely that the TNC will undertake to pay a more market-related price for the mineral, if it considers that the operation will then be worth continuing.

Case 2

The economic scale in this case is greater than in the first. The African country concerned relied for about half its foreign income on the export of a range of metals and minerals. All the local mining companies were wholly owned subsidiaries of TNCs based in the US, South Africa and Europe. Few sales were made directly to consumers from these local companies. Most sales were made through agents in tax havens, who in turn sold through sub-agents in consuming countries. These agents and sub-agents were receiving higher than market-rate commissions, in some cases three times the norm. Connections between many of the agents and sub-agents and the transnational mining companies were suspected, given the low prices paid to the TNC subsidiaries for mined products. The new government of the country decided to investigate.

This government was better equipped than many others in sub-Saharan Africa to investigate cases of transfer pricing, and set up a special unit consisting of trained officers from the Customs and Excise Department, tax officers, fraud squad police, lawyers and economists. The unit consisted of about ten persons plus a large auxiliary staff. Informal inquiries in trade circles revealed that the sales agencies were indeed owned by the very TNC mining companies operating in the country. If documentary evidence could have been compiled to prove this, various officials of the mining companies would have been liable to prosecution. Officially available information revealed only that the directors were local accountants and lawyers from the tax haven country, receiving considerable fees in addition to trade commissions, but with no knowledge of the minerals business and acting as nominees for the actual owners whose names could not be disclosed under that country's company law.

The unit recommended that the mining companies find other sales agents, but the companies and the Ministry of Mines declared that they were quite happy with the performance of these agents and saw no reason to make any change. Two agents were subsequently sacked, but were replaced by others. Several government officials were also dismissed, but the sales arrangements continued as before. The special unit had its budget cut and its most senior official was downgraded. The estimated annual loss of revenue to the country from transfer pricing is at least 15 per cent of the total value of mineral sales, and on some products more than 30 per cent. The impact on TNC profits is proportionately much more. The mining companies argue that they cannot pay higher wages or improve the living conditions of their workers, because, they say, the profits on the sale of minerals are too low.

This case offers a further insight of particular relevance. At the time that the special investigation unit was set up, the government was embroiled in an internal battle on the implementation of structural adjustment measures being strongly advocated by the IMF and the World Bank. Future loans and US aid were made conditional on the introduction of such measures. Government officials in favour of implementing the measures won. A senior government official opposing these was fired, apparently at the insistence of USAID, and replaced with a candidate of their choice receiving a hard currency salary six times the norm for such a post. Since the government's acceptance of the structural adjustment programme, no further investigations by the unit into this matter have taken place.

Case 3

The third case involves two neighbouring African countries. In one, a commercially viable mine was owned by TNC 'A', producing a particular ore, which was exported in an unrefined state. In the second, a marginally viable mine producing the same ore and a refinery for the ore were owned by TNC 'B'. The respective governments had the legal right to prevent trade in minerals if they were not satisfied that the trade was in the national interest and both imposed taxes on company profits rather than on export values. Company A had been selling its unrefined ore to associated subsidiaries in industrialised countries, but realised that refining the ore in the neighbouring country before export would cut transport costs. The value of the refined product was roughly triple that of the unrefined ore.

The simplest deal would have been for Company A to sell the ore to Company B and for Company B to sell the resulting refined product on to the world market. Company A knew Company B very well and both companies cooperated in trading in many other parts of the world. This arrangement would have been profitable for both companies; however, it would also have meant that they would have had high tax bills to pay to the host governments. Instead, Company A agreed to sell the unrefined ore to a dummy company in a tax haven. This dummy company then made a ten-year toll-refining deal (that is, refining for a fixed fee per tonne) with Company B. Just prior to this arrangement, Company B closed its marginally viable mine, sacking 1000 workers, and claimed that there was no work for the refinery unless the government agreed to the toll-refining deal. The fees from the toll-refining deal were only just sufficient to keep the refinery operating and so very little tax was payable.

The dummy company made it a condition of the deal that the African subsidiary of the mining TNC, Company B, should open a performance bond through a New York bank in its favour to the value of US$7 million, payable to the dummy company in the event that the refinery could not for any reason, including government action, fulfil any part of the contract. The government and Central Bank were forced to agree and could not annul the performance bond without forfeiting foreign exchange. The value of the ten-year contract was, coincidentally, an estimated US$7 million. The dummy company was then free to sell the refined product on to the world market at its true value without paying taxes on the profits, stripping both the African countries concerned of their rightful tax revenue. The contract is binding until 1994.

Case 4
The final sub-Saharan African case concerns a 50:50 joint venture mining company between a European TNC and an African government. The European parent company was appointed as the sole sales agent for the mine. The European company owned a small European mine producing the same product, but 'bagged up' the African product and sold it to customers as a European product. The company bought the material from the jointly owned African mine at about 30 per cent below the world market price and was paid a 5 per cent sales commission on all sales, even those made to itself. Few sales were made from Africa directly to the users. The price of this particular mineral varies substantially according to its grade, but, under the terms of the agreement, the European company had the sole right to assess the grade, and no disputes were permitted.

These examples of transfer pricing in the export of minerals from sub-Saharan Africa indicate that hundreds of millions of dollars of revenue are lost to African governments every year. It is reasonable to assume that many governments know what is going on and turn a blind eye, even if they do not actually gain from the abuse. It is often said that corruption is endemic in Africa. In the mining industry, as in many other industries in the Third World, TNCs justify their behaviour on the grounds that everyone does it. If they did not offer bribes, somebody else would. But the conditions in which corruption flourishes derive directly from the relative weakness of the African partners and the power of the foreign companies. African governments doubtless could do much to correct the situation by publishing stories of suspected abuse of transfer pricing and corruption; ongoing investigations of trading transactions could be facilitated by the UN and other agencies and financed from the recuperation of earnings. However, few of the *internal* measures that African governments could take would have a permanent effect if concomitant measures were not taken *outside* Africa to control the activities of third party companies based in countries whose legislation permits absolute financial secrecy. Political pressure at least equal to that being placed on sub-Saharan Africa to export its natural resources is needed to make these companies 'open their books' and to create the conditions under which trade ceases to be a trap and becomes a means to develop.

9. African Manufactured Exports

An after-effect of colonialism has meant that Third World countries have continued to export chiefly fuel and raw materials for the industries of the developed countries. Of all Third World regions sub-Saharan Africa has fared the least well since formal independence. The average income per head is lower than in any other region and 28 of the 42 Least Developed – that is, poorest – Developing Countries (LDDCs) are African. The small proportion which manufacturing contributes to GDP is one criterion for defining an LDDC. In 1975, Africa, excluding South Africa, contributed little more than 1 per cent to the 'non-communist' world total of manufacturing production. Between 1975 and 1981 Africa increased its output of manufactured goods by about 5 per cent a year, well in line with the performance of other developing countries in the Americas and the Middle East, but at half the rate of growth achieved in East and South-East Asia. Since 1981 African output has stagnated, while in all the regions of Asia manufacturing output has continued to grow at about 7 per cent a year – well ahead even of growth in the developed economies.

The absence of a developed manufacturing base in sub-Saharan Africa shows up clearly in the statistics for exports of manufactured goods. Comparisons in Chart 9.1 of the developing countries' share of world exports of manufactures and their populations show Africa trailing dismally and falling further behind the Asian 'dragons'. South Korea, Taiwan, Hong Kong and Singapore have greatly expanded their share of world trade, but they are the exceptions.

As we showed earlier, the success of the Asian dragons was not achieved by following the World Bank economic model. Moreover, the idea that all countries could have that success if only they tried hard enough is bizarre. It is almost impossible for dozens of countries at once to expand their exports of the same or similar products in this way. For a *reductio ad absurdum*, we may take the following extreme example. Today Singapore (Malaysia's *entrepôt*) exports about US$16 000 worth of goods *per capita* per year. If Indonesia, often cited as an apprentice Newly Industrialised Country (NIC) with a population of 171 million, were to export *per capita* the same amount as Malaysia/Singapore, Indonesia alone would export an amount equal to fully 75 per cent of *current* world trade![1] In the long run trade is not a 'zero-sum game' – that is, one in which if Indonesia 'wins' markets, the rest of the world 'loses' them – because trade is a process based on exchange. But the Asian model, while instructive for Africa, is not appropriate for current levels of African economic development and its weak purchasing power. World trade can in theory expand infinitely, but how far and how fast it expands will depend on what levels of production and consumption are sustainable in terms of the environment, non-renewable resources and human aspirations. So although the differences between the Asian and African economic experiences are instructive, that does not mean that the former should serve as a model for the latter.

Chart 9.1: Developing Countries' Regional Populations and Shares in World Manufactured Goods Exports, 1966–86

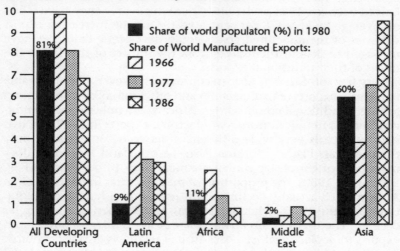

Source: UNCTC, M. Blomstroem, *Transnational Corporations and Manufacturing Exports from Developing Countries* (New York, 1990) Table 3.1; and for populations: UN, *Statistical Yearbook, 1985/6*

Manufactured goods are nearly one-third of Africa's total exports, but this figure includes output from the countries of North Africa, especially Algeria and Egypt, which both enjoyed considerable growth in the 1980s. Manufactured goods, moreover, include the first stages of processing tea, sugar and tobacco and refining copper and aluminium. That the proportion is as high as one-third, however, is more attributable to the fact that prices have fallen for primary commodities and risen for manufactures since 1985, than to any actual expansion in the volume of African manufactured exports. Our emphasis here on the stagnation and decline in the proportion of all Africa's exports of manufactures – now at levels below those of the 1980s – does not support the World Bank arguments for increasing exports of primary products (Annexe Table A37). Rather, it starkly demonstrates the flaw in the Bank's insistence on stepping up exports of primary commodities.

Between 1970 and 1980 the prices, or US dollar unit values, of African manufactures, raw materials and food rose roughly in line with each other. Prices then fell between 1980 and 1984, with raw materials' prices falling faster. After that the trends in prices for manufactures and for primary commodities diverged sharply. Since 1985 the unit values of manufactured goods in world trade have risen at 6 per cent a year, while the unit values of primary commodity exports of developing countries have fallen by over 2 per cent a year. Fuel prices rose thirteen-fold from 1970 to 1980 and were then halved between 1981 and 1986, since which time they have fallen on average by about 1 per cent a year. Only by increasing export volumes of manufactured goods could developing countries have managed to defend themselves from the impact of this fall in the prices of their traditional exports.

Very few sub-Saharan African countries, however, have been able to increase exports of manufactures and offset the collapse in earnings for their traditional commodities. Africa as a whole earned approximately US$19 billion from manufactured exports in 1989, but this figure conceals very wide differences between countries. In only three African LDCs – Burkina Faso, Lesotho and Rwanda – does manufacturing industry contribute more than 10 per cent of GDP. During the 1980s, the proportion of manufactures in the GDP of 16 African LDCs actually declined. This represents a further deterioration from the 1970s, when ten African LDCs experienced a similar decline.[2] The 1970s' fall in Africa's share of world manufactured goods exports took place against a backdrop of relatively strong economic growth in Africa. But this growth was underpinned by raw material exports, and left economic development exposed and undefended when commodity prices collapsed after 1975. The oil price rise protected oil producers like Nigeria, until that too dropped after 1983. Two decades (1970–90) of falling prices have, unsurprisingly, had a negative impact on *per capita* incomes.[3] The African oil producing countries lost the most in the 1980s, though these losses have to be set against the earlier gains of the 1970s. But all other sub-Saharan African countries also lost out: their falling income *per capita* throughout these two decades contrasted unhappily with major increases in East Asia and smaller advances in South Asia during this period.[4]

African countries were unable to make a major switch from exports of primary products to manufactures following the collapse of commodity prices. In contrast, Asian commodity producing countries, just like African countries, tried to make up for falling prices by increasing export volumes, but they also increased their manufactured exports. The development of manufacturing export capacity and markets enabled the East Asian region to reduce its debts and increase *per capita* incomes by a third. From 1980–6 Asia as a whole doubled the value of its manufactured exports. The performance of specific Asian countries and groupings is even more spectacular. By 1986 the four Asian 'dragons' almost trebled their total manufactured exports to a level exceeding the total manufactured exports of all other developing countries. By 1982 the value of Singapore's exports of manufactured goods was greater than those of all the African countries combined; Taiwan and South Korea each achieved levels three times those of all African countries combined. In the 1980s Malaysia and Thailand doubled exports of manufactures and India raised its total by 50 per cent.[5]

Two elements in this Asian switch have been missing from the African experience. The first concerns target markets. Although since 1986 African exports of manufactures have increased into EC and US markets at a rate of about 30 per cent a year and are reaching East Asian rates, Africa is barely represented in the Japanese market where East Asian and Chinese manufactured exports growth has been at 40–50 per cent a year.[6] The second concerns the type of manufacturing that is being developed for export. African manufactured exports are mainly of textiles, shoes and clothing – which appear under the classification of 'other manufactures' – and foods and beverages. For African LDCs, food, beverages and tobacco typically account for 50 per cent of the total of manufactured exports, and textiles and clothing for another 15 per cent (see Annexe Table A38). These exports are products of the first stage of industrialisation. Africa barely features in exports of more advanced manufactures – such as chemicals, machinery and transport equipment. It is a striking fact that over one-half of Asia's manufactured exports fall into this more advanced category.

Sub-Saharan Africa faces several problems in attempting to make an Asian-style switch and build a comparable manufacturing base. The outstanding problem is the size of the external debt. This was caused by the combination of falling commodity prices and rising interest rates. By 1990 African countries' debt service-to-export ratios and current account deficits on their foreign payments were far worse than those of other developing regions and the position of

African LDCs was worst of all. UNCTAD projections for the 1990s indicate only a slight fall in Africa's debt burden and a slower rate of economic growth than in any other developing country region (see Annexe Table A39).

Africa is also caught in a faulty analysis of the nature of its problem. The World Bank insists that the root of Africa's crisis lies not in external causes but internal blockages, such as flawed government policies. These, according to the Bank, can only be corrected by structural adjustment. Unfortunately, structural adjustment has a particularly significant impact on the development of manufacturing.[7] The Bank argues that when industry is developed on too small a scale with inadequate funds for importing capital goods, the result will be industries which can only survive with the aid of protectionism and subsidies, both of which the Bank uniformly opposes. It also opposes state-owned prestige projects,[8] but the Bank itself has financed many of these prestige projects over the years.[9]

Although individual sub-Saharan African countries depend on exporting only a few commodities, the region as a whole has a good 'mix' of both agricultural and mineral commodities, with probably a wider range than any other developing region. However, the commodity mix often coincides with the primary commodity resources of the existing or target markets in North America, Australasia, Europe and the former Eastern bloc.[10] All these regions are themselves producers of primary commodities and they based their own industrialisation on the raw material resources at their disposal.[11] In sub-Saharan Africa, industrialisation is minimal and standards of living so low that, except for foods, like sugar, tea, fish and meat, almost all production is exported. There is a large subsistence economy in food, fuel, building and clothing materials, but individual countries have tended to concentrate on the development of only two or three export commodities, resulting in a very weak mix of resources on which to build broader industrialisation.

What constraints and impediments do major African export commodities face if they are to become the basis for African industrialisation? The following case by case review does not imply approval of one strategy over another and the analysis has been undertaken within the confines of 'conventional wisdom'. 'Unconventional' solutions to Africa's problems will be the subject of a further TNI study.

Oil

Fuel oil accounts for a major share of export earnings in 15 sub-Saharan African countries and could provide a foundation for industrial development via petroleum-based products. In Nigeria this is already occurring. Historically, the main constraints on the development of petro-chemical industries have been the policies and strategic objectives of the foreign companies which initiated exploration and exploitation of African reserves. Today, problems of scale are retarding African oil-producing countries: efficient petro-chemical production requires economies of scale, but the local consumption of oil is not large enough to justify large-scale investment. Local consumption takes about one-tenth of production; average annual energy consumption is around 100 kg per head (compared with 10000 kg in the US [Annexe Table A31]). Without higher domestic demand, local refining and processing is unlikely to expand, so that further industrialisation, with its related rise in incomes and thus in demand for oil, will not occur. Without industrialisation, energy consumption in turn will remain low. The availability of oil is a decided advantage, but petro-chemical industrialisation demands more capital, stronger connections with a major export market and better transport systems – especially intra-African – and marketing facilities than are now available.[12]

Coffee

Coffee consumption in sub-Saharan Africa is low, about 160000 tonnes of the more than 1 million tonnes produced.[13] More than half of this is consumed in Ethiopia, and just five other countries, Madagascar, Zaïre, Nigeria, Cameroon and Kenya, account for most of the rest. The rest is exported, most of it as unprocessed, green coffee beans, for there are few manufacturers of soluble coffee within Africa. There are two soluble coffee processing plants in Tanzania, both built by Unilever – one for the government and one serving the South African market.[14] The largest coffee producers, Côte d'Ivoire, Ethiopia and Uganda, have no manufacturing facilities. A large proportion of the coffee consumed in three major industrialised country markets is soluble: 90 per cent in the UK, 50 per cent in Japan, 30 per cent in the US.[15] Just two companies – Nestlé and Philip Morris/Kraft General Foods – control three-quarters of the world market for soluble.[16] Coffee as a basis for industrialisation is not promising.

Copper

External factors that affect copper exports, such as competition and transport difficulties, would not negatively affect the development of African-based copper industries if development were led by domestic demand. Unfortunately, consumption of copper in Africa is negligible (see Annexe Table A22), so this product faces the same 'Catch 22' problem as oil – 'not enough domestic demand to lay the foundations for an industrialisation programme which would increase domestic demand'. In addition, TNC policies militate against further processing in Africa, as do the tariff structures for imports of worked-up copper into the EC, Japan and the US, which are the TNCs' main markets (see Annexe Table A40).

Diamonds

Diamond conversion takes place predominantly in the industrialised countries near the market for the final products – jewellery and industrial use. Since the appropriate craft skills exist in most African countries, and with a widespread illicit traffic in diamonds, it might seem surprising that a larger direct-sale market has not emerged. The issue here is legitimacy and authority: the de Beers' stamp ensures that high-value diamonds, particularly when purchased as an investment, are not false. No other African producer can quickly develop that credibility.

Cocoa

Sub-Saharan Africa exports about 67 per cent of all the cocoa beans entering world trade, but only 15 per cent of the cocoa butter and powder, and less than 1 per cent of the chocolate (see Annexe Table A15). Cocoa consumption in sub-Saharan Africa is so low that it does not feature in the UNCTAD *Commodity Yearbook*. The geographical concentration of African cocoa-producing countries – Benin, Cameroon, Côte d'Ivoire, Equatorial Guinea and Ghana – might favour joint manufacturing ventures. But currently a small number of companies – Nestlé/Rowntree, Cadbury-Schweppes and Mars – dominate the world market,[17] and escalating tariffs discriminate against processed imports in the EC and Japan (Annexe Table A40).

Timber

The largest proportion of African timber is exported as logs. A reduction in exports of logs from Côte d'Ivoire, the Congo and Ghana in favour of sawn wood had occurred by the mid-1980s, but not from two other exporters – Gabon and Liberia. The export levels of veneer and plywood, which are higher value products, have changed little. Asian producers have gradually shifted their timber exports away from logs to wood products, so that timber trade analysts have been recommending that African producers take over the role of log suppliers, especially to Japan,[18] eliciting strong protest from the environmental movement.[19] The timber market is not dominated by a few large companies and is at least partly open. Though import tariffs in potential markets rise with each stage of processing, Japan grants import concessions under the General System of Preferences (GSP) as does the EC, which also grants concessions under the ACP Lomé Convention for former European colonies. Tropical hardwood could be an appropriate basis on which to build new local industries.

African experience with pulp and paper mills has been particularly unhappy. A United Nations Industrial Development Organisation (UNIDO) study takes the Cellucam mill in Cameroon as an example and concludes, 'Some of Africa's major white elephants are pulp mills.'[20] Timber mills are capital-intensive and need large-scale markets for viable levels of production. The many separate African states and the poor transport facilities between them reduce the possibilities of widening markets. Paper manufacture suffers from an additional barrier to demand: illiteracy rates range from 42 per cent in the Seychelles to 91 per cent in Burkina Faso, with an average of 50 per cent.[21] Illiteracy and low incomes mean low consumption of packaging and paper-based products so the domestic foundation for industrial development is again lacking. In any case, African tropical hardwoods are ill-suited for paper production and too valuable a resource to be used for pulp. They have some potential for industrial development, at least for export, but forests would have to be far better managed and protected to ensure a steady and lasting supply.

Cane Sugar

Cane sugar is exported unrefined from sub-Saharan Africa. But African consumption is almost as high as production, so overall imports are greater than exports and include large quantities of refined sugar (see Annexe Table A41). Sub-Saharan African sugar exports, worth some US$700 million annually, are mainly concessionary exports to the EC under the Lomé Convention, tied to a refining agreement with Tate & Lyle in the UK.[22] Zimbabwe is the main supplier of refined sugar. There are three main barriers to bigger exports of refined sugar. First, the export quota agreements are conditional on working with TNCs as processors; if African producers challenged the big corporations, their markets would be closed. Next is the problem of escalating tariffs (10 per cent on refined sugar imports into the EC). Finally, although the US has lower tariffs,

African cane sugar must compete with subsidised local production.[23] Tariffs on sugar imports into Japan are higher for raw than for processed sugar and, at between 30 and 40 per cent are virtually prohibitive (Annexe Table A40). Demand is keenest in the domestic markets and investment in production for local consumption is being advanced through factories established by international companies like Bookers.

Meat and Live Animals

The EC, Japan and the US impose high tariffs on imports of meat, although the EC reduces these for ACP products. Hides and skins are an important resource for manufacturing. Annual exports of undressed hides and skins are worth approximately US$200 million, mainly from Namibia and Ethiopia. These indicate some scope for added value: the export of shoes and leather goods in place of these raw materials. World Bank experts have noted this sector as one in which the informal economy has begun to work.[24]

Cotton

The two major cotton exporters are in North Africa, Egypt and Sudan, but production is widely spread over more than 20 other countries. The market for cotton is not closed or dominated by a few companies, but access to markets in developed countries is subject to tariff and non-tariff barriers, including the very restrictive Multi-Fibre Arrangement (MFA). By the mid-1980s sub-Saharan Africa's exports of cotton consisted mostly of raw cotton lint – that is, it was not even spun into yarn – and African countries as a whole actually imported more yarn and fabrics than they exported (see Annexe Table A18). Exports of clothing – not all made of cotton – were about equal to the mainly synthetic imports. But since 1986 exports of textile yarn, fabrics and clothing have more than doubled. Mills in Nigeria and Zambia have increased their capacity utilisation to about 40 per cent.[25]

In this same period, exports of yarn, fabrics and clothing from Asia (excluding China) also doubled, but from levels which were already about 20 times higher than those of Africa.[26] The production of the raw material, cotton, in Africa is equal to that in India or in Pakistan, which together account for all Asian production outside China.[27] This output of the primary commodity provides the basis for a potential expansion of production to supply domestic markets; only if the MFA is dismantled will export opportunities also arise.

Iron Ore

Around 25 million tonnes of iron ore are extracted from three sub-Saharan African countries – Liberia, Mauritania and Zimbabwe. Almost all is exported as ore. The only processing before export is the 1 million tonnes converted in Zimbabwe, 3 million tonnes of pellets produced in Liberia and the products of the small plants in Nigeria. In contrast, iron ore production in South Africa goes roughly equally into local steel production and for export, while North African ore is all used for local iron and steel production. There are two obstacles to the development of iron and steel production in Liberia and Mauritania: the size of the local populations (about 2 million each), which means that domestic demand is low, and the closed nature of the international market, dominated by TNCs and consortia from North America, Western Europe and South Africa.

The ports in Liberia and Mauritania from which iron ore is exported are close to West African states, with much larger populations. Nigeria, to take the largest example, has 100 million inhabitants. But developing an iron and steel industry in Nigeria would require a major break in current commercial linkages.[28] The existing plants in Nigeria operate at less than a quarter of capacity.[29]

The remaining products in the range of sub-Saharan African commodities fall into three broad categories:

1. Commodities whose processing is undertaken in the different international operations of vertically integrated TNCs, for example, bauxite, the several 'exotic' minerals and natural rubber.
2. Commodities whose markets are more open or more conducive to local processing, whether for local markets or because the nature of the product demands immediate processing, for example, fish products, tobacco, tea, hard fibres and vegetable oils; but African consumption is small (see Annexe Tables A42 and A43).
3. Commodities which have no significant domestic market, such as rubber, or conversely, those for which there could be a strong domestic demand but which are valued more highly for their export earning potential, such as phosphate rock. Only South Africa has natural rubber-consuming industries as well as synthetic production.[30] The five sub-Saharan African rubber producers export all their production.

All these studies of manufacturing industry signal the failure of export-oriented production to contribute significantly to the development of local industries in Africa. When compared to the overall experience of developing countries, Africa's share in manufacturing production and export is particularly low (see Annexe Table A44). Lack of investment and market access are two fundamental reasons for this.

TNCs have shown virtually no real interest in investing in processing in Africa. The World Bank and the Fraser Expert Group attribute this reluctance to restrictive tax regimes and legislation that African governments impose on foreign investors, especially in mining. Yet mining legislation has been much amended and taxation has been relaxed throughout southern Africa without attracting an encouraging response from foreign investors.[31] TNCs have very demanding attitudes to local tax regimes, as we have seen in the evidence of their substantial and ongoing tax evasion.

Lack of Foreign Investment

Potential investors cite other reasons for not investing in Africa, some of which surfaced in interviews with traders. They note the absence of a local market. Then there is a general problem of viability. Metal-based industries require several mineral inputs, a wide range of human skills and a reasonable infrastructure of water supply, reliable electricity, transport and communication systems. Even where these are to be found, certain key skills and materials still have to be imported and the net result has often been that import costs exceed export receipts, otherwise known as 'input strangulation'. A UNIDO study cites such cases even in non-metal-based industries like cement manufacture and engineering.[32] Capital-intensive plant must operate at full capacity and this implies access to a wide enough market. Even if a sufficient market exists, for example in the construction industry or agricultural engineering, intermediate levels of technology may be more appropriate for the conditions. This factor has at times been recognised by World Bank experts.[33] But the emphasis of the Bank and Fraser Report on preparing the way for foreign investment[34] is to assume that major foreign investors will somehow see a long-term commercial interest in investing in intermediate and small-scale technology in Africa.

A large proportion of the extraction and marketing of African minerals is controlled by TNCs based in South Africa. To date this has kept down investment in manufacturing development, partly because the market in South Africa itself is extremely small, partly because South African products have been subject to international boycotts of varying severity for 25 years. TNCs are likely to see investment opportunities in manufacturing for already existing or expanding markets. Their attitudes towards an emerging democratic and multiracial South Africa remain to be seen.

The World Bank and the Fraser Expert Group assume that the diversification of exports through the development of a manufacturing industry can only be achieved through foreign direct investment.[35] Although this was certainly the case for the development of free trade zones like Singapore, Hong Kong, Manila and Colombo, it does not satisfactorily explain the 1980s' expansion of manufactured exports from Latin America or Asia. A recent study by the UNCTC shows that the share of manufactured exports from countries in these regions originating in US transnationals' majority-owned affiliates was quite small.[36] The US TNC affiliates' share in Latin America amounted to only 16 per cent in 1986, while in Asia it was no more than 6 per cent in 1986. The share was less than 2 per cent of the total exports of the four 'dragons'. The position of affiliates from Japanese and European TNCs appears to be no different. Thus foreign investment was not a key factor in the manufacturing successes of these countries.

US, EC and Japanese TNC investments have sought to increase sales from overseas plants, rather than increase exports from plants in the parent country. But they have achieved this through direct investment in the industrialised countries, not in developing countries, even Asian ones. Comparing the period 1985–90 with 1980–5, the UNCTC study shows that direct TNC investment flows more than doubled, but the proportion of this investment which went into developing countries fell from 25 per cent to 18 per cent of the total.[37]

If direct investment by TNCs in industrial development is not forthcoming, that does not necessarily mean industrialisation is impossible. The most successful of the newly industrialising countries, particularly South Korea and Taiwan, have established their own independent bases of capital accumulation. In 1985 six of the 600 top corporations worldwide with sales of over 1 billion dollars were South Korean.[38] Apart from Zimco in Zambia, which even now is being broken down into several different countries as part of a privatisation programme, the only other companies from developing countries which featured in the list of the top 600 were oil companies. South Korean companies have over 400 affiliates operating overseas and have themselves invested widely in Asia, partly in extractive industries on which Korea depends heavily, but also in labour-intensive subcontracting for the parent company. The technology used in Korean industry is from the US or Japan. It was not obtained by direct investment by US or Japanese TNCs in Korea, but under what are called Original Equipment Manufacturing (OEM) arrangements. Under OEM arrangements, long-term contracts are offered for the manufacture of components at below market prices; the deal is based on a combination of relatively cheap labour and the provision of technical know-how. Later the OEM contractor can break free and expand or develop this new technical base.[39]

African industrial development and diversification away from exports of unprocessed primary products depend on access to markets, but also on quality control, educational levels and infrastructure. For obvious historical and geographical reasons, Europe provides the largest market for most categories of African exports (see Chart 3.2). With the exception of fuel, North America on average is a market for only 15 per cent of other African commodities. Other markets for African exports are in Africa itself and other developing countries (for almost half of chemicals, machinery and transport equipment); the former Soviet bloc (for a third of textiles and yarns); South Africa (for 10 per cent of non-ferrous metals but little else). It is important to remember that sub-Saharan Africa as a whole represents less than 2 per cent of total world trade.

The historical trading relationship between Africa and Europe has been a mixed blessing for the development of manufactured exports. On the one hand, the Lomé Conventions, which cover nearly all African countries, have abolished or at least reduced otherwise highly prohibitive tariffs on imports to the EC. (Europe is generally more protective of its markets than are the US and Canada, and in some cases Japan [see Annexe Table A40]). The European market may be large, but still comprises only 30 per cent of the total world market. Europe takes just over 20 per cent of all developing countries' exports.[40] In other words, the main world markets do not lie in Europe; outside it, Africa's products must compete on equal terms with everyone else's. Even where links with the US, Canada or Japan have been forged, processed products all face escalating tariffs (see Annexe Tables A40 and A45). Here is the Fraser Report's conclusion on market access for African processed products:

> We judge, and recent IMF and World Bank studies give significant support to our judgment, that despite the benefits of the Lomé Convention and the preferences given to LDCs, developed countries do not provide the kind of market access that the developing countries of Africa need or which would be available if the developed countries refrained from narrowly self-interested protection policies and made the playing field more level.[41]

The Expert Group also tacitly acknowledges that foreign investors perceive this restricted access as a major disincentive to investment in Africa:

It is also clear that many multi-nationals believe that, despite a reduction in the overall level of formal protective measures imposed by developed countries, administrative protection, including safeguard clauses, anti-dumping measures, rules of origin and the like, are being used more readily and with greater arbitrariness, particularly by the US and the EC.[42]

First World Protection

Developed countries' tariffs on imports from developing countries can currently be modified or reduced under three schemes: the US's system of awarding Most Favoured Nation (MFN) status; the General System of Preferences (GSP); and the African, Caribbean and Pacific (ACP) countries' quotas agreed with the EC under the Lomé Convention. These are important concessions. MFN establishes the principle of non-discrimination. Any benefit awarded by a member state to one trading partner must be accorded to all. MFN status, once restricted to non-communist states, is now generally applicable and represents the 'base line' for developing country exports to the developed world. GSP status is granted for imports entering the EC, Japan, the former Soviet Union and Eastern Europe as part of aid schemes and mainly relates to imports from LDCs. The US granted special treatment to some LDC products in 1979, but later withdrew this and has been exploring duty-free access to US markets for LDCs as part of the GATT negotiations (Uruguay round).[43]

In practice the effect of any concessions to developing countries' exports has been limited, particularly because tariffs have remained high for products which compete with the developed countries' own production and because of their high residual tariffs and internal taxes on imports of manufactures – coffee (12 per cent), tobacco (67 per cent) and tropical fruit (13 per cent). In addition, reach has been indiscriminate. A 1987 study found that Hong Kong, South Korea and Taiwan together received 44 per cent of the total gains from the current GSP system and Brazil was the third biggest recipient, although none of these is a typical LDC and the Asian trio could arguably be termed developed countries.[44] ACP concessions have worked better, allowing duty-free entry for most products, although it is notable that several products on which tariffs remain directly affect prospects for diversifying African exports – namely, roasted coffee, margarine, canned fruits and meat.

A substantial non-tariff barrier is the universal system of quotas for clothing and textile imports, the Multi-Fibre Arrangement (MFA). The Fraser Expert Group recommends

> ... that the MFA should be discontinued or phased out as soon as possible after the expiry of the present agreement [in 1991]; that no government should apply tariff, non-tariff or administrative protective measures, to replace the measures previously in place under MFA; and that countries should not invoke safeguard procedures against imports from the least developed countries.[45]

Rules of Origin and other non-tariff measures were among those safeguards, all introduced to prevent disruption in the developed countries' textile and apparel industries by cheap labour in the developing countries. In analysing the impact and coverage of these measures (see Annexe Table A45) the Fraser Report makes the point that this protection can no longer be justified, since in some sections of the market, developing countries account for a smaller proportion of total trade than they did 20 years ago.

Although the fundamental purpose of GATT was to establish free trade principles in all international exchanges;[46] and though successive rounds of negotiation have reduced the levels of protection between developed countries' markets, access for developing countries to these markets has improved little. GATT, described by its first Secretary General as a 'collection of loop-holes held together by a few principles', does have some 'loopholes' which could have worked to the advantage of developing countries. For example:

- Article XII provides for general trade restrictions to be imposed to protect a country's balance of payments;
- Article XVIII allows infant industries to be protected;
- Article XIX permits *temporary* emergency protection against imports which cause or threaten 'serious injury' to domestic suppliers;
- Articles V and XVI provide for action against imports which are dumped or subsidised;
- Article XX provides for measures to safeguard patents, trade marks and copyrights;
- Article XXI provides for measures to safeguard public health and national security;

- Article XXIV provides for departures from the principle of non-discrimination to allow governments to form customs' unions or free trade areas.

Many of these articles have been deployed by developed countries against the developing world. As an Indian delegate to an early GATT meeting once observed, 'the GATT is a one-way street', down which developed countries can easily pass but which is blocked to those coming in the other direction.

A separate section on development was added to GATT provisions in 1964, which allowed special treatment for developing countries, especially under MFN treatment, that concessions made to them need not be accorded to all trading partners. At the start of the latest round of GATT negotiations begun in Uruguay in 1986, it was expressly stated by GATT officials that developing countries would have to increase their involvement in GATT's obligations. This was because a few of them had reached levels of economic development equal to that in countries of the North. In other words, the message was that, if they wanted more favourable treatment, they would have to make concessions; for example, if the MFA was to be phased out, they must open up their markets to the North. This was to apply especially to agricultural products and services, which were brought for the first time into GATT negotiations in the Uruguay round. But Third World farmers know that they still need protection from cheap, and often subsidised, food exports from the North and their governments know that they need to retain measures to develop an indigenous service sector. Secret deals may well be being done behind closed doors in these GATT negotiations at the expense of the developing countries,[47] but a total breakdown of the GATT would leave the developing countries at the mercy of uncontrolled beggar-my-neighbour policies; and it would put off for a long time the positive measures of trade development which were originally envisaged for an International Trade Organisation (ITO) before GATT was introduced to take their place. A resuscitated ITO to combine the work of UNCTAD and GATT has for long been the favoured option of the developing countries.[48]

The World Bank distinguishes between internal and external blockages or obstacles to economic development. It has generally insisted that internal blockages are at the heart of Africa's crisis. In fact, external factors influencing Africa's economic development are at least as important and indeed constitute almost insuperable obstacles. It has been exceedingly difficult for Africa to break out of the primary commodity straitjacket inherited from its colonial past and to end its reliance on TNCs – both processors and traders – whose objectives may not, and cannot be expected to, prioritise Africa's economic and social development. The protective barriers against imported manufactures and against the more processed stages of primary products defy most efforts to develop viable and independent industry. Of all developing regions, sub-Saharan Africa has fared the worst, because despite some duty-free access, African products with development potential, notably textiles, processed coffee and canned fruits, are still prohibitively taxed on entry to markets in developed countries. Finally, and most serious of all, there is a growing crisis of finance for Africa, as direct foreign investment bypasses Africa and the collapse in primary commodity prices and export earnings makes the already crippling foreign debt ever harder to service.

10. Export-led Growth and African Politics

Kabula Mboje held out a piece of her brightly coloured *kanga*, the garment traditionally worn by women and men in Tanzania. 'Look at this', she said. 'It was a cheap one, yet it cost me 800 shillings [£4.50 sterling]; not very much less than I earned from this year's cotton harvest.' It had been a bad year for cotton, yet even so Kabula had grown enough on her two-acre plot of land to make 720 *kangas* ... Kabula lives in Mwabuzo [West Central Tanzania] ... By law each adult member of the community is required to grow at least one acre of cotton. 'Cotton is the only cash crop we can grow around here. We have to grow something for cash so that we can pay our local taxes and buy essentials such as salt, clothes and shoes.' Kabula was disappointed with her year's cotton earnings, but relieved not to have made a loss. Some [in her community] did. [Kabula], like many people in the countries in which Oxfam works ... [has] been caught in the trade trap.[1]

Belinda Coote, *The Trade Trap: Poverty and the Global Commodity Markets*, 1992

Internal Problems

Most of the peoples of sub-Saharan Africa are caught in a commodity trade 'trap' and have been getting steadily poorer throughout the 1980s. The trap is the falling prices in world markets for African products. Yet the World Bank remains firmly convinced that Africa's main problems are internal.[2] It believes African governments spend too much and seek to raise excessive rents (or income) from production and exports; they protect inefficient industries in misguided attempts at import substitution; they interfere in the workings of the market by setting prices and they maintain exchange rates for their local currencies at levels which make their exports uncompetitive. Following the Bank's logic, these factors alone lie behind the failure to attract the foreign capital investment necessary for economic development in Africa. Asian countries have also faced

129

the problems of falling commodity prices, but have not only done better in exporting their primary commodities, they have also increased their exports from new manufacturing industries. This has simply not happened in Africa. Why? The World Bank's explanation has become increasingly self-critical. It spends large sums evaluating, monitoring and publishing its findings and recently these have been, perhaps through force of circumstances, less self-assured.[3] Former World Bank senior managers, like Percy Mistry, have announced frankly:

[In Africa the result of the] approach of the [World] Bank and the [International Monetary] Fund has been to worsen the problem. In Africa ... measures [to achieve external and internal account balances] have not worked out in the ways intended, except perhaps the measure of liberalising agricultural producer prices.[4]

Technical staff still working at the Bank have questioned the whole basis of structural adjustment programmes.[5] This book follows in their footsteps and aims to provoke some genuine debate, based on hard facts and realistic analysis. Among the internal obstacles which the Bank recognises are natural phenomena like drought, locust attacks, high winds, floods or earth movements, and man-made problems like *coups d'état*, urban riot and war. Policies may also contribute to falling terms of trade – that is, policies which reduce the value of primary exports relative to imports of manufactures.[6] Not all of these problems can be laid at the feet of African governments, although desertification and drought may result from excessive cash cropping and unsustainable forms of energy consumption. Political and ethnic conflicts are evidently man-made, and are exacerbated by many of the existing African political structures, but they are not the only cause of what is euphemistically called 'negative economic growth'.

Rent Seeking by Governments

World Bank criticism targets three particular government policies: the scale of rent taken on primary commodity exports, the excessive use of subsidies and absence of political pluralism.[7] In Africa, as elsewhere, rents are levied by governments through direct taxes and the operations of state marketing boards. The World Bank, among others, argues for privatisation in Africa on the basis that governments not only have a near-dominant position as one of the few buyers and revenue collectors, but that the rents are excessive and are diverted to non-productive uses.[8] The theory maintains that a private company will operate in direct competition with others and plough its profits back into more efficient operations.

Levels of government rents in Africa vary widely from state to state: from 6 to 36 per cent of GDP, with most lying in the range between 6 and 15 per cent.[9] High rents are believed to hinder economic growth because they divert resources from productive to unproductive activities and act as a disincentive to both capital and labour; the one is discouraged from investing, and the other from working. An econometric study by a World Bank economist looked at the effects of rent policies on economic growth in African states from 1975–81 and 1981–7.[10] The study considered five types of government 'rents' – tariff revenues, protection of domestic manufactures, monopolistic marketing boards, the allocation of foreign exchange and the use of investment funds for non-market related activities. Rents were then correlated not just with rates of macro-economic growth but also with:

- the proportion of rents in national income
- the level of *per capita* income
- the government share of spending in the GDP
- levels of capital investment, in particular in human resources such as education
- factors guaranteeing political pluralism and civil liberties

Some of the findings were not quite what the author had expected. For example, the expectation that more rent would be sought by less democratic regimes was not confirmed. Nor was there any firm evidence that the introduction of structural adjustment and the reduction of rents facilitated a transition to more pluralistic and democratic systems of government. The strongest correlations were between high spending by governments and rent comprising a large proportion of GDP and between high existing *per capita* incomes and a high degree of political pluralism.[11] There was some evidence that very high rents might cause political upheaval which, of course, is not conducive to economic growth.[12] Most African states have low growth, with little political pluralism and few civil liberties.[13] The study shows that in drawing up rules for economic reform it is unwise to be dogmatic.[14] Although high government spending was shown to be related to slow economic growth, the study concludes that government expenditure on the development of human resources and on other investment was shown to be an important source of growth. Non-productive spending like subsidies was, however, particularly damaging,[15] as the Bank always insists.

There is an irony in the World Bank's criticisms of African spending on subsidies given the high levels and many types of subsidy in Europe and North America, particularly for farmers with whom Third World farmers must compete. Economic subsidies interfere directly with the price 'signals' in the market which bring supply and demand into line. Under the EC's Common Agricultural Policy (CAP), for example, farmers grow more at higher prices than the market can take, leading to surpluses and dumping.[16] Subsidies can be justified by the need to protect disadvantaged social groups or threatened industries. The World Bank's structural adjustment conditions that force African governments to cut subsidies, particularly for food, have often been applied without discriminating between the different purposes of subsidies. In consequence, the burden has fallen on the poor. In 1989 the Managing Director of the IMF stated: 'In most countries the real costs of such cuts are being paid, disproportionately, by the poor and their children.'[17] At the same time, subsidised imported food means that local farmers cannot compete in the market and themselves go hungry.[18]

Much of the Bank's criticism of African governments has been directed against import substitution policies to encourage local industries. In Africa, inefficient local production – for example, plants operating at below capacity – has been sustained by subsidies and protective tariffs.[19] These result in a double loss: resources are diverted from productive uses and what is produced is too expensive and uncompetitive. But correctly timed and selective use of subsidies to support production and then to promote exports has helped generate rapid economic growth in other developing countries, like South Korea, Taiwan and Chile, when focused on industries with the capacity to develop efficiently.[20]

The study of the effects of rents on economic growth looks at the 1970s and 1980s; it does not consider the role of government before then, particularly under colonial rule when the system of marketing boards, tariffs and price controls was first established. It thus ignores the inheritance from the past which is a factor in shaping African economies. Since one of the strong correlations in the study was between high *per capita* incomes, high government spending and high rents, these high incomes could already have resulted from high governmental spending in colonial times. Nor does the study differentiate between the different trade structures of the several countries. Governments of African countries which rely on only one or two primary commodity exports have few opportunities for productive investment, and have no other sources of revenue in the short term. The multiple economic, marketing and transport problems involved in developing productive and viable industry, and thus an alternative tax base, have been illustrated in preceding chapters.

The World Bank's analysis lays the main blame for the general decline in Africa's terms of trade on one external factor – 'shock' induced by the fall in oil prices in the 1980s. But at the same time world prices for Africa's commodity exports also fell steadily while interest rates on external debts increased. These factors, also external, directly affected growth rates. Prices for almost all African commodities fell both absolutely and in relation to manufactured imports. An average of 26 per cent of export earnings had to be spent on servicing African countries' foreign debt, [21] worsening an already bad situation as falling prices cut national incomes. More capital left Africa than entered it. An economist writing in a 1990 National Westminster Bank *Quarterly Review* concluded: 'The economic development of debtor nations has been set back for at least a decade by the debt crisis and the burden of economic adjustment has fallen entirely on the poorest people of Africa and Latin America.'[22]

Commodity-based Development?

The World Bank's own forecasts predict little recovery in prices or demand for most of Africa's export commodities. Furthermore, the Bank is simultaneously encouraging other regions to increase production and exports as if oversupply had no effect on prices and market behaviour, and it has taken no account of market resistance to some African products. Yet, although the Fraser Report has argued that debt should be scaled down,[23] at the same time it continues to claim that the only solution to Africa's problems is increased commodity exports.[24] The Fraser Expert Group underlined the Bank's approach with an argument of quite breathtaking insouciance:

> During the course of economic development ... the relative importance of the commodities sector invariably declines over time. The speed with which it declines is a product of development itself. In the African context, the most obvious route to overall transformation is thus, *paradoxically* to strengthen the commodities sector.[25] (Emphasis added)

Of course, a country or region can only base its development on the resources at its disposal. But a review of the structure, ownership and marketing of sub-Saharan Africa's commodities shows clearly that exports are signally failing to contribute to the region's development. Receipts from commodity exports are falling because demand for some of them is declining and there is plentiful alternative supply. There is little diversification and second-stage processing, despite the eminent suitability of at least a few products for local manufacturing. Most sub-Saharan African countries have yet to reach even the early stages of industrialisation. The Fraser Expert Group did recognise that a commodity strategy should include both the attainment of food security at household, regional and national levels (that is, reduced dependence on food imports) and 'diversification to enlarge the export base and capture more value added, [so as to obtain] an increase in export earnings from primary and processed commodities'.[26]

Both the World Bank and the Expert Group believe that foreign investment by TNCs is the key to economic advance: diversification, value adding, larger market shares and so on. The fundamental obstacles to such an advance are, however, external: that is, they cannot be eliminated even by the most thoroughgoing internal reforms in African countries. The Expert Group does indeed have some doubts that World Bank and IMF policies can overcome these external obstacles; it is worth citing them at length:

> [Developing countries have been pursuing structural adjustment with] great courage and political determination. Over 30 [African] countries are now embarked on such programmes. Some countries have stuck to the programmes for five or six years and are determined to stick on the track. There is, however, *a high probability that such programmes will fail* unless the international community takes a wider view of its overall responsibilities.[27] (Emphasis added)

Then comes the crucial statement:

> The Fund and the Bank have addressed themselves to the macro-economic situation within particular countries, and resources have been provided subject to conditionality, a conditionality which is often regarded as excessively severe. The Fund and the Bank are not responsible for, and do not have direct authority for, direct foreign investment in such countries. Given their overall persuasive power, however, they have not taken sufficient steps to make sure that such countries embarking upon a diversified and expanded production base will gain *adequate access to markets in industrial countries*. Therefore, while attention is paid to the macro-

economic elements, the broader trade policy is not brought into the equation.[28] (Emphasis added)

The World Bank and the Fraser Expert Group see the fall in foreign investment in Africa during the 1980s as the main cause of Africa's economic decline. A 1990 study by the British Overseas Development Institute (ODI) provides a detailed analysis:

Sub-Saharan Africa accounted for only 14 per cent of the total developing country stock of foreign investment in 1985, falling from some 27 per cent in 1975. Whereas in real terms the stock of foreign investment in all developing countries increased over this period by 76 per cent, the stock value in sub-Saharan Africa fell by 8 per cent in real terms. It increased in all other sub-regions of the developing world.[29]

Foreign Investment in Africa Checked

Between 1985 and 1987, aid and other resource flows back into Africa restarted, but fell back again in 1990.[30] Direct investment as a proportion of all net resource flows into sub-Saharan Africa, however, fell from 5 per cent in 1980–2 to 1.3 per cent in 1985–7. This serious decline must be understood in the context of a starting level which was already comparatively low: it was less than for other low-income countries compared to an average for all developing countries of about 40 per cent.[31] Moreover, apart from a sharp drop in sub-Saharan Africa's relative share, what private foreign investment did occur is strikingly concentrated in primary production. Although the value of investment in sub-Saharan Africa rose, its share of total foreign direct investment virtually halved and 55 per cent of private foreign investment in the early 1980s was in primary production.[32]

The assumed benefits of foreign direct investment are summarised in the ODI study as follows: 'An expansion in productive and technological capacity, an increase in skill levels and employment, lower foreign exchange costs of goods now produced and previously imported, and an increase in foreign exchange earnings for goods exported.'

Unfortunately, in sub-Saharan Africa, none of these benefits has materialised and, according to the ODI, the impact of investment has been negligible. Its study concludes that technological transfer to Africa has been limited; local employment opportunities, other than for manual labour, are few and skill training is conspicuous by its absence; little or no attempt has been made to develop local sourcing of supplies, so that it often costs more in foreign exchange to produce goods locally than to import them. The contribution of foreign direct investment to economic growth

> has increasingly tended to be at the expense of negative flows on the balance of payments ... Further, the evidence in sub-Saharan Africa suggests that it is very unlikely that inflows on capital account, in the form of new equity investment, will offset these negative flows other than for an initial period and in exceptional years.

New forms of investment in sub-Saharan Africa are increasingly important because economic instability and weakness imply higher risks. The ODI study cites the example of Nigeria, where management agreements, patent and technology licensing agreements, production sharing contracts and other forms of subcontracting, made up an average 40 per cent share of overseas investment between 1976 and 1986, twice the figure estimated by the OECD for all developing countries. The largest portfolio of such projects is held by the UK-based Commonwealth Corporation which has invested in services to outgrowers in Malawi coffee, Kenya tea and sugar and other fields of agricultural production. Outgrowing contracts – which are replacing the more traditional vertically integrated TNC operations – place more of the risk and uncertainty on the growers, without any guaranteed increase in return of stable markets.

The Mauritius Export Processing Zone has been described as 'an industrial success story in Africa'.[33] The government set out in part to replace its single export commodity, sugar, with manufactured products. By offering a package of incentives to foreign companies, including free trade, tax exemption, free repatriation of capital and dividends and much local financial and infrastructure support, between 1970 and 1985 the government succeeded in attracting some 400 companies, with more than 50 per cent foreign equity participation. A strong Hong Kong connection helps explain this success: more than 80 per cent of production is of textiles and the foreign investors are mainly from Hong Kong. There was an active local Chinese business community in place, and the Hong Kong textile and garment industry was running up against the quota ceilings of the Multi-Fibre Arrangement (MFA) for its imports into industrialised countries. The other source of investment, although smaller, was France, which has continuing links with the francophone settler community and has lobbied for access for Mauritian products to the French market.[34]

The special combination of circumstances in Mauritius leads the authors of the ODI study to doubt whether its experience could become a model for every sub-region of Africa. In 1974 an Export Processing Zone was established in Senegal in which total exemption was assured from duty on imports and from direct or indirect taxation for 25 years. Despite this generous package and investment in efficient infrastructure, by 1985 there were only seven firms operating in the Zone and all were exporting to other countries in the region. For exporting to Europe, Senegal suffered from the high CFA/French franc rate of exchange in relation to other EC currencies. Export Processing Zones were being established in 1990 at Mombasa in Kenya and in Togo, but it remains to be seen how successful they will be.[35] Since 1989, even Mauritius's performance has been eroded as a result of pressure for higher wages, making its Export Zones less internationally competitive.[36] This illustrates how export-led growth based on Export Zones can work only as long as wages and working conditions can be kept at rock-bottom levels.

Original Equipment Manufacture (OEM) agreements, which played such an important role in South Korea's industrialisation, have not yet been tried in Africa, and very few sub-Saharan African states have reached a level of development that could justify such arrangements. Three countries might qualify, Nigeria, Kenya and Zimbabwe; they have recently liberalised their rules in the hope of attracting investors.[37]

The UN Expert Group believes the reason that foreign investment in Africa has declined is that:

... many multinationals believe that, despite a reduction in the overall level of formal protective measures imposed by developed countries ... [such measures] are being used more readily and with greater arbitrariness, particularly by the United States and the European Community. Against that background, international business will not provide considerable sums for export oriented investments in Africa if they believe that market access to industrialised countries, in particular, might be shut off. A doubt is sufficient to prevent the investment.[38]

The World Bank's structural adjustment programmes are intended to make countries adopting them more attractive to foreign investors, but in practice they are not helping foreign investors to overcome their doubts. In the 1980s, foreign-owned assets contributed close to 20 per cent of the GDP of many African economies. This was considerably lower than comparable figures for the 1960s and early 1970s, partly because of nationalisations of foreign capital in the intervening years.[39] The contribution of foreign direct investment to Nigeria's GDP fell from about 40 per cent in 1976 to 20 per cent in 1986. The ODI study also expresses doubts about whether structural adjustment programmes have brought in foreign investment, citing the case of Ghana, which has pursued one of the most vigorous programmes in the whole of Africa but where there has been little or no interest from foreign investors.[40] On the other hand Zambia and Zimbabwe have attracted foreign investors without economic reforms.

Not only is foreign investment being withdrawn from Africa, it is *bypassing* sub-Saharan Africa completely. Why? There are several explanations for this. First, rates of return on investment have fallen from over 30 per cent in the period 1961–3, to 13 per cent in 1973–80 and to just 2.5 per cent in 1980–7. Low growth rates over the last decade have left much existing plant operating well below capacity. Even a faster rate of growth in the near future would merely take up the slack and not necessarily require new equipment.[41] Second, several of the key elements of structural adjustment programmes deter potential investors because they can harm the operations of foreign companies. Examples include quotas and tariffs on imports that compete with local production, increasing local energy prices, depreciating the local currency, or raising local interest rates, all of which in turn increase the price of inputs.[42] Finally, cuts in government spending put at risk many of the services, or 'common goods', on which foreign companies rely – and do not expect to undertake themselves – like general infrastructure, transport, communications, water supply, sewerage and education.

Failure of Structural Adjustment

For all these reasons, the UN Economic Commission for Africa (UNECA) was able to demonstrate that, contrary to World Bank wisdom, the economies of sub-Saharan African countries which have pursued structural adjustment most strongly have declined in the period 1980–7. By contrast weak adjusters and non-adjusters experienced economic growth. The contrast is clear in Table 10.1. UNECA based its figures on weighted averages of the several countries: that is, they took into account the size of the national income in each, which figures published by the World Bank did not. The average annual growth rate over 1980–7 is 2 per cent for the weak adjusters, 3.5 per cent for the non-adjusters and -0.5 for the strong adjusters. Could the conclusion be clearer?

Table 10.1: Economic Growth, 1980-7

Country Group	1980/1	1981/2	1982/3	1983/4	1984/5	1985/6	1986/7	Average 1980-7
Strong adjusting	-3.01	0.33	-3.85	-4.31	6.33	2.82	-1.97	-0.53
Weak adjusting	5.44	3.46	0.66	-1.29	0.13	4.01	1.88	2.00
Non adjusting	3.92	3.35	3.53	3.68	6.40	3.62	-2.51	3.50
Sub-Saharan Africa	-1.05	1.01	-2.37	-2.94	5.44	3.09	-1.48	0.24
North Africa	-2.27	3.12	3.63	2.78	1.90	0.19	1.29	1.50
Africa Total	-1.52	1.81	-0.06	-0.66	3.98	1.92	-0.38	0.73

Notes: country coverage and classification of strong adjusting, weak adjusting and non-adjusting countries according to World Bank; average annual growth rates were calculated as arithmetic averages (preliminary)
Source: World Bank data files quoted in *Statistics and Policies ECA Preliminary Observations on the World Bank Report: Africa's Adjustment and Growth in the 1980s*, UNECA, 1989.

The Bank disputes the UNECA figures because, it argues, they make no allowance for the different dates when different countries began their adjustment programmes.[43] This actually cuts both ways. The ODI study, for example, concludes that the introduction of a structural adjustment programme causes confusion, uncertainty and often a flight of local and foreign capital. During the 1980s, even with structural adjustment programmes well under way, the decline of foreign investment continued.[44] British investment in sub-Saharan Africa fell from 4 per cent of its total foreign investment in the early 1980s to 0.5 per cent by 1986; the fall was in the industrial sector. French withdrawals were also recorded. Japanese investment in Africa fell from 4.5 per cent of Japan's total worldwide private investment to less than 1 per cent. US investment in Africa, always small, has remained at less than 1 per cent since 1985.

The ODI study concludes that structural adjustment programmes have not attracted direct foreign investment, and have, in part, been a cause of the decline. Moreover, the programmes cannot in any way influence several external factors that produce the decline or, more accurately, the diversion of foreign investment resources to other destinations. A UNCTC study examined the effects of changes in policy and regulations on foreign direct investment in 46 countries, including 26 developing countries, two-thirds of which they consider directly improved the investment climate for TNCs. But the study found that:

Despite [such] substantial changes in policies, flows of direct foreign investment to developing countries have increased only slightly, and these increases have tended to be concentrated in the largest and most rapidly growing developing countries ... For developing countries in the sample, except for the newly industrialising countries, the policy changes explained almost none of the flows of foreign investment. Instead the size of the host country market was the most important determinant of the analysis.[45]

To date, foreign investment has made sub-Saharan Africa neither ripe for industrialisation nor an attractive market. Since export-led growth depends on access to external markets, protectionism is a barrier not only to exports, but also to investment in further capacity where actual or expected trade barriers cannot at the same time be overcome. Europe is Africa's principal market and investment partner. Western Europe itself has many low productivity and labour-intensive industrial plants, and is displaying less interest in developing the first stages of industrialisation in Africa than are Japan or the US in their respective spheres of influence of East Asia and Latin America. This lack of Western interest has been compounded by the opening up of Eastern Europe for capital investment. Eastern Europe's labour-intensive industries are likely in time also to require protection from Third World competition.

Africa is being economically marginalised as never before, as the single European market, the American continental trade bloc and the Japanese Pacific Rim – the 'triad' – become the foci for capital investment and the target markets for the products of that investment. TNC corporate strategy is reinforcing these trends, by building 'regionally integrated, independently sustainable networks of overseas investments centred on a triad member'.[46] These networks tend to exclude developing countries. One example of this phenomenon cited in the UNCTC report is of the Nippon Electric Company (NEC), which has 25 overseas manufacturing affiliates, but not one in Africa. In the whole African continent there is only one sales and service office (out of 44 worldwide) and only three liaison offices (out of 24).[47] This pattern is not, in the UNCTC report's view, likely to change: 'The marginalisation of LDCs, most of which are located in Africa, is likely to continue since flows to developing countries are highly concentrated in newly industrialising and resource rich countries.'[48]

This diversion of investment away from Africa is extremely serious. Two decades have left Africa with very limited advanced technology and massive debt. Unless African countries cut themselves off from the world economy completely, end cash cropping for export, return to subsistence agriculture and conserve their mineral resources, they must have access to world markets and to resources they do not themselves possess. For that, foreign investment is essential. Countries which have successfully industrialised have always done so with the assistance of foreign capital. Britain was an exception, partly because it was the first to industrialise, but chiefly because tribute from overseas conquest took the place of foreign capital.[49] African industrialisation, although using foreign investment and foreign technology, need not take the same path as that in Europe, the Americas or Asia. From region to region, the process of industrialisation has differed; the most recent successes – the Asian 'dragons' – have been achieved with the aid of political repression and strategies amounting to economic warfare.

Africa's particular tragedy is that it needs to advance towards industrialisation just at a moment when the whole world economy has slowed down and the richer countries are adopting increasingly protective measures not only against Third World countries but against each other. The world economy has become a game of beggar-my-neighbour for economic survival. The division of the world into 'blocs' and the exclusion of substantial parts of sub-Saharan Africa must in the long run prove as disastrous for those inside the blocs as for those outside. Increasing inequalities can only mean reduced trade exchanges and finite markets, and this will rebound on the rich, industrialised countries.[50]

The evidence in this book leads inexorably to the conclusion that World Bank structural adjustment programmes will not improve sub-Saharan African countries' prospects for economic development. The 'solution' offered by the Fraser Expert Group is also deeply flawed. There are no markets for a much expanded production of Africa's primary commodities, agricultural or mineral. There will be no miraculous recovery of primary product prices after a decade of decline. Even if the industrialised countries emerge from the current world recession with more rapid rates of economic growth, demand for raw materials will grow only slowly, as substitutes replace natural products and rising incomes are spent on services rather than on goods. Diversification and local processing of Africa's export commodities will continue to be thwarted by protective barriers around First World markets. Without debt remission, a large share of export earnings will continue to be absorbed by debt servicing and will be unavailable to finance investment for economic growth.

A further conclusion is that the external obstacles to development in Africa far outweigh the internal problems which the World Bank has sought to address through its insistence on economic reforms in return for aid and loans. The colonial inheritance, a patchwork of over 50 separate sub-Saharan African states, has inhibited integrated development, resulted in a substantial need for investment in infrastructure, and has been exacerbated by the narrow perspective taken by foreign investors extracting Africa's natural resources. At least the Fraser Report acknowledges this: 'It is recognised that for many countries the colonial experience in Africa was in many ways a very damaging one.'[51]

African governments, predominantly undemocratic and unaccountable to all but their immediate economic and ethnic constituencies, are fighting to stay in power and to stave off political unrest, as they face the effects of declining world commodity prices and receipts, unemployment and economic collapse and as the debt continues to be serviced and foreign investment evaporates.

The Expert Group does give warnings and expresses concerns in its Report that the World Bank's export-based solution may fail.[52] But there is little real sense of conviction behind its references to 'the international community [taking] a wider view of its overall responsibilities'. For the economic reforms to work, the Group lists the external changes needed: better access to First World markets, an end to food dumping, debt cancellation, compensatory financing for falls in export earnings and additional resources to fill the savings gap of some US$27 billion in 1987 prices.[53] The World Bank and the other international aid and loan agencies do have influence over African governments and so the economic reforms will continue to be implemented. But without the external changes – beyond the power of even the most powerful multilateral agency to grant – the reforms will not deliver long-term economic growth to Africa and will continue to prove very damaging. A common view is that African governments need to cooperate more actively on both a regional and an international basis.[54] This and their many other political failures cannot be exonerated, despite the overwhelming external problems. But political change cannot be leveraged simply by the World Bank's economic conditionality. Africa can only avoid permanent political and economical marginalisation if there is an international commitment to a common programme to bring Africa back into the world polity. Meanwhile, it must look inwards, to the continuing strengths and astonishing resilience of Africans who have survived much before, and who – given half a chance – will survive well beyond this century which has brought them so little and taken from them so much.

References

Chapter 1: Africa in Crisis

1. This figure is the World Bank's projected figure for 1991 taken from the World Bank 1991 Debt Tables and includes all private and public (multi- and bilateral) creditors. Per man, woman and child, sub-Saharan Africans owe US$400 each, more than their average annual income.
2. Dr Alexander Yeats, *On the Accuracy of Observations: Do Sub-Saharan Statistics Mean Anything?* (International Economics Department, World Bank, 1989).
3. World Bank, *Beyond Adjustment: Towards Sustainable Growth with Equity in Sub-Saharan Africa*, Technical Report (11 November 1988) Chapter 1, para 3.
4. Ibid., Chapter 1, Table 1.1.
5. UNCTAD, *Trade and Development Report, 1990*, Tables 3 and 16, pp. 6, 32.
6. The research and compilation of this book have involved substantial amounts of statistical analysis. Where appropriate, general, illustrative and other related statistical tables and charts are presented in an Annexe at the end of the book for interested readers.
7. World Bank, *Beyond Adjustment*, para 1.16.
8. International Monetary Fund, *World Economic Outlook, 1985*, Table 36 and UNCTAD, *Trade and Development Report, 1990*, Table 9.
9. Paul Harrison, *The Greening of Africa* (Paladin, 1987) Chapter 3.
10. World Bank, *Beyond Adjustment*, para 1.14.
11. Ibid., para 1.16.
12. Ibid., para 1.16.
13. World Development Movement, *Disarm to Develop*, Briefing Paper (March 1990).
14. Study commissioned by a group of UK aid agencies for a memorandum submitted to the Foreign Affairs Select Committee of the British Parliament, April 1991 (ODI, London, 1991).
15. World Bank, *Social Indicators of Development, 1988*.
16. UNCTAD, *The Least Developed Countries Report, 1988*, p. 77.

Chapter 2: The Official Response

1. World Bank, *Adjustment Lending Policies for Sustainable Growth*, Policy and Research Series, no. 14 (1990).
2. United Nations Economic Commission for Africa (UNECA), *Statistics and Policies: ECA Preliminary Observations on the World Bank Report, Africa's Adjustment and Growth in the 1980s* (Addis Ababa, 1989).

3. UNECA, *African Alternative to Structural Adjustment Programmes (AA-SAP): A Framework for Transformation and Recovery* (Addis Ababa, April 1989).

4. Mohsin Khan, *The Macro-economic effects of Fund-Supported Adjustment Programmes*, IMF Staff Papers 37 (2) (June 1990).

5. Paul Mosley, Jane Harrigan and John Poye, *Aid and Power: The World Bank and Policy-based Lending* (Macmillan, 1991).

6. World Bank and United Nations Development Programme (UNDP), *Africa's Adjustment and Growth in the 1980s* (March 1989).

7. Robert Berg, *Towards Accelerated Development in Sub-Saharan Africa*, Committee on African Development (World Bank, 1981).

8. World Bank, *Report on Adjustment Lending* (August 1988).

9. World Bank, *Beyond Adjustment*.

10. World Bank and UNDP, *Africa's Adjustment and Growth*.

11. World Bank, *Sub-Saharan Africa: From Crisis to Sustainable Growth* (Washington, March 1989).

12. UN Secretary General's Expert Group, Fraser Report, *Africa's Commodity Problems: Towards a Solution* (New York, June 1990) p. ix.

13. World Bank, *Sub-Saharan Africa*, p. 3.

14. Ibid., p. 132.

15. R.A. Batchelor, R.L. Major and A.D. Morgan, *Industrialisation and the Basis for Trade* (Cambridge, 1980) p. 212 ff.

16. H. Ojima, quoted by John Eatwell in 'Whatever Happened to Britain?' BBC, 1982, and reproduced in B.J. McCormick, *The World Economy* (Philip Allan, Oxford, 1988) pp. 152–3.

17. Richard Caves, 'Export-led Growth and the New Economic History' in J. Bhagwati (ed.), *Trade, Balance of Payments and Growth* (North Holland, 1971).

18. International Monetary Fund, *International Financial Statistics Yearbook, 1989*, Country Tables.

19. World Bank, *Capital Accumulation and Economic Growth: The Korean Paradigm*, Staff Working Papers, no. 712 (Washington, 1985).

20. Ibid., p. 9, quoting Paul Streeten, 'Development Dichotomies', in *Pioneers in Development* (Oxford, 1984) p. 346.

21. Ibid., p. 9.

22. Ibid.

23. Ibid., p. 24.

24. Quoted in James Pickett and Hans Singer, *Towards Recovery in Sub-Saharan Africa* (Routledge, 1990) pp. 40–1.

Chapter 3: Africa's Resources

1. *Oxford Economic Atlas of the World*, 4th Edition (Oxford University Press, 1972) Commodity Tables.

2. UNCTAD, *Commodity Yearbook* (New York, 1989), p. 97 ff.

3. Compare Annexe Table A1 and Table 3.1.

4. International Monetary Fund, *International Financial Statistics Yearbook, 1990*, Country Tables.

5. World Bank, *World Tables, 1988–89*, and UNCTAD, *Statistical Pocket Book, 1989*.

6. Food and Agricultural Organisation (FAO), *Yearbook, 1990,* Tables 1 and 3.
7. Ibid., Table 4.
8. Ibid., Tables 4 and 5.
9. UNCTAD, *Commodity Yearbook* (New York, 1991).
10. FAO Yearbooks.
11. Percy Mistry, *The Present Role of the World Bank in Africa* (Institute for African Alternatives, London, 1988).
12. Harriet Friedmann, 'The Origins of Third World Food Dependence' in H. Bernstein *et al.* (eds), *The Food Question* (Earthscan, 1989).
13. Maureen Mackintosh, *Gender, Class and Rural Transition: Agribusiness and the Food Crisis in Senegal* (Zed Press, 1989).
14. FAO *Yearbook, 1990,* Tables 4 and 5.
15. Percy Mistry, *World Bank in Africa.*
16. World Bank, *Africa's Adjustment and Growth,* Tables on Comparative Compensation Patterns, para 1.8.

Chapter 4: What Future for Export Crops?

1. UNCTAD, *Commodity Yearbook* (New York, 1989).
2. UNCTAD, *Statistical Pocket Book, 1989,* Table 2.4.
3. Ibid., Table 3.9.
4. World Bank, *Sub-Saharan Africa.*
5. Ibid., p. 173.
6. World Bank, *African Adjustment and Growth,* p. 3.
7. Ibid.
8. Henk Kox, *Export Constraints for Sub-Saharan Africa,* Serie Research Memoranda (Free University of Amsterdam, 1990) Table 8.
9. Ibid., Table 9.
10. Overseas Development Institute (ODI), *Biotechnology and the Third World,* Briefing Paper (London, September 1988).
11. Henk Hobbelink, *New Hope or False Promise: Bio-technology and Third World Agriculture* (ICDA, Brussels, 1987) p. 14 ff.
12. UNCTAD, *Statistical Pocket Book, 1989,* Table 2.3.
13. World Bank Working Paper S348, *Recent Trends and Prospects for Agricultural Commodity Exports in Sub-Saharan Africa* (December 1989) Table 12.
14. 'Unrelieved Gloom for African Commodities', *African Recovery,* vol. 5, no. 4 (December 1991).
15. World Bank, *Sub-Saharan Africa.*

Chapter 5: Which Cash Crops?

1. World Bank, *Sub-Saharan Africa,* p. 132.
2. Foreign Agricultural Service, US Department of Agriculture (FAS/USDA), *Production Estimates and Assessment,* June 1990.
3. International Coffee Organisation (ICO) statistics, reproduced by Robert Stainer in *South* magazine, May 1989, p. 26.
4. World Bank, *Recent Trends and Prospects,* p. 30 ff.
5. The quotes appearing in this chapter are from off the record interviews with commodity traders carried out as part of the research for this book.

6. ICO statistics, via *South*, May 1989.
7. Ibid.
8. UNCTAD, *Commodity Yearbook, 1991*.
9. World Bank Paper, *Recent Trends and Prospects*.
10. FAS/USDA, *Production Estimates*, June 1990.
11. Rex E.T. Dull, Horticultural and Tropical Division, FAS/USDA, *Report*, June 1990.
12. ODI, *Biotechnology and the Third World*.
13. *Coffee and Cocoa International*, no. 6, 1989.
14. World Bank, *Recent Trends and Prospects*, p. 24.
15. Gill & Duffus, *Cocoa Statistics*, November 1989 and see Annexe Table A15.
16. World Bank, *Recent Trends and Prospects*, Figure 7.
17. Ibid.
18. *Financial Times*, 6 April 1989.
19. *Financial Times*, 12 October 1989.
20. Gill & Duffus, *Cocoa Statistics*, November 1989.
21. *Coffee and Cocoa International*, no. 1, 1990, p. 54.
22. Public Ledger's *Commodity Week*, 10 August 1991.
23. Information supplied to Cameron Duncan by the Rural Advancement Fund International, Pittsburgh, North Carolina, July 1990.
24. Dr Russell Larson, Science Adviser, American Cocoa Research Association 'Cocoa Raw Product – Production and Problems' in *Cocoa Biotechnology*, 1986, p. 13.
25. Gill & Duffus, *Cocoa Statistics*.
26. Robin Stainer in *Guardian*, 9 February 1990.
27. *Financial Times*, 19 December 1989.
28. World Bank, *Recent Trends and Prospects*, pp. 35–6.
29. Rural Advancement Fund International via Cameron Duncan.
30. World Bank, *Recent Trends and Prospects*, p. 46.
31. UNCTAD, *Commodity Yearbook, 1991*. The Fraser Report makes a mistake in showing Africa's share of the total world supply of palm oil as over 18 per cent. See UN Expert Group (Fraser Report), *Africa's Commodity Problems*, Table 4.
32. World Bank, *Recent Trends and Prospects*, pp. 46–7.
33. Ibid.
34. *Grocer*, 19 May 1990.
35. Ibid.
36. World Bank, *Recent Trends and Prospects*.
37. 'Due diligence' is the legal term given to the procedures companies are reasonably expected to undertake to ensure that the product they are dealing with is both safe and healthy by the time it reaches the consumer.
38. World Bank, *Recent Trends and Prospects*.
39. Belinda Coote, *The Hunger Crop, Poverty and the Sugar Industry* (Oxfam, 1987) Chapter 5.
40. UNCTAD, *Commodity Yearbook, 1989*.
41. Public Ledger's *Commodity Week*, 10 August 1991.
42. Landell Mills, *Commodities Studies: Sugar*, London, July 1990.

43. Interviews with sugar traders, July 1990.
44. *Tropical Timbers*, January 1989.
45. Paul Melly in *South* magazine, March 1990.
46. Ibid.
47. Ibid.
48. Ibid.
49. Simon Counsell, *Courier*, March–April, 1990, p. 92.
50. Christine McGourty quoting the Environment Department of the World Bank in *Nature*, 29 January 1987.
51. C.M. Peters, 'Valuation of an Amazonian Rain Forest', *Nature*, 29 June 1989.
52. Simon Counsell, *Courier*.
53. Interviews with veneer companies, July 1990.
54. UNCTAD, *Commodity Yearbook, 1989*.
55. World Bank, *Recent Trends and Prospects*, p. 43.
56. Ibid.
57. UNCTAD, *Commodity Yearbook, 1989*.
58. Ibid.
59. World Bank, *Recent Trends and Prospects*, Figure 8.
60. Ibid.
61. Tea Association of the USA, *Tea World*, Spring 1987, p. 3.
62. World Bank, *Recent Trends and Prospects*, pp. 39–41.
63. Ibid.
64. Ibid., p. 29 and p. 41.
65. Belinda Coote, *The Trade Trap: Poverty and the Global Commodity Markets* (Oxfam, 1992) p. 96.
66. UNCTAD, *Commodity Yearbook, 1989*.
67. Ibid.
68. Ibid.
69. Christopher Stevens, *ACP Export Diversification: Jamaica, Kenya and Ethiopia*, ODI, Working Paper no. 40, London, 1990 and Roger Riddell, *ACP Export Diversification: The Case of Zimbabwe*, ODI Working Paper no. 38, London, 1990.
70. Interview with P.J. Woodhouse, Agronomist and Specialist in African fruit and vegetable production, Institute of Development Policy and Management, University of Manchester.

Chapter 6: Africa's Mineral Wealth
1. G. Lanning and M. Mueller, *Africa Undermined* (Penguin, 1979) p. 53.
2. Ibid., p. 71.
3. Ibid., p. 107.
4. HM Treasury, *UK Balance of Payments*, 1970.
5. M. Barratt Brown, *After Imperialism* (Heinemann, 1962) Table XIII.
6. World Bank, *Sub-Saharan Africa*, p. 10.
7. World Bank statistical data published with *From Crisis to Sustainable Growth*, summarised by Henk Kox, *Export Constraints on Sub-Saharan Growth*, Table 38.

8. Paul Noel Giraud, *Consumption of Eight Mineral Resources: Retrospective Analysis 1950–85 and Lessons for Forecasting* (CERNA, Paris 1986).
9. ODI Briefing Paper, *Commodity Prices: Investing in Decline?* (London, March 1988).
10. Ibid.
11. UNCTAD, *Commodity Yearbook, 1989.*
12. Public Ledger's *Commodity Week,* 14 September 1991.
13. World Bank, *World Development Report* and *Long Term Outlook for the World Economy,* 1990.
14. UNCTC, *Transnational Corporations in World Development; Trends and Prospects* (Washington, 1988) pp. 300–5.
15. A.C. Warhurst, 'A Bug Turns Waste to Profits', *South* magazine, February 1983, p. 42.
16. UNCTAD, *Commodity Yearbook, 1989.*
17. *Metal Bulletin,* London, 19 April 1990.
18. *Metal Bulletin,* London, 17 May 1990.
19. Peter M. Fozzard, 'Mining Developments in Sub-Saharan Africa', World Bank *Technical Papers,* November 1989.
20. Fraser Report, *Africa's Commodity Problems,* 1990, pp. 50–60.
21. *Metal Bulletin,* London, 26 March 1990.
22. *Engineering and Mining Journal,* London, January 1990.
23. *Metal Bulletin,* London, 26 March 1990.
24. *Engineering and Mining Journal,* London, March 1990.
25. *Metal Bulletin,* London, 30 April 1990.
26. L. Pagni, 'Zambian Copper: a Fickle Friend', *The Courier,* 1990.
27. *Metal Bulletin,* London, 24 May 1990.
28. *Metal Bulletin,* London, 19 April 1990.
29. *Metal Bulletin,* London, 30 April 1990.
30. James Capel, quoted in *Financial Times,* 24 January 1990.
31. Cameron Duncan, interview with Simon Hunt, April 1990 issue of *Pay Dirt,* Washington.
32. UNCTAD, *Commodity Yearbook, 1989.*
33. J.W.F. Rowe, *Primary Commodities in International Trade* (Cambridge, 1965) pp. 154–5.
34. Interviews with commodity analysts, Washington, August 1990.
35. Commodities Research Unit, *Copper Greenfield Projects in the 1990s,* London, 1990.
36. Norbert Broderson, Chairman, International Wrought Copper Council meeting, Lucerne, September 1989, reported in *Metal Bulletin,* London, 24 May 1990.
37. UNCTAD, *Commodity Yearbook, 1989.*
38. UNCTC, quoted in J. Raumolin and L. Siitonen (eds), *Problems Related to the Transfer of Technology and Mineral-Based Industrialisation,* University of Helsinki, 1988, p. 86 ff.
39. Ibid., pp. 88–9.
40. World Gold Council, *Gold Supply Forecasts,* London, 1990.
41. Ibid.

42. Goldfields Mineral Services, *Gold 1990*, London 1990.
43. UNCTAD, *Commodity Yearbook, 1989.*
44. *Metal Bulletin*, London, 13 September 1990.
45. US Department of Commerce statistics collated by Cameron Duncan.
46. *Metal Bulletin*, London, 23 August 1990.
47. Bird Associates, *Aluminium Annual Review*, quoted in *Financial Times*, 3 April 1990.
48. *Metal Bulletin*, London, 9 July 1990.
49. Public Ledger's *Commodity Week*, 14 September 1991.
50. UNCTAD, *Commodity Yearbook, 1989.*
51. Ibid.
52. *Metal Bulletin*, London, 2 July 1990.
53. *Metal Bulletin*, London, 12 July 1990.
54. UNCTAD, *Commodity Yearbook, 1989.*
55. Ibid.
56. Ibid.

Chapter 7: Africa's Fuel and Energy Resources

1. 'Production of Selected Energy Commodities', *UN Statistical Yearbook, 1985/86*, Table 134.
2. World Bank, *Sub-Saharan Africa*, p. 3.
3. Ibid., p. 13.
4. Martin Quinlan, 'West Africa: Exploration Interest', *Petroleum Economist*, May 1989, pp. 143–5.
5. Ibid.
6. Martin Quinlan, 'Nigeria: Taking Advantage', *Petroleum Economist*, May 1989 and July 1990.
7. Information from Nigerian oil economist, Abubakar Siddique Muhammad, July 1991.
8. Martin Quinlan, *Petroleum Economist*, May 1989.
9. Nigerian National Petroleum Corporation (NNPC), *Monthly Petroleum Information*, 1977–88.
10. R. Vielvoye, 'Oil and Natural Gas Production in Nigeria', *Oil and Gas Journal*, 26 February 1990, p. 27.
11. Martin Quinlan, *Petroleum Economist*, May 1989.
12. Mark Gallagher, *Rent-Seeking and Economic Growth in Africa* (Oxford, Westview Press, 1991).
13. 'Memorandum of Understanding', signed in Lagos, 17 January 1986, between the Federal Military Governor of Nigeria and selected international oil companies.
14. Summary of 'Memorandum' communicated by Abubakar Siddique Muhammad.
15. Information from Abubakar Siddique Muhammad, July 1991.
16. NNPC, *Monthly Petroleum Information*, 1977–88.
17. NNPC, *Understanding the Nigerian Oil Industry*, Lagos, 1987.
18. *Energy Trends*, UK Department of Energy, October 1990.
19. UN *Statistical Yearbook, 1985/6*, Table 134.
20. Ibid.

21. OECD, International Energy Agency, *World Energy Statistics and Balances, 1971–87.*
22. *Marchés Tropicaux*, Paris, 6 January 1989, quoted by Abubakar Siddique Muhammad.
23. Information from Abubakar Siddique Muhammad, 1991.
24. Ibid.
25. NNPC, *The Role of Refineries in Nigeria: Today and Tomorrow*, Lagos 1987.
26. G.A. Adams, General Managing Director, NNPC, 'Investment Opportunities in the Oil and Gas Industries of Nigeria', speech at the Benin Stock Exchange, 12 April 1989.
27. NNPC, *The Role of Refineries in Nigeria*, 1987.
28. G.A. Adams, 'Investment Opportunities', Benin, 1989.
29. Laurence Cockcroft, *Africa's Way*, I.B. Tauris, 1990, pp. 162–5.
30. World Bank Staff Working Papers, no. 712, *Capital Accumulation and Economic Growth*, 1985.
31. Information from Abubakar Siddique Muhammad, July 1991.
32. Ibid.
33. Bruno Papillone, 'La Demande de l'Energie dans les Nouveaux Pays Industrialisés d'Asie et l'Asean', *Energie Internationale* (Paris, Economica, 1990).
34. Energy Information Administration, *Annual Energy Outlook 1989*, 'Long-term Projections', US Department of Energy, Washington, p. 51.
35. World Bank, unpublished article *A Perspective on Prices, January 1986–January 1987*, quoted by Abubakar Siddique Muhammad.
36. NNPC, *Annual Statistical Bulletin*, 1988.
37. UK Department of Energy, *Energy Trends*, October 1990.
38. Information from Abubakar Siddique Muhammad, July 1991.
39. Ibid.
40. *International Herald Tribune*, 1–2 February 1992.
41. Bruno Papillone, *Energie Internationale*.
42. UNCTAD, *Statistical Pocket Book, 1989*, Table 2.1.
43. Martin Quinlan, *Petroleum Economist*, May 1989.
44. Bruno Papillone, *Energie Internationale*.
45. International Energy Agency, *Crude Oil and NGL Production, 1980–1990*, 1991.
46. Information from Abubakar Siddique Muhammad.

Chapter 8: What does Africa get out of its Trade?

1. Colin Leys, *Underdevelopment in Kenya: The Political Economy of Neo-Colonialism, 1964–71* (Heinemann, 1975) p. 160 ff., and Laurence Cockcroft, *Africa's Way*, especially Chapters 8 and 10.
2. Interviews with traders in London and New York, July 1990.
3. F. Clairmonte and J. Cavanagh, *Merchants of Drink* (Third World Network, Penang, 1988) p. 59, Table 4.1.
4. UNCTC, *Transnational Corporations and Non-fuel Primary Commodities in Developing Countries*, New York, 1987, p. 43 ff.
5. M. Barratt Brown, *Economics of Imperialism* (Penguin, 1974) Chapter 7.

6. World Bank, Staff Working Papers, no. 574, *The Japanese and Korean Experiences in Managing Development*, Washington, 1983.
7. Robin Murray, 'Underdevelopment, International Firms and the International Division of Labour', in *Towards a New World Economy*, Rotterdam, 1972.
8. Interview with trader, London, July 1990.
9. Consumer-led 'development' campaigns, based on a 'trade not aid' message, are underway in the Netherlands, Belgium and the United Kingdom to ensure the producer receives a reasonable price for coffee (and other commodities). Such 'fairly traded coffee' accounted for 2.2 per cent of the large Dutch market in 1991. Similar estimates of market share are projected for schemes in six European countries.
10. Jon Morris, 'What Goes Wrong' in *Extension Alternatives* (ODI, London, 1991).
11. Henk Kox interview with Paul Elshof, Centre for Research on Multinational Corporations (SOMO), Amsterdam, July 1990.
12. UNCTC, *TNCs and Non-fuel Primary Commodities*, p. 18.
13. UNCTAD, *Market Access Conditions and Other Factors and Conditions Pertinent to the Development of Viable Diversification Programmes*, Geneva, 1989, p.14.
14. World Bank, *Development Report, 1989*, Washington.
15. Clairmonte and Cavanagh, *Merchants of Drink*, pp. 119–20.
16. Kox, *Export Constraints for Sub-Saharan Growth*, p. 50.
17. *Financial Times*, 27 June 1990.
18. Kox, interview with Paul Elshof, SOMO, Amsterdam, July 1990.
19. Mike Hall, 'Blending Tea with Technology in Malawi', *Financial Times*, 14 March 1989.
20. Julian Ozanne, 'Uganda Blends Tea with Technology', *Financial Times*, 7 November 1989.
21. *World Tobacco Directory, 1990*, International Trade Publications, Redhill.
22. Barbara Dinham and Colin Hines, *Agribusiness in Africa* (Earth Resources Research Bureau, London, 1983) p. 33.
23. Commonwealth Secretariat, *Guidelines for Exporters of Selected Vegetables to the UK Market* and *Guidelines for Exporters of Avocados, Mangoes, Pineapples, Papayas and Passion Fruit to the UK Market*, 1989, appendices on 'Costs to Reach Market'.
24. Ibid.
25. Dalgety plc, *Annual Report and Accounts, 1990*.
26. Robert Corzine, 'Harmony Mined from Seam of Goodwill', *Financial Times*, 7 July 1991.
27. M. Faber, 'The Volta River Project' in J. Picket and H. Singer (eds), *Towards Economic Recovery in Sub-Saharan Africa* (Routledge, London, 1990) pp. 65–92.
28. UNCTC, *TNCs and Non-fuel Primary Commodities*, Tables III.4 and III.5.
29. Ibid., with mineral prices updated to end of 1991.
30. Ibid., pp. 56–60.
31. OECD, *Transfer Pricing and Multinational Enterprises*, Paris, 1979, Chapter 2; and Robin Murray, 'Introduction' and 'Transfer Pricing and its

Control', in Robin Murray (ed.), *Multinationals Beyond the Market* (Harvester Press, 1981) pp. 147–76.

32. See, for example, BBC TV programme 'Trade Slaves', an Inside Story documentary about the operations of Alu-Suisse in Sierra Leone, broadcast in September 1991.
33. See for example K.M. Lamaswala, 'The Pricing of Unwrought Copper in Relation to Transfer Pricing', in Murray (ed.), *Multinationals Beyond the Market,* pp. 77–85.
34. This happened in the case of the Alu-Suisse operations revealed in the BBC TV programme on Sierra Leone, 'Trade Slaves', September 1991.

Chapter 9: African Manufactured Exports

1. Walden Bello and Stephanie Rosenfeld, *Dragons in Distress: Asia's Miracle Economies in Crisis* (San Francisco, Institute for Food and Development Policy, 1990).
2. UNCTAD, *The Least Developed Countries: 1988 Report* (New York, 1989) p. 50 ff. and Table A-10.
3. UNCTAD, *Trade and Development Report, 1989* (New York, 1990).
4. UNCTAD, *Statistical Pocket Book, 1989.*
5. M. Blomström, *Transnational Corporations and Manufacturing Exports from Developing Countries* (UNCTC, New York, 1990).
6. UNCTAD, *Trade and Development Report, 1989*, p. 63 ff.
7. World Bank, *Sub-Saharan Africa*, pp. 2–3.
8. World Bank, *Beyond Adjustment*, Chapter 1.
9. Conceded by the World Bank itself, see *World Development Report, 1990*, summarised in *Economist*, 12 October 1991.
10. The point is argued at length in a paper by Lev Gonick, of Wilfred Laurie University, Ontario, Canada, dated March 1991, entitled 'Wretching the Earth: the Contradictions of Export-Led-Growth Strategies in Africa', and written after Gonick conducted a number of interviews with North American commodity brokers and tobacco, sugar, lumber and food importers for this project.
11. A. Maizels, 'Patterns of Industrial Growth' in *Industrial Growth and World Trade* (Cambridge, 1963) Chapter 2.
12. UNIDO, *Industry and Development: Global Report 1990–91* (Vienna, 1991) p. 67.
13. UNCTAD, *Commodity Yearbook, 1989.*
14. *Coffee and Cocoa International*, issue 6, 1989, p. 4.
15. Interviews with traders, July 1990.
16. Clairmonte and Cavanagh, *Merchants of Drink*, Chapter 6.
17. Ibid.
18. *South* magazine, March 1990.
19. Simon Counsell, of Friends of the Earth, 'The International Trade in Tropical Timber', *Courier*, March–April 1989.
20. UNIDO, *Industry and Development, 1990/91*, p. 67.
21. UN, *Statistical Yearbook, 1985/6*, Table 52.
22. UNCTAD, *Market Access Conditions* (Geneva, 1989).
23. Interviews with traders, 1990.

24. World Bank, *Beyond Adjustment*, Chapter 4, 'Fostering African Entrepreneurship'.
25. UNIDO, *Industry and Development, 1990–1*, p. 64.
26. UN, *Monthly Bulletin of Statistics*, June 1991.
27. UNCTAD, *Commodity Yearbook, 1989*.
28. Faysal Yachir, 'The Strategies of the Transnationals' in *Mining in Africa Today* (UN University and Zed Press, 1988).
29. UNIDO, *Industry and Development 1990–1*, p. 67.
30. UNCTAD, *Commodity Yearbook, 1989*.
31. Raumolin and Siitonen, *Problems Related to Transfer of Technology*, pp. 78–9.
32. UNIDO, *Industry and Development, 1990–1*, p. 64.
33. World Bank, *Beyond Adjustment*, para 3.89.
34. World Bank, *Sub-Saharan Africa*, pp. 2–3 and Fraser Report, *Africa's Commodity Problems*, p. 37.
35. World Bank, *Sub-Saharan Africa*, pp. 2–3; and Fraser Report, *Africa's Commodity Problems*, p. 84.
36. UNCTC, *World Investment Report, 1991* (New York, 1991) Table 3, p. 10.
37. Ibid., Table 4, p. 11.
38. UNCTC, *Transnational Corporations in World Development* (New York, 1988) Annexe Table B.1, p. 535 ff.
39. Ibid., p. 163 ff.
40. UN's *Monthly Bulletin of Statistics*, June 1991.
41. Fraser Report, *Africa's Commodity Problems*, p. 30.
42. Ibid., p. 31.
43. M.J. Roarty, 'Protectionism and the Debt Crisis', in *Quarterly Review*, National Westminster Bank, February 1990.
44. UNCTAD, *The Least Developed Countries, 1988 Report*, p. 121.
45. Fraser Report, *Africa's Commodity Problems*, pp. 80-1.
46. Hugh Corbet, 'Agricultural Issue at the Heart of the Uruguay Round', *Quarterly Review*, National Westminster Bank, August 1991.
47. At the time of writing in mid-1992.
48. Jan Pronk, *A World of Difference* (South Commission, September 1990).

Chapter 10: Export-led Growth and African Politics

1. Coote, *The Trade Trap*, pp. 1–3.
2. World Bank, *Sub-Saharan Africa*, pp. 2–3.
3. World Bank, *World Development Report, 1990*.
4. Percy Mistry, *World Bank in Africa*, p. 19.
5. Gallagher, *Rent-Seeking and Economic Growth*.
6. World Bank, *Africa's Adjustment and Growth*, p. 33 ff.
7. World Bank, *Beyond Adjustment*, para 3.9.
8. UNCTAD, *Trade and Development Report, 1989*, p. 157 ff.
9. Gallagher, *Rent-Seeking and Economic Growth*, Figure 4.5, p. 101.
10. Ibid.
11. Ibid., p. 120 ff.
12. Ibid., pp. 129–30.

13. Ibid., Figures 4.7 and 4.8, pp. 109–10.
14. Ibid., pp. 132–3.
15. Ibid., p. 122.
16. M.J. Roarty, 'The Impact of the Common Agricultural Policy on Agricultural Trade and Development', *Quarterly Review*, National Westminster Bank, February 1987.
17. M. Camdessus, Managing Director of the IMF, quoted in *UNICEF Report 1989*, pp. 17–18.
18. Clive Robinson, *Hungry Farmers* (Christian Aid, 1989) Chapter 6.
19. UNCTAD, *The Least Developed Countries: 1988 Report*, p. 22 ff.
20. UNIDO, *Industry and Development, 1990/91*, pp. 79–83.
21. UNCTAD, *Statistical Pocket Book, 1989*, Table 4.5.
22. Roarty, 'Protectionism and the Debt Crisis', p. 46.
23. Fraser Report, *Africa's Commodity Problems*, p. 85.
24. Ibid., p. 36.
25. Ibid., p. 35.
26. Ibid., p. 36.
27. Ibid., p. 30.
28. Ibid., p. 31.
29. Laurence Cockcroft and Roger C. Riddell, *Foreign Direct Investment in Sub-Saharan Africa* (ODI, London, 1990).
30. *Economist*, 12 October 1991.
31. Cockroft and Riddell, *Foreign Direct Investment*, p. 4.
32. Ibid.
33. UNIDO, *Industry and Development, 1990/91*, pp. 68–9.
34. Cockcroft and Riddell, *Foreign Direct Investment*, pp. 31–3.
35. Ibid., p. 32.
36. Ibid., p. 33.
37. UNIDO, *Industry and Development, 1990/91*, p. 70.
38. Fraser Report, *Africa's Commodity Problems*.
39. Cockroft and Riddell, *Foreign Direct Investment*, p. 12.
40. Ibid., pp. 22–3 and p. 17.
41. Ibid., p. 36.
42. Ibid., pp. 14–15.
43. World Bank, *Comments on ECA's Response*, May 1989, p. 10.
44. Cockcroft and Riddell, *Foreign Direct Investment*, p. 34.
45. UNCTC, *World Investment Report 1991: The Triad in Foreign Direct Investment* (New York, July 1991) p. 28.
46. Ibid.
47. Ibid., p. 43.
48. Ibid., p. 13.
49. M. Barratt Brown, *After Imperialism* (Heinemann, 1962) Chapters 1 and 2, reproduced in Part One of the Open University Development Studies course, 1980, revised 1990.
50. See Susan George, *The Debt Boomerang: How Third World Debt Harms us All* (Pluto Press with the Transnational Institute, 1992).

51. Fraser Report, *Africa's Commodity Problems*, p. 39.
52. Ibid., p. 3.
53. Ibid., pp. 83–7.
54. Fraser Report, *Africa's Commodity Problems*, pp. 93–4 and Cockcroft and Riddell, Foreign Direct Investment, p. 51.

Statistical Annexe: Tables and Charts

Table A1: Developing Countries of Africa: Indices of Development, 1988/89 (by groups in order of GDP/head)

Country	Population (millions)	Pop. Growth % ('70–88)	Pop. Density /km²	GDP per head (US$) in '88	'60–70	Change % '70–80	'80–89	Exports (US$ millions) 1989	Imports (US$ millions) 1989
North Africa									
Libya (a)	4.2	4.3	2	5417	20.0	-1.1	-8.8	6.8	5.1
Algeria (a)	23.7	3.1	10	2284	-0.7	3.7	-0.3	8.6	8.4
Tunisia (a)	7.8	2.4	48	1287	2.2	4.2	0.8	2.9	2.9
Morocco	23.8	2.5	53	922	1.1	2.8	1.5	3.3	5.5
Egypt	50.1	2.3	50	681	2.0	5.0	2.5	2.6	7.4
Sudan (see LDCs below)									
Total (5)	109.6							24.2	29.3
Average (including Sudan)		2.7	16	2140	1.0	3.0	-0.9		
Middle and Low Income Africa									
Réunion	0.6	1.5	230	3931*	8.2	4.4	2.6	0.1	1.7
Seychelles	0.1	2.6	300	3511	1.4	3.4	-0.7	–	0.2
Gabon (b)	1.1	4.4	4	3030	6.1	4.0	-4.0	1.2	1.0
Mauritius	1.1	1.4	568	1843	-0.6	4.9	5.0	1.0	1.3
Cameroon (b)	11.1	2.9	23	1136	3.2	2.5	0.7	0.9	1.3
Congo (b)	2.1	3.0	6	1007	3.3	-0.4	0.3	0.9	0.5
Côte d'Ivoire (d)	11.2	4.0	35	876	4.0	2.5	-3.2	3.0	2.4
Senegal (d)	6.9	2.9	35	717	-1.9	-0.7	0.3	0.6	1.2
Zimbabwe (f)	9.1	3.1	23	690	1.3	-1.6	-0.3	1.3	1.1
Liberia (c)	2.4	3.2	22	484	2.2	-0.8	-4.4	0.4	0.2
Angola (f)	9.5	3.0	8	495*	3.1	-9.4	0.3	1.4	0.5
Kenya	22.5	3.8	39	375	4.8	1.8	0.4	1.1	2.1
Ghana (e)	14.1	2.8	59	369	0.0	-2.3	-0.7	1.0	0.9
Zambia	7.9	3.6	10	346	5.2	-2.0	-2.8	1.4	0.9
Nigeria (e)	101.9	3.3	110	296	1.4	1.3	-3.9	9.0	3.6
Zaïre (g)	33.5	3.0	14	193	0.0	-3.1	-1.3	1.3	0.8
Madagascar	11.3	2.9	19	167	0.9	-2.1	-2.1	0.3	0.3
Total (17)	246.5							24.9	20.0
Average		3.0	22	520	2.5	0.2	-1.3		

continued

156

Country	Population (millions)	Pop. Growth % ('70–88)	Pop. Density /km²	GDP per head (US$) in '88	Change % '60–70	'70–80	'80–89	Exports (US$ millions) 1989	Imports (US$ millions) 1989
Least Developed Countries (LDCs)									
Botswana (f)	1.2	3.8	2	1654	2.9	9.7	7.2	1.4	1.0
Cape Verde (e)	0.3	1.5	87	748	1.9	0.7	6.6	–	0.1
Djibouti	0.4	4.7	18	589	6.0	-2.9	1.4	–	0.2
São Tomé	0.1	2.6	120	548	-2.9	2.7	-6.3	–	–
Mauritania (d)	1.9	2.5	2	522	5.9	-1.1	-0.7	0.2	0.2
Sudan	23.8	3.1	10	461	0.3	2.2	-1.1	0.7	1.2
Guinea (c)	5.4	1.9	22	446	-1.7	2.9	-3.8	0.4	0.5
Eq. Guinea (b)	0.3	0.8	14	438	–	–	-1.9	–	–
Benin (d)	4.4	2.7	39	410	2.1	-0.3	-1.2	–	0.3
Togo (e)	3.3	2.8	59	408	6.3	1.4	-1.9	0.2	0.5
Comoros	0.5	3.6	237	402	4.2	-4.4	0.0	–	0.1
Cent. Africa (b)	2.9	2.5	5	388	-0.6	-0.2	-0.5	0.1	0.2
Rwanda (g)	6.8	3.4	258	340	1.5	0.8	-2.0	0.1	0.3
Niger (d)	7.3	3.2	6	329	2.0	-1.5	-4.2	0.3	0.4
Sierra Leone (c)	4.0	2.2	55	297	5.3	-0.5	-2.7	0.1	0.2
Gambia (e)	0.8	3.2	72	271	1.0	2.2	0.7	–	0.2
Uganda	17.5	3.3	74	243	1.1	-4.9	-1.3	0.5	0.7
Somalia	7.0	3.7	11	239	-0.6	0.9	-0.8	0.1	0.1
Lesotho (f)	1.7	2.6	55	232	2.0	6.0	0.1	–	0.4
Mali (d)	8.7	2.6	7	223	-1.9	2.4	0.5	0.3	0.5
Burkina Faso (d)	8.5	2.4	31	218	2.7	1.4	2.5	0.1	0.4
Burundi (g)	5.2	2.2	186	211	-4.4	1.2	1.5	0.1	0.2
Chad (b)	5.4	2.2	4	169	-1.6	-2.8	1.3	0.1	0.4
G. Bissau (e)	0.9	3.2	26	159	4.7	-2.2	1.8	–	0.1
Malawi	8.2	3.4	69	146	2.2	2.8	-0.9	0.3	0.5
Tanzania (f)	25.5	3.6	27	123	4.7	-0.3	-1.2	0.3	0.8
Ethiopia	46.1	2.6	38	121	1.9	-0.2	-0.6	0.4	1.1
Mozambique (f)	14.9	2.6	19	84	1.3	-4.9	-4.9	0.1	0.7
Total (28)	214.2							6.0	11.2
Average		2.8	32	340	1.7	0.6	-0.4		
All Developing Africa									
Total (50)	570.0							55.1	60.5
Average (unweighted)		2.9	19	650	2.3	0.7	-0.8		
All Sub-Saharan Africa									
Total (40)	460.0							30.9	31.2
Average (unweighted)		3.0	27	430	2.0	0.4	-0.7		

Notes: 1. Asterisked figures (*) are for 1986; 2. Regional Groupings: (a) Maghreb (b) UDEAC (c) MARIUN (d) CEAO (e) other ECOWAS (f) SADCC which also comprises Namibia not listed above (g) CEPGL
Source: UNCTAD, *Handbook of International Trade and Development Statistics, 1990*

Table A2: African Countries' Outstanding Debt and National Income, 1988-9

Country	Population (millions) '87	'88	GDP (US$) per head '87	'88	Total debt (US$ billions) '87	'89	Debt (US$) per head '87	'89	Debt/ exports '87	Debt service/ exports '89
NORTH AFRICA (5)										
Libya	3.7	4.2	5479	5417	–	–	–	–	–	–
Algeria	22.5	23.7	2713	2284	27.9	26.1	1018	1110	218	62
Tunisia	7.2	7.8	1222	1287	6.9	6.9	958	890	182	20
Egypt	48.0	50.1	776	681	40.3	48.8	840	970	343	44
Morocco	22.5	23.8	657	922	20.7	20.8	920	875	382	34
Subtotal	103.9	119.6			90.8	102.6				
Averages			1196	2120			909	961	281	40
MIDDLE/LOW INCOME (17)										
Réunion	0.5	0.6	3931	–	–	–	–	–	–	4
Gabon	1.2	1.1	2882	3030	2.1	3.2	1750	2900	148	10
Seychelles	0.1	0.1	2680	3511	0.12	–	1500	–	82	11
Mauritius	1.1	1.1	1365	1843	0.78	0.8	709	720	64	14
Cameroon	10.1	11.1	1077	1136	4.0	4.7	400	427	190	31
Congo	1.8	2.1	1033	1007	4.6	4.3	2555	2040	444	38
Côte d'Ivoire	11.2	11.2	920	872	13.6	15.4	1333	1370	374	59
Liberia*	2.3	2.4	723	484	1.6	1.8	696	745	324	12
Zimbabwe	9.1	9.1	583	690	2.5	3.1	275	342	152	26
Senegal*	6.6	6.9	564	717	3.7	4.1	567	595	286	28
Angola	9.0	9.5	495	–	–	–	–	–	–	–
Nigeria	99.0	101.9	473	296	28.7	32.8	290	320	369	34
Ghana*	14.1	14.1	407	369	3.1	3.1	274	220	324	55
Kenya*	21.6	22.5	333	375	5.9	5.7	273	254	342	34
Madagascar*	10.3	11.3	259	167	3.4	3.6	330	319	813	63
Zambia*	6.9	7.9	257	346	6.4	6.9	927	875	670	12
Zaïre*	30.9	33.5	180	193	8.6	8.8	324	264	447	20
Subtotal	234.6	246.4			89.1	98.3				
Averages			545	1002			813	814	333	22
LEAST DEVELOPED COUNTRIES (LDCs) (28)										
Botswana	1.1	1.2	997	1654	0.5	0.5	454	415	28	5
Djibouti*	0.5	0.4	471	589	0.2	–	360	–	–	17
Mauritania*	1.9	1.9	413	1522	2.0	2.0	1053	1050	430	29
CAR	2.6	2.9	391	388	0.6	0.7	231	240	318	14
Sudan	22.2	23.8	382	461	11.1	13.0	500	547	1562	45
Comoros*	0.5	0.5	356	402	0.2	–	400	–	676	2
Cape Verde*	0.3	0.3	353	748	0.1	–	333	–	–	18
Somalia*	5.5	7.1	351	239	2.5	2.1	454	296	1988	90
São Tomé*	0.1	0.1	347	548	0.1	–	1000	1000	950	19
Benin*	4.2	4.4	335	410	1.1	1.2	262	273	537	6
Togo*	3.0	3.3	322	408	1.2	1.2	400	363	280	29
Sierra Leone*	3.7	4.0	309	297	0.7	1.1	189	273	390	12
Rwanda*	6.2	6.8	297	340	0.6	0.7	97	103	331	12
Niger*	6.3	7.3	294	329	1.7	1.6	159	219	523	39

continued

Country	Population (millions)		GDP (US$) per head		Total debt (US$ billions)		Debt (US$) per head		Debt/ exports	Debt service/ exports
	'87	'88	'87	'88	'87	'89	'87	'89	'87	'89
Eq. Guinea*	0.4	0.3	294	438	0.2	–	*500*	–	490	15
Uganda*	16.0	17.5	278	243	1.4	1.8	87	103	378	49
Guinea*	6.2	5.4	267	446	1.8	2.2	*290*	410	–	35
Burundi*	4.9	5.2	266	211	0.8	0.9	163	173	686	30
Tanzania*	23.0	25.5	214	123	4.3	4.9	187	191	966	25
Gambia*	0.7	0.8	213	271	0.3	–	*428*	–	277	17
Burkina Faso*	7.1	8.5	205	218	0.9	0.8	128	95	175	10
Mali*	8.3	8.1	188	223	2.0	2.2	*241*	*272*	620	25
Guinea-Bissau*	0.9	0.9	185	159	0.4	–	*444*	–	1783	48
Lesotho*	1.6	1.7	181	232	0.2	0.3	150	175	72	5
Chad*	5.1	5.4	178	169	0.3	0.4	59	74	187	4
Malawi*	7.2	8.2	170	146	1.4	1.4	*194*	*171*	448	31
Mozambique*	14.4	14.9	138	84	3.6	4.7	*261*	*315*	1726	53
Ethiopia*	44.6	46.1	119	121	2.6	3.0	58	65	319	34
Subtotal	199.5	212.5			42.9	46.7				
Averages			260	356			364	3190	539	26
TOTAL	538.0	578.5			222.8	247.6				
Averages			666	950			695	700	384	30

Notes: * = eligible for IMF Structural Adjustment Funds; LDCs are according to the UN designation; emphasis is added where debt *per capita* is greater than GDP *per capita*; CAR = Central African Republic
Source: World Bank, *World Debt Tables, 1988–9*

Chart A3: Fluctuations in Sahel Rainfall, 1900–80

Sahel rainfall, percentage above and below normal. The recent 15-year drought was the worst on record, but precipitous fluctuations are frequent.

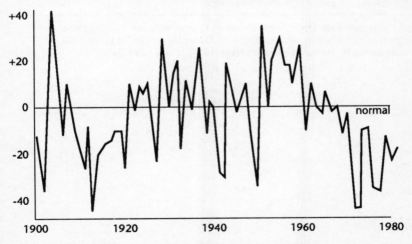

Source: Sharon Nicholson, *The Sahel: A Climatic Perspective*, OECD Paris 1982

**Table A4: Types of Export Incentives and Dates of Operation 1950–75
Republic of Korea**

Type of Export Promotion Scheme	Dates Applicable
Tariff exemptions on imports of raw materials and spare parts*	1959–75
Tariff and tax exemptions granted to domestic suppliers of exporting firms	1965–75
Domestic indirect and direct tax exemptions	1961–72
Accelerated depreciation	1966–75
Wastage allowance subsidies	1965–75
Import entitlement linked to exports	1951-55
	1963–65
Registration as an importer condition on export performance	1957–75
Reduced rates on public utilities	1967–75
Dollar-denominated deposits held in Bank of Korea by private traders	1950–61
Monopoly rights granted in new export markets	1967–71
Korean Trade Promotion Corporation	1965–75
Direct export subsidies	1955–56
	1961–64
Export(s) targets of industry	1962–75
Credit subsidies	
Export credit	1950–75
Foreign exchange loans	1950–54
	1971–75
Production loans for exporters	1959–75
Bank of Korea discount of export bills	1950–75
Import credits for exporters	1964–75
Capital loans by medium industry bank	1964–75
Offshore procurement loans	1964–75
Credits for overseas marketing activities	1965–75

* Note: tariff exemptions were shifted to to a rebate system in July 1974
Source: A.O. Krueger, *The Development Role of the Foreign Sector and Aid*,
distributed by Harvard University Press, 1979, p. 93, Table 24

Chart A5: Africa's Declining Shares in the World Market 1970 and 1987: selected commodities

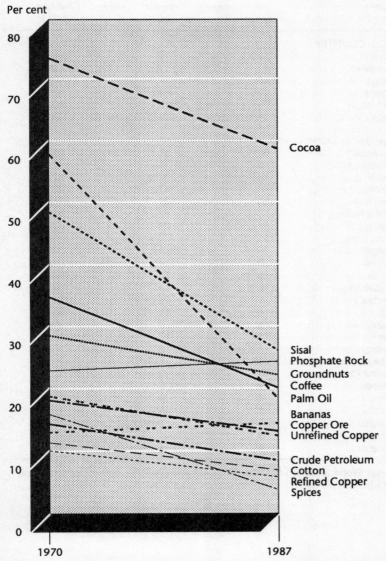

Note: Commodities that representaed a share of more than 10 per cent in 1970.
Source: UNCTAD, *Commodity Yearbook, 1991*

Table A6: African Primary Commodity (PC) Export Earnings as Percentage of GNP (averages of 1983 and 1987) and GNP per head (US$), 1987

Country	All Exports	Fuel	Non-fuel PC	Other	GNP/head (US$)
A. OIL COUNTRIES					
Gabon	50	40	10	–	2882
Seychelles	42	28	3	11	2680
Congo	40	35	5	–	1033
Nigeria	29	28	1	–	473
Cameroon	22	8	12	2	1071
Benin	16	4	6	10	335
B. NON-OIL COUNTRIES					
Botswana	66	–	31	34	997
Mauritania	45	–	44	1	413
Liberia	40	–	39	1	723
Zambia	38	–	37	1	257
Mauritius	36	–	26	10	1365
Côte d'Ivoire	33	–	27	6	920
Togo	31	1	27	3	322
Zaïre	25	–	23	2	180
Senegal	20	–	15	5	564
Malawi	19	–	16	3	170
Ghana	18	–	16	2	407
Zimbabwe	18	–	13	5	583
Gambia	16	–	15	1	213
CAR	16	–	11	5	391
Niger	14	–	14	–	294
Mali	13	–	10	3	188
Madagascar	11	–	8	3	259
Sierra Leone	11	–	5	6	309
Burkina Faso	10	–	10	–	205
Burundi	9	–	8	1	268
Rwanda	8	–	8	–	297
Somalia	8	–	8	–	351
Ethiopia	8	–	7	1	119
Sudan	8	2	6	–	382
Tanzania	8	–	6	2	214

Source: World Bank, *World Tables, 1988–89* and UNCTAD, *Statistical Pocket Book, 1989* for GDP/head

Table A7: African Land Use, Agricultural Production and Population, 1972–87 (millions of hectares and percentages)

1. LAND USE Region (total land area)		1972	1977	1982	1987	Change % 1972–87
All Africa (2964)	Arable	155	160	163	167	+7.7
	Perm. Crops	16	18	18	19	+19
	Pasture	793	792	789	787	-1
	Forest	731	715	701	686	-6
North Africa & RSA (516)	Arable	31	32	34	32	+3
	Perm. Crops	3	4	4	5	+70
	Pasture	153	155	157	159	+4
	Forest	15	15	15	15	–
Sub-Saharan Africa (2446)	Arable	124	128	129	135	+9
	Perm. Crops	3	14	14	14	+8
	Pasture	640	637	632	628	–
	Forest	718	700	686	671	-7

2. PRODUCTION ALL AFRICA (1979–81 = 100)		1972	1977	1982	1987	Change 1972–87
TOTAL	Agriculture	85	93	104	114	+34 (1988=118)
	Food Prod.	85	93	104	114	+34
	Crops	87	95	103	114	+31
	Livestock	80	91	107	118	+47
	Cereals	87	90	101	108	+24 (1988=123)
PER HEAD	Agriculture	110	102	98	93	-16
	Food Prod.	110	102	98	93	-16

3. POPULATION (millions and %) Region		1972	1977	1982	1987	Change % 1972–87
All Africa	Population	400	430	530	592	+48
	% in Agric.	72	70	67	65	–
North Africa & RSA	Population	94	112	123	139	+48
	% in Agric.	50	45	40	37	–
Sub-Saharan Africa	Population	306	318	407	453	+48
	% in Agric.	78	75	72	70	–
Nigeria	Population	62	69	85	102	+64
	% in Agric.	71	69	67	66	–

Source: FAO, *Yearbook: Production*, vol. 42, 1988

Table A8: African Food Imports and Exports, 1969–89 (all figures in US$ millions)

Region	IMPORTS			EXPORTS			of which in 1989 Tropical Beverages
	1969	1980	1989	1969	1980	1989	
All Africa (50)	1667	14 747	14 419	3491	10 213	9193	4016
Sub-Sahara (total)	1040	7567	6385	2790	9031	7483	4016
OIL EXPORTERS	432	6577	5666	749	743	305	–
North Africa (total)	254	3517	4296	193	120	35	–
Algeria	158	2202	2995	192	120	35	–
Libya	96	1315	1301	1	–	–	–
Sub-Sahara (total)	178	3059	1370	556	623	287	208
Angola	49	373	498	162	170	17	12
Congo	15	82	112	15	15	28	2
Gabon	13	117	121	2	14	20	5
Nigeria	101	2487	639	377	424	222	189
NON-OIL EXPORTERS	1235	8170	8753	2742	9570	8888	3808
North Africa (total)	373	3682	3738	508	1062	1404	–
Egypt	198	2348	2368	201	207	236	–
Morocco	104	852	712	255	696	884	–
Tunisia	71	482	658	52	150	284	–
Sub-Sahara (total)	862	4498	4247	2234	8408	7776	4158
Sub-Sahara major FOOD EXPORTERS (total)	529	2628	3021	1663	6434	5599	3402
Cameroon	27	128	350	148	638	331	287
Côte d'Ivoire	68	557	643	278	1955	1569	1243
Ethiopia	9	97	250	97	315	314	292
Ghana	58	161	143	246	789	523	480
Kenya	33	203	151	134	591	689	514
Mozambique	40	121	174	83	165	90	1
Réunion	40	230	346	41	116	113	–
Senegal	84	281	361	83	205	506	–
Sudan	37	394	239	81	257	190	7
Swaziland	9	38	50	26	204	172	–
Tanzania	26	162	63	120	320	210	124
Uganda	23	45	30	145	340	273	272
Zaïre	64	153	284	79	195	155	149
Zimbabwe	10	58	39	102	354	464	33
Sub-Sahara remainder (total)	333	1870	1954	571	1974	1597	406

Source: UNCTAD, *Commodity Yearbook, 1991*

Table A9: African Countries' Dependency on Individual Primary Commodities, 1970s–80s. Only individual products comprising 10 per cent or more of exports are shown.

Producing Country	Products	Dependency (%)		Non-fuel Exports (US$ millions)	
		1972–6	1982–6	1974	1986
NORTH AFRICA					
Algeria	Fuel Oil & Gas	85	98		
	Other	15	2	740	260
Egypt	Fuel Oil	13	61		
	Cotton	50	20		
	Other	37	19	1454	1170
Libya	Fuel Oil	100	100		
Morocco	Phosphates	44	23		
	Fish	6	10	1690	2314
	Fruit	10	7		
	Other	40	60		
Tunisia	Fuel Oil	38	41		
	Veg. Oil	15	4	541	1041
	Cotton	10	2		
	Other	37	53		
SUB-SAHARAN OIL STATES					
Angola	Fuel Oil	53	83		
	Coffee	24	4	n.a.	n.a.
	Other	23	17		
Cameroon	Fuel Oil	–	38		
	Coffee	27	23	447	677
	Cocoa	30	20		
	Timber	12	9		
	Other	31	10		
Congo	Fuel Oil	66	91		
	Timber	22	5	32	127
	Other	12	4		
Gabon	Fuel Oil	76	82		
	Timber	12	6	186	454
	Other	12	12		
Nigeria	Fuel Oil	92	96		
	Other	8	4	607	209
Seychelles	Fuel	0	69		
	Fish	6	11		
	Copra	25	6	3	5
	Spices	39	3		
	Other	30	11		

continued

Producing Country	Products	Dependency (%)		Non-fuel Exports (US$ millions)	
		1972–6	1982–6	1974	1986
COFFEE PRODUCERS					
Burundi	Coffee	87	87		
	Other	13	13	29	147
Central African	Coffee	26	31		
Republic	Diamonds	21	33	45	98
	Timber	29	23		
	Cotton	17	11		
	Other	7	2		
Madagascar	Coffee	30	39		
	Cloves	13	13	198	285
	Vanilla	7	17		
	Other	50	31		
Rwanda	Coffee	67	73		
	Tin	12	12		
	Livestock	11	0	51	165
	Other	10	15		
Tanzania	Coffee	22	40		
	Cotton	16	13	292	285
	Hard Fibres	13	6		
	Other	49	41		
Uganda	Coffee	73	95		
	Cotton	13	2	315	441
	Other	14	3		
COCOA PRODUCERS					
Côte d'Ivoire	Cocoa	23	35		
	Coffee	28	23		
	Palm Oil	24	17	1070	2782
	Fuel Oil	0	10		
	Other	25	15		
Equat. Guinea	Cocoa	68	54		
	Timber	5	41	na	31
	Coffee	16	5		
	Other	11	0		
Ghana	Cocoa	70	59		
	Bauxite	8	24	615	868
	Timber	13	2		
	Other	9	15		
São Tomé	Cocoa	61	76		
	Other	39	24	na	na

continued

Producing Country	Products	Dependency (%)		Non-fuel Exports (US$ millions)	
		1972–6	*1982–6*	*1974*	*1986*
COTTON PRODUCERS					
Benin	Cotton	32	35		
	Cocoa	19	28	72	39
	Palm Oil	24	17		
	Fuel Oil	2	10		
Burkina Faso	Cotton	29	48		
	Veg. Oil	22	15		
	Livestock	31	12	61	125
	Groundnuts	12	0		
	Other	6	25		
Chad	Cotton	44	29		
	Livestock	31	12	39	100
	Other	25	59		
Mali	Cotton	40	39		
	Livestock	42	57	57	134
	Other	18	4		
Sudan	Cotton	51	42		
	Veg Oil	29	14	421	441
	Livestock	2	12		
	Groundnuts	10	6		
	Other	10	16		
GROUNDNUT PRODUCERS					
Gambia	Groundnuts	94	45		
	Other	6	55	44	63
Guinea-Bissau	Groundnuts	65	24		
	Cashews	2	29		
	Palm Oil	12	13	na	na
	Other	18	34		
Senegal	Groundnuts	45	20		
	Fish	10	32		
	Phosphates	19	10	416	594
	Fuel Oil	4	n.a.		
	Other	12	n.a.		
FISHERIES					
Cape Verde	Fish	41	65		
	Bananas	8	16		
	Fruit	8	16	na	na
	Other	43	3		
Mauritania	see below				
Mozambique	Fish	4	27		
	Prawns	4	16		
	Sugar	14	6	na	na
	Cotton	13	8		
	Other	65	43		
Senegal	see above				

continued

Producing Country	Products	Dependency (%)		Non-fuel Exports (US$ millions)	
		1972–6	1982–6	1974	1986
SUGAR PRODUCERS					
Mauritius	Sugar	86	65		
	Other	14	35	315	686
Réunion	Sugar	83	74		
	Other	17	26	na	na
Swaziland	Sugar	36	39		
	Fruit	7	13		
	Iron Ore	10	0	179	278
	Other	47	48		
TOBACCO PRODUCERS					
Malawi	Tobacco	46	55		
	Tea	20	20		
	Sugar	10	9	119	250
	Other	24	17		
Zimbabwe	Tobacco	14	20		
	Other	86	80	260	1323
LIVESTOCK PRODUCERS					
Djibouti	Livestock	12	25		
	Fuel Oil	2	10	16	20
	Other	86	65		
Somalia	Livestock	53	76		
	Bananas	15	11		
	Fruit	15	11	64	89
	Other	17	2		
Mali	see above				
MINERAL PRODUCERS					
Botswana	Diamonds	28	78		
	Meat	66	17	142	852
	Other	6	5		
Guinea	Bauxite	83	89		
	Other	17	11	n.a.	n.a.
Liberia	Iron Ore	70	64		
	Rubber	13	17	394	408
	Other	17	19		
Mauritania	Iron Ore	74	45		
	Livestock	11	11	187	419
	Fish	7	42		
	Other	8	2		
Niger	Uranium	51	85		
	Livestock	24	12		
	Groundnuts	16	0	81	330

continued

Producing Country	Products	Dependency (%)		Non-fuel Exports (US$ millions)	
		1972–6	*1982–6*	*1974*	*1986*
Sierra Leone	Diamonds	61	32		
	Cocoa	6	17		
	Coffee	7	13	143	126
	Bauxite	4	13		
	Other	22	25		
Togo	Phosphates	61	47		
	Cocoa	17	13		
	Cotton	2	12	215	273
	Coffee	10	10		
	Other	10	18		
Zaïre	Copper	67	58		
	Coffee	11	19	1521	1844
	Fuel Oil	2	18		
	Other	20	5		
Zambia	Copper	92	98		
	Other	8	2	1396	797

Sources: Fraser Report, *Africa's Commodity Problems*, 1990 Table 2, pp. 103–13;
and IMF, *International Financial Statistics, Yearbook, 1989*

Table A10: Sub-Saharan Africa's Main Commodity Exports by Product Groups: Earnings and Prices 1988/89 relative to 1980

Commodity	Value 88/89 US$ million	Earnings 88/89 as % 1980	Prices 88/89 as % 1980	Share of world market (%) 88/89
Fuel Oil	10 949 (a)	60	44	7.2
Food products of which	7965	66		2.8
coffee	1988	94	68	20
cocoa beans & products	1812	106	55	42
fish products	985	330	94 (b)	3
sugar	685	90	40	6.5
live animals & meat	487	79	na	1.5
tobacco	478	113	117	11
tea	344	140	84	15
groundnuts & oil	146	48	108	18
palm oil & nuts	69	70	67	3
Agricultural materials of which	2505		95	3
timber	807	120	108 (c)	6
cotton & yarn	395 (d)	51	74 (e)	3
rubber	293	260	74	6
hides & skins	224	87	108	3
Mineral ores & metals (excluding gold & diamonds) of which	4680		114	4
copper: refined	1489	130	122	16
copper: unrefined	557	111	124	10
bauxite	447	142	131	2
iron ore	419	87	85	5
phosphate rock (f)	235	170	88	13
manganese	150	150	138	31
Diamonds	1600 (g)	na	112	40
Gold	250 (h)	na	67	na

Notes: (a) including North Africa = $19 880 million; (b) fish meal c.i.f. Hamburg; (c) logs; (d) including North Africa = $1164 million; (e) cotton only; (f) estimate; (g) including North Africa = $760 million; (h) estimate for Zimbabwe.
Source: UNCTAD, *Commodity Yearbooks, 1987* and *1991*

Table A11: Developing Countries' Export Markets, 1970–80 and 1980–7 (average annual changes, percentages)

Commodities	Years	World	Developed All	EC	Developing
a. DEVELOPING COUNTRIES' EARNINGS FROM EXPORTS					
All Countries					
All Commodities	1970–80	25.7	25.5	22.9	28.5
	1980–87	-1.5	-2.4	-4.1	-0.6
Food	1970–80	15.5	13.0	12.8	20.9
	1980–87	1.2	2.4	1.7	0.4
Agric. Materials	1970–80	13.7	12.9	11.4	16.6
	1980–87	-0.8	-1.3	0.3	0.3
Ores & Metals	1970–80	13.8	12.7	11.6	22.0
	1980–87	0.8	-1.2	-3.7	5.7
Fuels	1970–80	34.7	34.5	30.0	35.0
	1980–87	-12.2	-14.1	-14.2	-7.8
Manufactures	1970–80	16.2	25.0	19.8	27.2
	1980–87	27.4	16.6	26.3	7.8
Sub-Saharan Africa					
All Commodities	1970–80	19.7			
	1980–87	-5.7			
b. VOLUMES OF EXPORTS FROM DEVELOPING COUNTRIES					
All Countries					
All Commodities	1960–70	7.5			
	1970–80	0.5			
	1980–88	3.2			
Sub-Saharan Africa					
All Commodities	1960–70	6.3			
	1970–80	-0.6			
	1980–88	-1.1			
Agric. Prods. only	1973/75–78/80	-5.3			
	1978/80–85/87	0.8			
c. UNIT VALUES OF EXPORTS FROM DEVELOPING COUNTRIES					
All Countries					
All Commodities	1960–70	-0.4			
	1970–80	25.9			
	1980–88	-5.3			
Sub-Saharan Africa					
All Commodities	1960–70	1.7			
	1970–80	21.5			
	1980–88	-4.3			
Agric. Prods. only	1973/5–1978/80	25.0			
	1979/80–1985/7	-7.6			

Source: UNCTAD *Statistical Pocket Book, 1989,* Tables 2.5 and 3.9

Table A12: World Bank 1988 Forecasts of Real Commodity Prices

	1961	*1970/1*	*1980/1*	*1986/7*	*1990*	*1995*	*2000*
Bananas	–	–	100	82.3	–	83.1	77.7
Coffee*	(77)	(85)	100	92.8	(58)	68.1	68.5
Tea*	(135)	(114)	100	72.5	(120)	73.7	78.8
Cocoa*	(44)	(54)	100	73.3	(36)	46.4	51.3
Sugar*	(30)	(40)	100	23.6	(50)	46.6	52.7
Palm Oil*	(28)	(38)	100	43.5	(140)	59.2	53.6
Coconut Oil	–	–	100	49.7	–	71.4	62.8
Tobacco*	(62)	(79)	100	72.7	(70)	67.1	64.7
Rice	–	–	100	40.5	–	39.4	37.9
Cotton*	(110)	(100)	100	58.0	(75)	66.0	62.2
Jute	–	–	100	85.3	–	87.0	84.5
Rubber	–	–	100	60.6	–	83.7	76.8
Logs	–	–	100	86.6	–	90.9	93.4
Sawnwood	–	–	100	67.4	–	62.3	62.5
Aggregate of starred * products	(62.5)	(68.5)	(100)	(66.5)	(60.5)	(65.5)	(70.5)

Note: Figures in brackets from World Bank, 1989
Sources: (1) World Bank, 1988 via C. Stevens and D.C. Faber, *The Uruguay Round and Europe 1992*, ECDPM, 1990 p. 57; (2) World Bank, *Trends and Prospects*, 1989

Table A13: Effects of World Bank Projections for Sub-Saharan Non-fuel (NF) Commodity Exports

Commodity	Actual 1982/87 NF comm. exports		Implications of World Bank projections (2000) in 1990 US$ billions earnings per commodity (c)					
	Share in total exports (a)	US$ billions	Central case	Variant				
				1	2	3	4	
Coffee	17.1	2.38	4.41	4.80	4.04	4.69	3.95	
Cocoa beans	12.2	1.64	3.05	3.32	2.79	3.24	2.73	
Copper	13.9	1.87	3.47	3.77	3.17	3.69	3.11	
Timber (logs)	5.5	0.74	1.38	1.50	1.26	1.47	1.24	
Cotton	5.0	0.68	1.25	1.37	1.15	1.34	1.12	
Sugar	4.0	0.53	0.99	1.07	0.90	1.05	0.88	
Iron ore	3.5	0.47	0.87	0.95	0.80	0.93	0.78	
Tobacco	3.1	0.42	0.77	0.84	0.71	0.82	0.69	
Tea	2.5	0.34	0.63	0.68	0.57	0.67	0.56	
Bauxite	3.1	0.41	0.76	0.83	0.70	0.81	0.68	
Rubber	1.2	0.16	0.30	0.33	0.28	0.32	0.27	
Phosphate rock	1.1	0.15	0.28	0.30	0.25	0.30	0.25	
Manganese	0.9	0.12	0.22	0.24	0.20	0.24	0.20	
Groundnut oil	0.6	0.09	0.16	0.18	0.15	0.17	0.14	
Palm oil	0.4	0.05	0.09	0.10	0.08	0.10	0.08	
Groundnut cake	0.3	0.04	0.07	0.08	0.07	0.08	0.06	
Sisal	0.2	0.03	0.05	0.06	0.05	0.06	0.05	
Subtotal	75.2	10.10	18.73	20.38	17.15	19.93	16.77	
Other NF commodities	24.8	3.33	6.17	6.72	5.65	6.57	5.53	
Agricultural total	52.7	6.94	13.15	14.33	12.04	13.84	11.77	
1. Total NF exports	100.0	13.43	24.90	27.10	22.80	26.50	22.30	
2. Total exports		28.0	56.50	56.50	51.80	60.20	50.60	
3. (1) as % of (2)		48%	44%	48%	44%	44%	44%	
Agric. % of subtotal	70.1	69.0	70.00	70.00	70.00	69.00	70.00	
Growth rates (1987–2000)								
Total NF exports		-3.4(b)	4.9	5.6	4.2	5.4	4.0	
Total exports		-3.1(b)	5.6	5.6	4.8	6.1	4.7	
Agric. prices		-7.5(b)	3.0	3.0	3.0	3.0	3.0	

Note: (a) average commodity share (1983–7) in total non-fuel commodity exports (%). For the five metals an average of 1982–4 is used, with a correction for price increases since then.

(b) Average growth rates 1980–7.

(c) The commodity composition of total non-fuel commodity exports is assumed to be the same as the average of the period 1982/87. Amounts are in US$ billions.

Sources: Statistical Annex Table 37, Tables 1,3; *Sub-Saharan Africa: From Crisis to Sustainable Growth*, UNDP/World Bank (1989); World Bank (1989a); own calculations, Henk Kox, *Export Constraints for Sub-Saharan Africa*, Free University of Amsterdam, 1990

Table A14: Export Value and Volume Projections for Selected Commodities

Year	Cocoa		Coffee		Cotton		Groundnut Oil	
	Volume	Value	Volume	Value	Volume	Value	Volume	Value

				SSA				
1988	1.13	1295	0.93	2044	0.65	659	0.15	64
1989	1.14	1039	1.05	1901	0.67	824	0.14	75
1990	1.17	805	1.05	1487	0.70	875	0.14	65
1991	1.19	837	1.03	1548	0.72	895	0.14	65
1992	1.21	871	1.01	1605	0.75	914	0.14	66
1993	1.24	905	0.99	1659	0.77	932	0.14	67
1994	1.26	940	0.96	1708	0.80	949	0.15	67
1995	1.28	976	0.94	1753	0.82	965	0.15	68
1996	1.29	1079	0.94	1799	0.84	974	0.15	69
1997	1.30	1183	0.94	1846	0.86	982	0.16	70
1998	1.31	1289	0.94	1893	0.88	990	0.16	70
1999	1.32	1396	0.95	1939	0.90	997	0.16	71
2000	1.33	1505	0.95	1986	0.92	1003	0.16	72

				World				
1988	1.97	2268	4.00	8794	5.03	5080	0.59	254
1989	2.02	1842	4.49	8135	5.05	6212	0.60	327
1990	2.06	1421	4.54	6399	5.10	6375	0.60	281
1991	2.10	1479	4.56	6834	5.15	6360	0.61	287
1992	2.14	1538	4.57	7272	5.21	6343	0.63	293
1993	2.18	1598	4.59	7713	5.26	6325	0.65	300
1994	2.22	1660	4.61	8157	5.32	6305	0.67	306
1995	2.27	1722	4.63	8604	5.37	6283	0.69	311
1996	2.30	1916	4.66	8886	5.45	6288	0.70	315
1997	2.33	2115	4.69	9171	5.53	6291	0.71	319
1998	2.36	2318	4.72	9459	5.61	6291	0.72	322
1999	2.39	2526	4.75	9749	5.69	6289	0.74	325
2000	2.42	2738	4.78	10043	5.76	6284	0.75	329

continued

Year	Palm Oil		Sugar		Tea		Tobacco		Total
	Volume	Value	Volume	Value	Volume	Value	Volume	Value	Value
				SSA					
1988	0.20	63	1.66	270	0.27	36	0.18	267	4697
1989	0.20	52	1.70	351	0.28	39	0.18	275	4555
1990	0.20	50	1.75	436	0.28	42	0.17	281	4040
1991	0.20	52	1.80	428	0.30	44	0.18	277	4147
1992	0.19	53	1.85	419	0.31	47	0.18	273	4248
1993	0.19	55	1.91	408	0.32	49	0.18	269	4343
1994	0.18	57	1.96	397	0.34	51	0.19	264	4432
1995	0.18	58	2.01	384	0.35	53	0.19	259	4516
1996	0.16	52	2.07	409	0.37	56	0.19	260	4698
1997	0.15	46	2.13	434	0.38	59	0.19	261	4881
1998	0.13	40	2.19	460	0.40	62	0.20	262	5066
1999	0.12	35	2.25	487	0.42	65	0.20	263	5253
2000	0.10	30	2.31	515	0.44	68	0.20	264	5442
				World					
1988	6.53	2070	27.83	4537	1.77	230	1.36	2049	25 281
1989	7.34	1923	27.53	5671	1.80	248	1.35	2089	26 447
1990	7.58	1886	27.72	6902	1.82	272	1.33	2139	25 673
1991	8.04	2120	28.08	6667	1.87	280	1.35	2105	26 131
1992	8.51	2368	28.45	6423	1.92	288	1.37	2070	26 596
1993	8.98	2629	28.81	6171	1.97	296	1.38	2034	27 066
1994	9.45	2904	29.18	5911	2.01	305	1.40	1995	27 542
1995	9.91	3192	29.54	5642	2.06	313	1.42	1955	28 024
1996	10.28	3257	29.94	5911	2.11	324	1.44	1963	28 860
1997	10.65	3317	30.35	6185	2.17	334	1.46	1971	29 702
1998	11.01	3374	30.75	6464	2.22	345	1.47	1978	30 550
1999	11.38	3427	31.15	6748	2.28	355	1.49	1984	31 404
2000	11.74	3476	31.56	7037	2.33	366	1.51	1990	32 264

Source: World Bank Paper, *Recent Trends and Prospects for Agricultural Commodity Exports in Sub-Saharan Africa* December 1989
Note: Volume in million tonnes, value in 1985 US$ millions

Table A15: Sub-Saharan Africa (SSA): Shares in World Cocoa Production and Exports ('000 tonnes and percentages)

Production/ Export Stage	1971–3			1979–80			1987–9		
	World	SSA	%	World	SSA	%	World	SSA	%
Production:									
raw cocoa	1470	1014	69	1628	1022	62	2300	1250	54
grindings	na	na	–	1500	142	9	1970	167	8
Export:									
beans	1192	950	80	991	730	74	1530	1022	67
cocoa butter	159	48	30	171	41	24	275	41	15
powder & cake	111	19	17	168	42	25	268	37	14
paste & liquor	63	47	75	136	21	15	148	44	29
Manufacture:									
chocolate	365	3	0.8	544	8	1.4	922	6	0.7

Source: ICCO, *Quarterly Bulletin of Statistics*; Gill & Duffus, *Cocoa Statistics*, November 1989

Chart A16: Stages in Chocolate Production

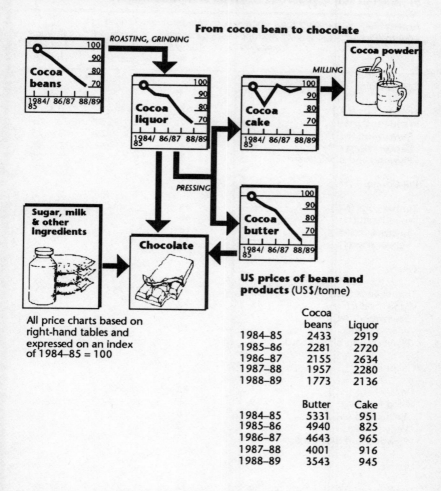

From cocoa bean to chocolate

All price charts based on right-hand tables and expressed on an index of 1984–85 = 100

US prices of beans and products (US$/tonne)

	Cocoa beans	Liquor
1984–85	2433	2919
1985–86	2281	2720
1986–87	2155	2634
1987–88	1957	2280
1988–89	1773	2136
	Butter	Cake
1984–85	5331	951
1985–86	4940	825
1986–87	4643	965
1987–88	4001	916
1988–89	3543	945

Source: Richard Natkiel Association for Gill & Duffus: USDA via *South* magazine, April 1990

Table A17: Share of Processed Wood Products in Total Wood Exports of Selected Major Exporters of Tropical Hardwoods

In percentage of country's total wood exports and tonnage exported

Country/Product	Average 1967/71 %	Average 1982/86 %	Average 1973/75 tonnes	Average 1985/87 tonnes
Côte d'Ivoire				
Timber Logs (NC)	84	67	2332	1317
Wood Products	16	33		
Sawnwood (NC)	13	4		
Veneer sheets	3	4		
Plywood and block board	1	3		
P R Congo				
Timber Logs (NC)	76	54	232	231
Wood Products	24	46		
Sawnwood (NC)	3	13		
Veneer sheets	21	33		
Ghana				
Timber Logs (NC)	55	41	753	155
Wood Products	45	59		
Sawnwood (NC)	37	49		
Veneer sheets	0	10		
Plywood and block board	8	1		
Gabon				
Timber Logs (NC)	81	82	989	814
Wood Products	19	18		
Sawnwood (NC)	1	0		
Veneer sheets	3	2		
Plywood and block board	16	17		
Liberia				
Timber Logs (NC)	99	94	215	na
Wood Products	1	6		
Sawnwood (NC)	1	6		

Note: NC = non-coniferous
Source: UNCTAD, *Market Access Conditions,* Paper TD/B/C.1/AC/6 (Geneva, 1989) Annex Table 9 via Henk Kox, *Export Constraints for Sub-Saharan Africa* (Free University of Amsterdam, 1990) Annex Table 37

Table A18: African Production, Consumption, Export and Import of Cotton, averages for 1985–8

Product	AFRICA TOTAL	RSA	EGYPT	SUDAN	OTHER N. AFRICA	OTHER S-SAHARA
Quantities ('000 tonnes)						
Cotton Lint						
Production	1370	60	350	150	–	810
Consumption	715	75	280	15	70	375
Exports	780	–	140	180	–	460
Yarn						
Exports	89	4	70	–	5	10
Imports	20	2	–	–	6	12
Export Values (US$ millions)						
Natural fibres	1355	185	350	170	–	650
Cotton and yarn	1515	15	700	170	30	600
Cotton	1095	–	340	170	–	585
Yarn	420	15	360	–	30	15
Textile yarn and fabric	1400	na	na	na	na	na
Clothing	1500	na	na	na	na	na
Import Values (US$ millions)						
Natural fibres	350	45	–	–	80	225
Cotton and yarn	285	35	–	–	60	190
Cotton	235	30	–	–	60	145
Yarn	50	5	–	–	–	45
Textiles yarn and fabrics	3070	370	na	na	na	na
Clothing	995	70	na	na	na	na

Sources: FAO, *Production Yearbook, 1988*; UNCTAD, *Commodity Yearbook, 1991*; and UN, *Monthly Bulletin of Statistics*, May 1991

Table A19: Commodity Trade of the Different Africas, 1988 (US$ billions and percentages)

Commodity		ALL AFRICA	RSA	NORTH AFRICA (incl. Egypt)	S-S AFRICA
All merchandise	$bn	65.9	12.7	24.6	28.6
exports	%	100	100	100	100
Fuels	$bn	30.6	1.2	14.3	15.1
	%	46	4	58	53
Non-fuels	$bn	35.3	11.5	10.3	13.5
of which	%	54	96	42	47
Agric.Prods	$bn	18.0	2.2	6.4	8.3
	%	27	17	26	29
Minerals (a)	$bn	5.9	1.2	0.8	3.9
	%	9	9	3	14
Manufactures	$bn	11.4	8.1	2.3	1.0
	%	17	64	9	3
Gold	$bn	9.8	8.9	–	0.9
Diamonds	$bn	2.8	1.2	–	1.6

Note: (a) excluding gold and diamonds, but including non-ferrous metals
RSA = Republic of South Africa
Source: UNCTAD *Commodity Yearbook, 1989*; UN, *Monthly Bulletin of Statistics*, May 1990; IMF, *International Financial Statistics, 1990*

Table A20: African Minerals: Prices and World Bank Forecasts, 1970–2000 (US$ current and constant 1985 prices)

Commodity	Values	1970	1980	1985	1987	1989	1990	1991	1995	2000
Gold per oz.	current	36	608	318	446	381	360	394	408	489
	constant	99	583	318	347	277	250	260	222	222
Copper tonne	current	1413	2182	1417	1783	2848	1380	1800	2300	2700
	constant	3887	2092	1417	1385	2070	1000	1188	1252	1227
Iron ore tonne	current	15.2	26.7	22.7	22.2	26.3	26.0	28.9	31.0	37.9
	constant	41.8	25.6	22.7	17.2	19.1	18.0	19.1	16.9	17.2
Phosphate rock tonne	current	11	47	34	31	41	42	47	58	72
	constant	30	45	34	24	30	29	31	32	32
Coal tonne	current	–	43	47	36	41	39	42	48	62
	constant	–	41	47	28	29	27	28	26	28
Chrome tonne	current	–	(53)	45	42	62	60	70		
	constant	–	(54)	45	33	45	42	45		
Manganese mtu	current	–	(1.37)	1.39	1.28	2.9	3.2	3.9		
	constant	–	(1.38)	1.39	0.99	2.1	2.2	2.9		
Uranium lb.	current	–	(17.8)	15.5	16.8	10.2	8.7	9.5		
	constant	–	(18.0)	15.5	13.1	7.4	6.0	7.1		
Platinum oz.	current	–	(359)	293	559	512	450	394		
	constant	–	(363)	293	406	372	310	295		

Notes: Chrome = 44% Cr_2O_3, Manganese = 48–50% Mn, Uranium = Ur_3O_8, Figures in brackets are for 1984
Sources: World Bank, *Revision of Commodity Price Forecasts*, December 1989; *Metal Bulletin*, 1990, 1991

Table A21: Major Metals and Minerals Consumption: Average Growth Rate by Regions

	Steel		Aluminium		Copper		Lead		Zinc		Tin		Nickel		Phosphates	
	50–73	74–85	50–73	74–85	50–73	74–85	50–73	74–85	50–73	74–85	50–73	74–85	50–73	74–85	50–73	74–85
World	5.8	(0.4)	9.2	1.7	4.3	1.6	4.0	1.2	5.2	(1.4)	2.3	(-0.5)	5.9	(1.4)	7.6	0.8
Western world	5.2	(-0.6)	9.0	(1.1)	4.6	(1.0)	3.2	(1.1)	4.7	(1.2)	1.6	-0.8	6.7	1.1	nd	nd
OECD	4.9	(-1.6)	8.6	(1.0)	4.2	(1.0)	3.0	(0.6)	4.2	(0.2)	1.5	-1.2	6.6	(0.6)	4.9	(0.2)
Eastern world	7.0	0.4	9.5	3.9	4.1	3.7	6.8	1.5	6.4	1.2	4.0	1.3	nd	2.5	nd	nd
LDCChina	9.2	5.5	18.1	6.1	13.4	6.2	8.4	3.7	10.9	6.0	9.3	0.75	16.3	7.1	15.5	4.5
Japan	14.6	(1.1)	20.1	3.0	9.9	3.4	10.7	4.1	12.7	1.7	9.9	(-0.0)	24	(2.6)	5.9	(1.0)
W. Europe	5.6	-2.1	8.5	2.0	2.6	(0.4)	3.4	(0.7)	4.2	(0.5)	1.2	-2.8	8.0	(1.2)	nd	(0.5)
US	2.4	-2.7	7.5	(-0.4)	3.5	(0.5)	1.6	(-0.4)	2.1	(-1.3)	(0.1)	-0.1	3.3	(-1.4)	4.5	(-1.0)

Note: ( ) means correlation coefficient not satisfactory   nd = not available

Source: Pierre-Noel Giraud, Director of CERNA (Centre d'Economie de Resource Naturelle), Ecole Nationale Superieure, Paris, from a paper entitled 'Consumption of Eight Mineral Resources: Retrospective Analysis 1950–85', presented at seminar held in Jakarta, November 1986

Table A22: African Copper Production, Exports and Consumption, 1989 (in '000 tonnes and US$ millions)

Process Stages		Zambia	Zaïre	Zimbabwe	Botswana	RSA
Ore						
Production	tonnes	500	441	16	22	197
Exports	tonnes	–	16	–	21	3
	$m	–	30	–	42	5
Blister						
Production	tonnes	485	424	23	–	185+37
Exports	tonnes	–	221	13	–	34+33
	$m	–	382	30	–	85+71
Refined						
Production	tonnes	466	255	24	–	144
Exports	tonnes	456	202	–	–	79
	$m	1194	401	–	–	209
Consumed tonnes		9	2	14	–	72

Notes: RSA = Republic of South Africa + Namibia
Source: UNCTAD, *Commodity Yearbook, 1991*

Table A23: African Diamond Exports, 1984–8 (all figures in US$ millions)

Country	1984	1985	1986	1987	1988
South Africa	669	880	na	na	na
Botswana	435	535	648	1350	988
Namibia	110	130	na	na	na
Zaïre	160	185	210	170	100
Sierra Leone	40	35	45	43	40
Central African Republic	40	35	41	50	45
Angola	40	30	na	na	na
Liberia	30	20	6	11	na
Ghana	20	40	na	na	na
Guinea	15	20	na	na	na
Total Sub-Sahara (estimate)	890	1030	944	1624	1173
Total de Beers	2500	3000	3500	4000	4000

Notes: The smaller figures are estimates of value based on carats. De Beers' sales through the Central Selling Organisation (CSO) do not include $1000 million probably produced in the USSR, of which only $1 million entered the CSO in 1988.
Source: IMF, *International Financial Statistics Yearbook, 1990* and UN, *Statistical Yearbook, 1985/86*

Table A24: Gold Supply and Demand in the West, 1980–9 (tonnes)

	1980	1981	1982	1983	1984	1985	1986	1987	1988	1989
SUPPLY										
mining	962	985	1031	1116	1167	1236	1296	1383	1551	1653
net CPE/EIT sales (a)	90	280	203	93	205	210	402	303	263	296
recovery of scrap	492	242	243	294	291	304	474	407	328	304
net official sales (purchases)	-230	-276	-85	142	85	-132	-145	-72	-285	225
Total	1313	1231	1392	1645	1747	1618	2027	2021	1857	2477
DEMAND										
fabrication	945	1219	1279	1232	1483	1487	1688	1605	1866	2207
investment outside Europe & N. America	23	274	294	73	332	306	214	258	459	516
net implied investment in Europe & N. America	346	-261	-181	340	-68	-175	126	157	-468	-246
Price (US$/oz)	612	460	375	424	361	317	368	446	437	381

Note: (a) CPE/EIT = Centrally Planned Economies/Economies In Transition
Source: Gold Fields Mineral Services Ltd, 1990

Table A25: African Bauxite and Aluminium Production and Export, 1988/9 (all figures in '000 tonnes or US$ millions)

Process Stage			Guinea	Ghana	Sierra Leone	Cameroon
Bauxite	Production	(weight)	17 600	265	1,450	–
		(alumina content)	3,950	70	290	–
	Export	(weight)	14 000	310	1500	–
		(alumina content)	3200	75	290	–
		(dollar value)	405	12	28	–
Alumina	Production	(weight)	275	–	–	–
	Export	(alumina content)	305	–	–	–
Aluminium	Production	(weight)	–	165	–	85
	Export	(weight)	–	130	–	–
		(dollar value)	–	220	–	–
	Consumption	(weight)	–	8	–	20

Note: South African production of aluminium in 1985–8 was 170 000 tonnes and consumption of aluminium, primary and secondary, was 120 000, of which 80 000 was exported – valued at US$120 million
Source: UNCTAD, *Commodity Yearbook, 1991*

Table A26: African Iron Ore Production, Processing and Export, 1987–9 (million tonnes and US$ millions)

Process Stage		Unit	Liberia	Mauritania	Zimbabwe	S-SA Total	RSA
Iron Ore Production	– weight		13.4	10.5	1.5	25.4	25.2
	– fe.wt.		9.0	6.6	0.8	16.4	17.0
	– pellets/ sinter		3.2	–	0.2	3.4	–
Exports	– weight		13.2	10.0	–	23.2	11.2
	– fe.wt.		9.0	6.9	–	15.9	7.1
	– value ($m)		210	152	–	362	160
Pig Iron Production	– weight		–	–	0.5	0.5	6.3
Crude Steel Production	– weight		–	.005	0.6	0.605	9.0

Notes: RSA = Republic of South Africa; S-SA = Sub-Saharan Africa; fe. wt. = ferrous content
Source: UNCTAD, *Commodity Yearbook, 1991*

Table A27: African 'Exotic' Mineral Exports, 1987 (in US$ millions)

Mineral	Exporting Country/ies	Exports by country	Value US$ millions S-SA Total	RSA
Chrome	Zimbabwe	50		
	Others	25	70	1300
Cobalt	Zaïre	60		
	Zambia	40	100	–
Lead	Namibia	20	20	26
Manganese	Gabon	132		
	Ghana	20	152	89
Nickel	Botswana	64		
	Zimbabwe	50	114	79
Phosphate	Senegal	52		
	Togo	87		
	Zimbabwe	–	139	45
Silver	Namibia	5		
	Zaïre	3		
	Zambia	1		
	Zimbabwe	2	11	11
Tungsten	Namibia	1		
	Rwanda	1	2	–
Uranium	Gabon	22		
	Namibia	92		
	Niger	78	192	76
Zinc	Zaïre	82		
	Zambia	28	110	–
TOTAL			910	626

Notes: RSA = Republic of South Africa. Phosphate rock produced in Zimbabwe is not exported. Morocco's exports of phosphates are valued at $400 millions
Sources: UNCTAD, *Commodity Yearbook* and various press cuttings

Table A28: Africa: Oil Production, Reserves and Exports, 1987/8

COUNTRY	RESERVES (million barrels) 1988	PRODUCTION (barrels/ day) 1988	EXPORTS (millions tonnes 1987	SHARE OF COUNTRY EXPORTS (% of earnings) 1982–6
1. WEST AFRICA				
Nigeria	16 000	1514 000	57.4	96
Angola	1200	455 000	15.6	83
Gabon	1100	165 000	6.7	82
Cameroon	500	167 000	6.5	38
Congo	750	135 000	5.5	91
Zaïre	100	28 600	1.0	18
Côte d'Ivoire	100	15 000	0.1	11
Benin	100	5000	0.4	9
Ghana	–	0	0.0	8
Total	20 000	2484 600	75.8	–
2. NORTH AFRICA				
Algeria	16 000	1000 000	29.6	72
Egypt	4000	3000 000	24.5	61
Libya	40 000	4000 000	40.0	100
Morocco	1000	100 000	–	4
Total	61 000	8100 000	94.1	–
3. WORLD				
Total	700 000	65 000 000	1170.0	–
of which				
Developing	575 000	33 700 000	848.0	–
Developed	58 000	16 200 000	156.0	–
Socialist	67 000	15 100 000	166.0	–

Note: 7.5 barrels to a tonne make 100 000 barrels a day into 5 million tonnes a year, so that sub-Saharan African oil producers export 76 million tonnes out of the 125 million tonnes they produce each year.

Sources: *Petroleum Economist*, May 1989, plus UNCTAD, *Commodity Yearbook* for world exports and Fraser Report for shares of country exports

Table A29: Oil Exploration in Africa by Multinational Companies

Company Name	Countries where Company is Participating in Exploration	Comments
Agip (Italy)	Somalia, Kenya, Madagascar, Tanzania	–
Amoco (US)	Mauritania, Morocco, Sierra Leone, Liberia, Ghana, Kenya, Tanzania, Mozambique	associated with Petrofina in Kenya; with Arco in Tanzania and in Ghana
British Petroleum & subsidiary Britoil (UK)	Guinea-Bissau, Sudan, Ethiopia	associated with Sun in Sudan and the SFI (World Bank) in Ethiopia
British Gas (UK)	Mozambique, Sudan	associated with Marathon in Sudan
Atlantic Richfield (Arco) (US)	Ghana, Tanzania	associated with Amoco in Tanzania; associated with Pecten (Shell) and Unocal in Ghana
Chevron – Standard Oil of California (US)	Morocco, Chad, Sudan, Ghana	associate of Shell in Sudan and Chad
Conoco (US), Dupont de Nemours group	Sudan, Somalia	associated with Phillips Petroleum in Somalia and in another block with Murphy, Lundin and Neste Oil
ELF-Snea (France)	Guinea-Bissau, Niger, Equatorial Guinea	associated with Pecten in Guinea-Bissau and Esso in Niger
Burmah Oil (UK)	Senegal	associated with Ocelot, Domson Mines, Diamond Shamrock (US)
Hunt (US)	Chad	associated with Chevron
Husky Oil (Canada)	Senegal, Somalia	associated with Marathon and Walter in Senegal
Energy Resources (US)	Liberia	–
International Petroleum Ltd (Canada) financial group	Djibouti, Benin	–
Lundin (Sweden)		
Japan National Oil Co.	Morocco	–
Marathon (US)	Morocco, Senegal, Sudan, Kenya	associated with Husky, Walter in Senegal; British Gas in Sudan; and Total in Kenya
Mobil (US)	Kenya, Madagascar	associated with Total in Kenya

continued

Company Name	Countries where Company is Participating in Exploration	Comments
Murphy (US)	Somalia	associate of Conoco, Neste Oil and Lundin
Neste Oil (Finland)	Somalia	associate of Conoco
Ocelot (Canada)	Senegal, Sudan	associate of Burmah in Senegal and Sun in Sudan
Occidental (Oxy) (US)	Madagascar	like other contractors in Madagascar, in association with the government organisation, OMNIS
Petro Canada International Assistance Corp (PIAC)	Morocco, Senegal, Gambia, Ghana, Tanzania, Madagascar, Botswana	technical assistance contracts with local companies
Phillips Petroleum (US)	Somalia	associated with Conoco
Samedan (one-time USSR)	Morocco	–
Petrofina (Belgium) or American subsidiary APEX	Morocco, Tanzania, Kenya	associate of Amoco in Kenya and Tanzania
Panoco (Switzerland)	Sudan	associate of Conoco in a block in the Red Sea
Exxon or Esso (US)	Morocco, Niger, Chad, Mozambique, Madagascar, Somalia	associated with Shell in Somalia and Mozambique; with Elf in Niger; with Chevron in Chad
Shell (or its subsidiary Pecten) (UK and Netherlands)	Chad, Guinea-Bissau, Somalia, Mozambique	associate of Esso in Somalia and Mozambique; with Elf in Guinea-Bissau; with Hunt and Chevron in Chad
Sun Oil (US)	Sudan	associated with Sun, Conoco, Panoco, Yukong
Taurus (US) (Swedish interests)	Morocco	associated with the sté financière Oil Exploration (Liechtenstein)
Texaco	Mauritania	–
Total (Cie Francaise des Pétroles) (France)	Kenya, Sudan	associated with Marathon and Kufpec (Kuwait) in Sudan; with Mobil and Marathon in Kenya
Tullow Oil (Ireland)	Senegal	–
Trilogy (Canada)	Benin, Togo	associated with Simmons (Canada)
Unocal (Union Oil of California) (US)	Ghana	associated with Arco and Pecten

continued

Company Name	Countries where Company is Participating in Exploration	Comments
Walter (one-time USSR)	Morocco, Senegal	associated with Samedan in Morocco; and Husky and Marathon in Senegal
Wintershall (Federal Republic of Germany)	Guinea-Bissau	associate of Pecten (Shell) and Elf in Guinea-Bissau
Yukong (South Korea)	Sudan	

Source: *Marchés Tropicaux,* 18 August 1989

Table A30: Petroleum Taxation and Royalty in Sub-Saharan Africa

Country	Royalty rate (%)	Income Tax rate (%)
Benin	12.5	50
Cameroon	nil	57.8
Congo	concession – 15 production – 0	60.0
Gabon	20	concession – 73 production – 56.25
Ghana	12.5	65
Côte d'Ivoire	12.5	50
Nigeria	20	85
Zaïre	12.5	50
Chad	12.5	50
Ethiopia	12.5	51
Madagascar	20	45
Niger	12.5	50
Senegal	1.25	33.33
Sudan	12.5	50
Tanzania	not specified	50+
CAR	not specified	not specified
Equat. Guinea	10	not specified
Gambia	12.5	50
Guinea	12.5	46
Guinea-Bissau	20	52.5
Liberia	12.5	50
Malawi	not specified	50
Mauritania	12.5	50
Seychelles	12.5	55
Sierra Leone	12.5	50
Somalia	15	67
Togo	1	50
Uganda	not specified	not specified
Burkina Faso	5	not specified
Zambia	not specified	45

CAR = Central African Republic

Note: The table below shows the comparative effect of increases in royalty and income tax.

	Royalty 12.5% Tax 50%	Royalty 16.5% Tax 50%	Royalty 12.5% Tax 55%
Revenue	10000000	10000000	10000000
Royalty	1250000	1650000	1250000
	8750000	8350000	8750000
Costs	7000000	7000000	7000000
Pre-Tax Profit	1750000	1350000	1750000
Tax	875000	675000	962500
After-Tax Profit	875000	675000	787500

Source: World Petroleum Tax and Royalty Rates, Barrows Inc., New York

Table A31: Sub-Saharan Africa's Energy Balances, 1987 (in million tonnes oil equivalent, except for consumption per head)

Country	Production			Consumption		Trade	
	Oil	Gas	Hydro	Total	per head (kg)	Exports	Imports
OIL PRODUCERS							
Angola	18.0	0.1	0.3	1.0	60	16.0	–
Benin	0.4	–	–	0.2	30	0.4	0.2
Cameroon	9.0	–	0.5	1.5	180	7.2	–
Congo	6.1	–	0.1	0.4	300	5.9	0.1
Côte d'Ivoire	1.0	–	0.3	1.5	130	0.4	1.5
Gabon	8.0	0.1	0.2	0.9	660	7.2	–
Ghana	0.1	–	1.0	2.0	60	0.1	1.1
Nigeria	63.0	2.0	0.1	10.1	120	57.2	–
Zaire	1.1	0.1	0.3	1.2	42	1.0	0.8
Subtotal	106.7	0.3	2.8	18.8	176	95.4	3.7
NON OIL EXPORTERS							
Burkina Faso	–	–	–	0.1	18	–	0.1
Burundi	–	–	–	0.0	10	–	0.0
CAR	–	–	–	0.0	18	–	0.0
Chad	–	–	–	0.0	12	–	0.0
Ethiopia	–	–	0.1	0.5	12	0.2	0.8
Gambia	–	–	–	0.0	70	–	0.05
Guinea	–	–	–	0.3	50	–	0.3
Liberia	–	–	–	0.2	100	–	0.2
Madagascar	–	–	–	0.2	24	–	0.2
Malawi	–	–	–	0.2	26	–	0.2
Mali	–	–	–	0.1	15	–	0.1
Mauritania	–	–	–	0.2	90	–	0.2
Mauritius	–	–	–	0.2	240	–	0.2
Mozambique	–	–	–	0.3	18	–	0.3
Niger	–	–	–	0.2	30	–	0.2
Réunion	–	–	–	0.2	500	–	0.2
Rwanda	–	–	–	0.1	18	–	0.1
Senegal	–	–	–	0.6	84	–	0.9
Sierra Leone	–	–	–	0.1	42	–	0.2
Somalia	–	–	–	0.3	66	–	0.4
Sudan	–	–	–	0.9	42	–	1.1
Togo	–	–	–	0.1	36	–	0.1
Uganda	–	–	–	0.2	18	–	0.2
Zambia	–	–	0.7(a)	1.2	180	0.2	0.5
Zimbabwe	–	–	0.2(a)	3.5	410	0.1	1.1
Subtotal	–	–	1.0	10.3	87	0.4	10.2
TOTAL (b)	106.7	0.3	3.8	29.1	108	95.8	13.9

Notes: (a) Coal production in Zambia and Zimbabwe adds about the same as Hydro; (b) Fuel wood totalling some 75 million tonnes is excluded.
Sources: UN, *Statistical Yearbook* and OECD, International Energy Agency, *World Energy Statistics and Balances, 1971–1987*

Table A32: The World Oil Market, Exports and Imports, 1989 (all figures in US$ billions)

Region	Exporting Total	Importing North America	West Europe	Japan	Developing Countries	East Europe & China
Total	292	54	99	38	64	30
OPEC	113	22	32	22	31	2
Developed	79	17	44	5	9	1
Developing	163	36	38	32	48	4
Mid-East	75	8	16	18	30	2
Africa	30	8	18	–	3	3
Americas	28	17	3	1	5	3
CP	50	1	17	3	8	25

Notes: Exports exceed imports because Oceania is excluded and the destination of some exports is not revealed. CP = formerly Centrally Planned and includes China.
Source: United Nations *Monthly Statistical Bulletin*, May 1991

Table A33: Producers' Share and Foreign Margins on Selected Primary Commodities in the 1970s (percentage of retail price)

A. COTTON

	Denim dungarees US 1974	Denim jeans UK 1975	Shirt, 35% cotton FRG 1976
Raw material producer	8.4	8.4	3.5
Textile manufacturer	19.6	48.6	18.7
Apparel manufacturer	30.0		29.8
Wholesaler/retailer	42.0	43.0	48.0
Retail price	100.0	100.0	100

B. TOBACCO

	Cigarettes US 1972
Growers' gross returns	5.7
Manufacturing: total	30.1
of which (i) materials and services	15.7
(ii) employee compensations	2.9
(iii) gross profit	11.5
Wholesaler/retailer	23.0
Taxes	41.2
Retail price	100.0

C. BANANAS

	1969	1980
Producer countries, retained value	12.7	14.2
Freight and insurance	7.0	15.9
Jobber-ripener	31.9	21.5
Retailers	36.3	35.2
Others	12.1	13.2
Total	100.0	100.0

D. COFFEE

	year	Imports c.i.f.	tax	Other costs and margins	Total	Retail Price Index
FRG	1975	26	35	39	100	100
	1978	44	30	26	100	132
France	1975	39	7	54	100	100
	1978	49	7	44	100	223
UK	1975	37	63	–	100	100
	1977	64	36	–	100	266
US	1975	68	32	–	100	100
	1977	72	28	–	100	245

E. TEA

	Bags US 1978	Bags Canada 1975	Packets UK 1977	Packets India 1977
Grower	15(a)	27(a)	47	62
Freight & insurance	3	4	12(a)	–
Importer or auction charges	1	2	3	–
Blender	60	49	26	20
Wholesaler	17	18	10	–
Retailer	4			4
Excise & sales tax	–	–	–	14
Total	100	100	100	100

Notes: (a) including export and other duties; cif = cost, insurance, freight; FRG = Federal Republic of Germany
Source: UNCTC, *Transnational Corporations and Non-fuel Primary Commodities in Developing Countries* (New York, 1987) pp. 44–5

Chart A34: Cost Breakdown of a Coffee Dollar

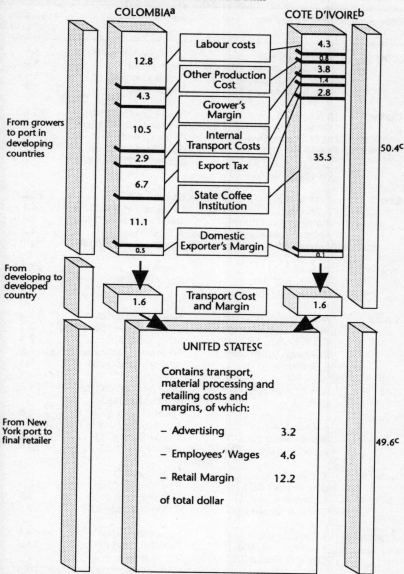

Notes: (a) 1979; (b) 1976– 79; (c) 1980

Source: Designed and computed from data supplied by International Coffee Organisation and US Department of Commerce. From Clairmonte and Cavanagh, *Merchants of Drink* (Third World Network, Penang, 1988).

Table A35: Major Food Traders and Processors, 1980

Commodity	Leading Traders	Leading Processors	1980 sales (US$bns)
Sugar	Tate & Lyle (UK)	Gulf & Western (US)	5.3
	Sucres et Denrées (France)	Lonrho (UK)	5.0
	Engelhard (Philipps) (US)	Tate & Lyle (UK)	3.4
	E.D. & F. Man (UK)	Amstar (US)	1.8
Coffee	J. Aron (US)	Nestlé (Switzerland)	13.8
	Volkart (Switzerland)	Proctor & Gamble (US)	11.2
	ACLI International (US)	General Foods (US)	6.4
	Socomex (US)	Coca Cola (US)	5.9
	General Foods and Proctor & Gamble (US)	Jacobs (FRG)	1.6
Corn	Continental (US)	Cargill (US)	25.0
	Louis Dreyfus (France)	CPC International (US)	4.1
	Bunge & Born (Brazil)	Standard Brands (US)	3.0
	André (Switzerland)	ADM (US)	3.2
	Cargill (US)	Bunge & Born (Brazil)	na
Rice	Connell (US)	Cargill (US)	25.0
	Continental (US)	Continental (US)	na
	'Six Tigers' (Thailand)		
Cocoa	ACLI International (US)	Nestlé (Switzerland)	13.8
	Volkart (Switzerland)	Cadbury-Schweppes (UK)	2.7
	Gill & Duffus (UK)	Mars, Inc (US)	2.3
	Internatio (US/Holland)	Rowntree-Mackintosh (UK)	1.5
	J. H. Raynor (US)	Hershey Foods (US)	1.3
Tea	Allied-Lyons (UK)	Unilever (Liptons) (UK)	24.3
	Unilever (UK)	Associated British Foods (Twining) (UK)	5.8
	J. Finlay (UK)	Allied-Lyons (UK)	5.0
	Brooke Bond (UK)	Brooke Bond (UK)	1.6
	Associated British Foods (UK)	James Finlay (UK)	na
Bananas	R. J. Reynolds (Del Monte) (US)	R. J. Reynolds (Del Monte) (US)	10.4
	United Brands (US)	United Brands (US)	3.9
	Castle & Cooke (US)	Castle & Cooke (US)	1.7
Pineapples	Mitsubishi (Japan)	Mitsubishi (Japan)	66.1
	R. J. Reynolds (US)	Nestlé (Libby) (US)	13.8
	Castle & Cooke (US)	R.J. Reynolds (Del Monte) (US)	10.4
		Castle & Cooke (US)	1.7

Source: From a paper presented by F. Clairmonte and J. Cavanagh at a Consumer Association of Penang Conference, Malaysia, 1981.

Table A36: Ownership Structure in the SADCC Mining Industry (%)

| Mineral | Company | | Ownership | |
	Local	Parent	Private	State
COPPER				
Zambia	ZCCM	Anglo American Corp (AAC)	40	60
Zimbabwe	MTD	Individuals	45	55
	LSM	Individuals	35	65
	Corsyn	Lonrho	100	
	BNC	AAC	100	
Botswana	BCL	Botswana RST Ltd	85	15
Mozambique	MAGMA			100
COBALT				
Zambia	ZCCM	AAC	40	60
Zimbabwe	BNC	AAC	100	
Botswana	BCL	Botswana RST Ltd	85	15
LEAD/ZINC				
Zambia	ZCCM	AAC	40	60
NICKEL				
Botswana	BCL	Botswana RST Ltd	85	15
Zimbabwe	BNC	AAC	100	
CHROMITE				
Zimbabwe	Zimalloy	AAC	100	
	Zimasco	Union Carbide	100	
GOLD				
Zimbabwe	Various	Small private owners	100	
Zambia	ZCCM	AAC	40	60
DIAMONDS				
Botswana	Debswana	De Beers	50	50
Angola	Diamang	Société Générale	23	77
Tanzania	Williams	De Beers	50	50
COAL				
Zimbabwe	Wankie	AAC	20	80
Zambia	Maamba			100
Botswana	Morupule	AAC	93	na
Mozambique	Carbomoc			100
ASBESTOS				
Zimbabwe	S&M	Turner Newall	100	
Swaziland	Havelock	Turner Newall & Gencor	100	
OIL				
Angola	Cabcog	Chevron	49	51

Source: Government and company data from *Problems Related to Transfer of Technology and Mineral-Based Industrialisation*, Report 16 B, Helsinki University Institute of Development Studies, 1988.

Table A37: Africa's Exports of Manufactures and Primary Products, 1966–89

Commodities	Commodity Shares				Price Changes per year		
	1966	*1977*	*1986*	*1989*	*1970-80*	*1980–4*	*1985–9*
All exports (US$bn)	8.2	48.0	46.8	57.4	+21	-4	-4
per cent	100	100	100	100			
Fuel	18	64	56	53	+34	-7	-1
All non-fuel	82	36	44	47	+11	-3	+3
Primary Products	42	16	20	15	+11	-3	-2
Manufactures of which	40	20	24	32	+11	-3	+6
Food products	18	11	11	9			
Chemicals	1	1	2	2			
Metal products	13	4	3	3			
Machinery & transport equipment	–	–	–	1			
Other manufactures of which	7	4	7	15			
Textiles	–	–	2	2			
Clothing	–	–	2	4			

Note: these figures are for all developing Africa, including North Africa
Source: UN, *Monthly Bulletin of Statistics,* June 1991

Table A38: Structure of Manufacturing in Selected Least Developed Countries, 1985 (values as percentage of gross output)

ISIC number	Gross output (US$mn)	Food, beverage & tobacco 31	Textiles and apparel 32	Chemicals & petro-refinery 351–353	Metal products 381	Machinery & Transp. equipment 382–384	Other
Bangladesh	2024	22	30	29	10	6	3
Benin	178	57	17	4	6	0	16
Botswana	49	51	12	0	0	0	37
Burkina Faso	344	61	15	1	0	6	23
Burma	3662	71	7	0	4	3	15
Burundi	87	75	11	5	0	0	9
CAR	100	40	20	6	0	0	34
Ethiopia	1381	40	17	23	5	0	15
Gambia	44	70	2	2	2	0	24
Lesotho	28	29	11	0	0	0	60
Malawi	126	49	13	11	0	2	25
Rwanda	260	77	1	12	0	0	10
Somalia	132	30	14	15	2	0	39
Sierra Leone	71	37	4	38	0	0	21
Sudan	1052	35	12	33	3	0	17
Tanzania	1016	30	21	9	5	11	24
Total	10 554	48	15	14	4	4	14

Source: UNCTAD Secretariat calculations based on data from UNIDO, World Bank and other sources. Taken from UNCTAD, *The Least Developed Countries 1988 Report*, p. 51

Table A39: Baseline Projections of GDP Growth, Debt Service and External Balances of Developing Countries, 1900–2000 (per cent)

	1990		*2000*
ALL DEVELOPING COUNTRIES			
GDP Growth (a)	–	3.6	–
Debt/exports	106.4		58.0
Interest payments/exports	7.4		3.4
Current account balance/exports	-4.2		-5.4
LATIN AMERICA			
GDP Growth (a)	–	2.6	–
Debt/exports	222.9		73.9
Interest payments/exports	19.2		5.8
Current account balance/exports	-4.5		-5.8
AFRICA			
GDP Growth (a)	–	2.4	–
Debt/exports	320.7		194.2
Interest payments/exports	17.3		9.4
Current account balance/exports	-28.6		-18.8
ASIA			
GDP Growth (a)	–	4.5	–
Debt/exports	45.5		38.8
Interest payments/exports	2.8		2.2
Current account balance/exports	-1.1		-3.8
Memo item			
LEAST DEVELOPING COUNTRIES			
GDP Growth (a)	–	2.9	–
Debt/exports	460.3		363.0
Interest payments/exports	11.4		8.4
Current account balance/exports	-68.4		-54.4

Note: (a) average annual rate for 1991–2000
Source: UNCTAD Secretariat calculations based on SIGMA projections from
UNCTAD, *Trade and Development Report, 1990*, p.67

Table A40: Tariffs on Selected Commodities in Major World Markets by Degree of Processing, 1986 (per cent ad valorem)

Item	EC MFN	EC GSP	ACP	Japan MFN	Japan GSP	US MFN
Coffee						
Raw	9.0	6.5	1.3	0.0	–	0.0
Roasted, ground	6.5	12.0	3.3	20.0	10.0	0.0
Extracts, preparations	18.0	9.0	0.0	24.2	7.5	0.0
Tea						
In bulk	0.0	–	–	12.5	2.5	0.0
For retail sale	5.0	0.0	0.0	20.0	14.0	0.0
Extracts, essence	12.0	0.0	0.0	17.3	8.0	0.0
Cocoa						
Beans	3.0	–	0.0	0.0	–	0.0
Paste	15.0	11.0	0.0	15.0	7.5	0.0
Butter	12.0	8.0	0.0	2.5	0.0	0.0
Powder	16.0	9.0	0.0	21.5	10.5	0.5
Chocolate	–	–	–	30.0	12.5	1.9
Sugar						
Raw	–	–	–	37.5	–	14.5
Processed	10.0	–	–	28.4	–	4.2
Molasses	–	–	–	28.1	–	4.5
Spices						
Unground, unprocessed	7.5	4.4	0.0	1.21	0.0	0.7
Ground, processed	11.8	4.0	0.0	6.6	0.0	4.7
Essential oils						
Essential oils	4.5	0.0	–	3.9	0.0	0.9
Mixtures	5.3	0.0	–	6.6	0.0	4.4
Preparations	6.6	0.0	–	7.2	0.0	5.3
Vegetable plaiting materials						
Raw	0.5	0.0	0.0	5.0	5.0	2.8
Plaits	3.4	0.0	–	5.8	0.8	5.2
Basketwork, wickerwork	6.2	0.0	–	9.4	0.0	6.6
Oilseeds, vegetable oils						
Oilseeds	0.0	–	–	1.0	–	3.4
Vegetable oils	7.2	7.2	1.0	8.5	8.3	4.3
Fatty acids, fatty alcohols	8.8	4.4	0.9	5.4	0.9	4.4
Margarine	25.0	–	5.0	35.0	–	0.0
Soaps	6.9	0.0	–	6.5	0.0	4.1

continued

Item	EC			Japan		US
	MFN	GSP	ACP	MFN	GSP	MFN
Tobacco						
Unmanufactured	24.4	14.8	0.0	0.0	–	72.6
Manufactured	78.8	67.0	0.0	14.3	–	11.0
Rice						
Unmilled	12.0	–	2.4	0.0	–	5.1
Milled, processed	–	–	–	16.7	–	16.4
Manioc, roots, tubers						
Fresh, dried	6.0	–	3.0	11.3	–	13.5
Flour	–	–	0.0	12.5	–	–
Meals; starches	30.0	–	0.0	22.8	–	0.0
Bananas						
Fresh	20.0	0.0	0.0	25.5	14.3	1.7
Flour, prepared	17.0	0.0	0.0	–	–	5.9
Tropical nuts						
Unshelled, crude	2.2	0.0	0.0	7.9	1.5	5.2
Shelled, prepared	15.0	6.0	0.0	21.0	8.3	7.6
Tropical fruit						
Fresh, dried	8.0	2.3	0.0	9.1	4.0	8.7
Preserved	13.4	3.7	0.9	21.0	8.9	–
Prepared, fruit juices	24.0	13.1	4.6	27.5	11.4	46.7
Tropical wood						
In the rough	1.3	–	0.0	0.4	0.0	3.4
Simply worked	3.1	0.0	–	2.6	1.3	2.0
Veneers, plywood	4.0	0.0	0.0	8.4	0.1	4.4
Wood articles	4.9	0.0	–	–	–	6.3
Fish						
Fresh, chilled, frozen	13.5	5.2	0.0	6.1	–	0.6
Dried, smoked	12.7	7.5	0.0	11.9	5.0	2.4
Prepared, preserved	17.2	8.4	0.4	13.7	6.8	9.1
Meat						
Fresh, chilled, frozen	11.6	1.7	0.0	11.8	–	6.4
Salted, dried, smoked	19.5	–	1.0	19.8	–	9.8
Prepared, preserved	18.1	11.5	3.1	19.2	6.4	3.9
Molluscs, crustaceans						
Fresh, chilled, frozen	10.7	4.3	0.0	6.5	6.7	3.7
Preparations	18.0	6.0	0.0	12.4	5.7	5.3

continued

Item	MFN	EC GSP	ACP	Japan MFN	GSP	US MFN
Rubber						
Natural rubber	0.0	0.0	–	0.0	–	0.0
Simple manufactures	3.7	3.7	0.0	3.5	0.0	4.7
Tyres, tubes	3.6	3.6	–	3.2	0.0	3.1
Other articles	4.8	0.0	–	3.5	0.0	5.2
Jute						
Raw	0.0	–	–	0.0	–	0.0
Processed	–	–	–	–	–	0.3
Yarns	5.3	0.0	0.0	10.0	0.0	4.1
Woven fabrics	8.7	0.0	0.0	20.0	0.0	1.3
Made-up articles	7.7	0.0	0.0	11.2	0.0	3.8
Sisal, henequen						
Raw	0.0	–	–	0.0	–	0.0
Processed	–	–	–	–	–	8.0
Twine, cordage	12.0	12.0	0.0	6.5	0.0	4.2
Aluminium						
Bauxite	–	–	–	0.0	–	0.0
Alumina	–	–	–	5.4	0.0	0.0
Aluminium, unwrought	–	–	–	3.0	0.0	1.3
Aluminium, worked	7.3	0.0	0.0	7.1	0.0	3.9
Copper						
Copper ores and concentrates	–	–	–	0.0	–	0.3
Copper, blister	–	–	–	7.3	0.0	1.0
Copper, refined	–	–	–	7.6	0.0	–
Copper and copper alloys, worked	5.2	0.0	0.0	6.8	0.0	4.9
Iron						
Iron ores and concentrates	0.0	–	–	0.0	–	0.0
Pig iron, cast iron and spiegeleisen in pigs, blocks, lumps and similar forms	2.7	–	–	3.7	0.0	0.3
Iron or steel powders, shot or sponge	3.0	0.0	0.0	3.7	0.0	0.9
Ingots of iron and steel	3.5	0.0	0.0	5.7	0.0	3.9
Lead						
Lead ores and concentrates	–	–	–	0.0	–	6.1
Lead and lead alloys, unwrought	–	–	–	–	–	–
Lead and lead alloys, worked	5.8	0.0	0.0	7.2	0.0	4.8

continued

| Item | EC | | | Japan | | US |
	MFN	GSP	ACP	MFN	GSP	MFN
Phosphate						
Phosphate rock	0.0	–	–	0.0	–	0.0
Phosphoric acids	11.0	0.0	0.0	4.9	0.0	0.0
Superphosphates	4.8	0.0	0.0	2.9	–	0.0
Tin						
Tin ores and concentrates	–	–	–	0.0	–	0.0
Tin and tin alloys, unwrought	–	–	–	–	–	–
Tin and alloys, worked	3.7	0.0	0.0	3.4	0.0	2.5
Zinc						
Zinc ores and concentrates	–	–	–	0.0	–	0.0
Zinc and zinc alloys, unwrought	–	–	–	–	–	–
Zinc and zinc alloys, worked	7.1	0.0	0.0	5.4	0.0	5.7
Petrochemicals						
Hydrocarbons	7.1	0.0	0.0	4.7	0.0	7.0
Acrylic, cycl. alcohol	7.8	0.0	0.0	8.6	0.8	6.7
Carboxylic 4	8.2	0.0	0.0	6.2	0.0	7.9
Nitrogen function	8.1	0.0	0.0	6.2	0.3	10.7
Other	7.5	0.0	0.0	5.6	0.0	11.1
Condensation polyc. and polyadci	7.9	0.0	0.0	6.0	0.0	6.4
Polimerization and copol	11.9	0.0	0.0	7.0	0.0	7.5

Notes: – = Tariff rate not available or inapplicable. MFN = Tariff rate applied under the most-favoured-nation principle. ACP = Tariff rate applied by the EEC to African, Caribbean and Pacific countries under the Lomé Convention. GSP = Tariff rate applied under General System of Preferences. LDC rates applied by EEC and Japan are zero. GSP and Caribbean Basin Initiative rates applied by US are zero.
Source: The Fraser Report, 1990

Table A41: Africa's Sugar Balance, average 1987–8 (all figures in '000 tonnes)

Sugar Output		All Africa	Egypt	Sub-Sahara	South Africa
Cane		73 360	9010	42 950	20 600
Centrifuge Production		7985	1015	4250	2250
Exports –	Raw	2580	–	1600	980
	Refined	142		120	22
Imports –	Raw	915	–	365	–
	Refined	2350	–	1480	–
Consumption		8560	1715	3670	1405

Sources: FAO *Production Yearbook, 1989,* and UNCTAD, *Commodity Yearbook, 1991*

Table A42: African Tobacco Production, Trade and Consumption, average 1987–8, by Countries in Relation to World Totals (in '000 tonnes)

Country/region	Production	Exports	Imports	Consumption
World	6350	1350	1350	6000
Africa	314	179	130	230
South Africa	31	4	20	47
North Africa	13	1	21	96
Sub-Saharan	270	174	89	87
of which				
Zimbabwe	122	105	na	3
Malawi	65	58	na	1
Tanzania	13	8	na	6
Kenya	8	1	na	6
Nigeria	8	–	na	9
Zaïre	8	–	na	5
Others	46	3	na	57

Sources: FAO *Production Yearbook, 1988*; UNCTAD *Commodity Yearbook, 1991*

Table A43: African Tea Production, Trade and Consumption, average 1987–8, by Countries in Relation to World Totals (in '000 tonnes)

Country/region	Production	Exports	Imports	Consumption
World	2450	1130	1130	2270
Africa	270	236	170	212
South Africa	10	1	12	22
North Africa	–	–	15	127
Sub-Saharan	255	235	143	63
of which				
Kenya	160	146	na	18
Malawi	33	35	na	2
Tanzania	15	11	na	4
Zimbabwe	16	11	na	3
Others	31	32	na	36

Sources: FAO *Yearbook of Production 1988*; UNCTAD *Commodity Yearbook, 1991*

Table A44: Raw Material Output Processed by Stages, 1987/88. All Developed Countries and African Countries (all figures in '000 tonnes)

Commodity	Country or Group	Primary production	Processed Output Stage 1	Stage 2	Stage 3
Aluminium	All developing	10 410	4541	3311	2515
	Africa – Guinea	3881	294	–	–
	Ghana	64	–	161	8
	Egypt	–	–	180	79
Copper	All Developing	4067	3300	3007	1526
	Africa – Zambia	502	477	468	9
	Zaïre	469	446	282	2
Iron	All Developing	176 830	70 502	107 834	na
	Africa – Liberia	8936	–	–	–
	Mauritania	6562	–	6	–
Nickel	All Developing	287	157	72	na
	Africa –Botswana	20	–	–	–
	Zimbabwe	12	18	–	–

Source: UNCTAD *Commodity Yearbook, 1991*, Annex Table A5

Table A45: Coverage of Non-tariff Barriers (NTBs) on African Exports, 1986

Country	Trade Coverage (%)		Frequency Coverage (%)
EC	Primary:	23.6	26.8
	Manufactured	48.2	19.3
US	Primary:	0.8	5.3
	Manufactured	16.3	2.6
Japan	Primary:	27.1	29.2
	Manufactured	2.0	16.5
Australia	Primary:	0.0	0.9
	Manufactured	15.6	13.8
Canada	Primary:	5.3	8.5
	Manufactured	31.3	20.1

Note: *Trade coverage* is calculated as the percentage of the value of all exports affected by NTBs; *Frequency Coverage* is the percentage of the number of all export products affected by NTBs
Source: *The Fraser Report*, 1990

Index of Authors and Sources

(Entries in italic appear in the Statistical Annexe)

Subject Index

(Entries in italic appear in the Statistical Annexe)